MANDELSTAM

Oleg Lekmanov

Studies in Russian and Slavic Literatures, Cultures and History

Series Editor: Lazar Fleishman (Stanford Universtity)

MANDELSTAM

Oleg Lekmanov

Translated from Russian by Tatiana Retivov
Edited by Lazar Fleishman

Boston
2010

Library of Congress Cataloging-in-Publication Data

Lekmanov, O. A.
  [Osip Mandel'shtam. English]
  Mandelstam / Oleg Lekmanov ; translated from Russian by Tatiana Retivov.
    p. cm. — (Studies in Russian and Slavic literatures, cultures and history)
  Includes bibliographical references and index.
  ISBN 978-1-934843-28-4
  1. Mandel'shtam, Osip, 1891-1938. 2. Poets, Russian — 20th century — Biography. I. Title.
  PG3476.M355Z74613 2010
  891.71'3 — dc22
  [B]
                    2009054033

The book is supported by Mikhail Prokhorov Foundation
(translation program TRANSCRIPT).

Copyright © 2010 Academic Studies Press
All rights reserved

ISBN 978-1-934843-28-4

Book design by Ivan Grave
On the cover: Photograph by Moisei Nappel'baum ©, 1925.

Published by Academic Studies Press in 2010
28 Montfern Avenue
Brighton, MA 02135, USA
press@academicstudiespress.com
www.academicstudiespress.com

Contents

Introduction 1

Chapter One
    BEFORE THE FIRST "STONE" (1891-1913) 5

Chapter Two
    BETWEEN "STONE" (1913) AND "TRISTIA" (1922) 41

Chapter Three
    BETWEEN "TRISTIA" (1922) AND "POEMS" (1928) 81

Chapter Four
    BEFORE THE ARREST (1928-1934) 101

Chapter Five
    THE FINAL YEARS (1934-1938) 133

Epilogue
    NADEZHDA IAKOVLEVNA 165

Bibliography 168

Index of Names 179

List of illustrations

Osip Mandestam. 1895	11
Osip Mandestam. Early 1910-s	17
Nadezhda Mandelstam. 1923	66
Olga Arbenina-Gil'debrandt. 1920-s	73
Osip Mandestam. 1923	85
Olga Vaksel	92
Boris Kuzin. 1930-s	112
Boris Pasternak	112
Vladimir Maiakovsky	112
Aleksandr, Emil, Nadezhda and Osip Mandelstam, Maria Petrovykh, Anna Akhmatova. 1934	128
Osip Mandestam. 1934	137
Osip Mandelstam. 1938. A photograph from his case	160

Introduction

Let us cite two of Osip Emil'evich Mandelstam's poetical statements "about time and about myself":

> *No, never have I been anyone's contemporary,*
> *Such honor does not become me.*
> *Oh how I loathe a namesake,*
> *It was not I, it was another.*

It is with these lines that the poet began one of his poems in 1924. Seven years later, in 1931, he took back his own words:

> *It's time for you to know, I too am a contemporary,*
> *I am a person from the Moskvoshvei era,*
> *See how my jacket puckers on me,*
> *How well I take a step and speak!*
> *Just try and tear me away from this century,*
> *Believe me, you will wring your own neck!*

These two declarations appear to be in striking contradiction to one another, and invite some sort of explanation. It is likely in the first poem, the "contemporary" refers to the pre-revolutionary past, whereas the second one is an affirmation of Mandelstam's identification with the Soviet present. Thus, the circumstances of the poet's life enable us to decipher his enigmatic poetic statements. Throughout his whole life, Mandelstam desired to be understood by the present and his contemporaries (thus: "It's time for you to know, I too am a contemporary…"). However, the *raznochinets* aspiration "to be like everybody" was combined in Mandelstam with an acute sense of his own specialness, his not being like anyone else (thus: "No, never have I been anyone's contemporary…"). The urge "to be and play with people" alternated in him with the wish to stay aloof from his milieu.

INTRODUCTION

The poet's willingness to march "in step with the company" was not as apparent as his desire to make a stand for his own originality. This is why, in the memoirs of his contemporaries, Mandelstam often appears to be an uncouth eccentric who does not have any sense of the basic laws and rules of human conduct. "Mandelstam would rush in without any greeting, looking for a "Maecenas" willing to pay for his cab. Then he would drop into an armchair and demand some cognac in his tea in order to get warm, and then immediately drop the cup onto the rug or desk" (G. Ivanov 1994: 223); "Mandelstam was hysterically crazy about sweets. Even in hardship conditions, without boots, in the cold, he managed to remain spoiled. His somewhat feminine dissoluteness and birdlike frivolity were not lacking in a system. He had the real airs of an artist, and an artist lies in order to be free for his only occupation, he was like the monkey, which, according to the Hindu, does not speak so that no one makes it work" (Shklovsky: 231); "He would make the impression of someone very weak, thin, with reddish, chick-like fluff growing on his head instead of hair" (Sedykh: 45); "The full extent of his unusual mismatch with daily life became especially apparent to me in the summer of 1922" (N. Chukovsky: 153); "Extremely vain, suspicious, he would sometimes exhibit an unpleasant presumptuousness most likely as a result of his 'being at loose ends'."

In such a way, an unreliable or distorted portrait of the mythical Osip Mandelstam was created.

A major role in rectifying the picture was played by the poet's widow, Nadezhda Iakovlevna Mandelstam. In one of her letters, she gave a harsh summing up evaluation of most of the memoir writers about her husband: "They tried to force him into their prearranged ideas about a 'poet.' One should not forget about who his contemporaries were and what they did" (Shumikhin: 10). Nadezhda Mandelstam's as well as Anna Akhmatova's memoirs were created with the polemical intent of repudiating the legends that were current at the time. "Now we must all write down our recollections about him. Otherwise you know what kind of stories will be told: "tuft of hair...short...restive...a scandalist," Anna Akhmatova said to Emma Gershtein (Gershtein: 415). "Stop 'the memoirs'"—Mandelstam himself would beg of his contemporaries in his drafts of the "Egyptian Stamp" (III: 574).

INTRODUCTION

And yet, some of the mythical episodes in accounts of Mandelstam's life should not always be so readily dismissed as Nadezhda Iakovlevna and Anna Andreevna had chosen to do. Sometimes they are supported by the real facts of Mandelstam's biography.

Let's take just two examples. Referring to the memoirs of Nikolai Chukovsky, which, indeed are full of inaccuracies; Nadezhda Iakovlevna made the following indignant comment: "Nikolai Chukovsky <...> wrote, for example, that O. M. looked like Pushkin and was aware of it, and thus once appeared dressed as Pushkin at a masquerade. Whereas he did not look like Pushkin, did not quote Pushkin's name in vain, and never dressed up as Pushkin" (Iz Perepiski: 154). However, this episode recorded by N. Chukovsky can be found in other memoirs as well, including those of D. Slepian, which we have no reason to doubt: "I remember how among those dressed up for the masquerade there appeared Osip Mandelstam dressed "as Pushkin," in colored tails with a jabot, a wig with side-whiskers, and a top hat. At that time he was <...> very popular, and at that event in one of the overflowing reception rooms I saw Mandelstam standing on the marble window sill of a huge mirrored window facing a classical Petersburg square, reading his poems into the white night. The lights were faded, the curtains were drawn open, and his entire figure in masquerade standing against such a background, as if in an engraving, was unforgettable, most likely, for all those present" (Slepian: 196-197).

It's understandable why the portrait of Mandelstam in the role of Pushkin did not make Nadezhda Iakovlevna happy, for such a fact was very much in keeping with the myth of the eccentric poet. But since the event actually did take place, one should admit that the "mythical" Mandelstam did bear some kind of resemblance to his "real" prototype.

A second example is perhaps even more striking, though perhaps less indisputable. Readers of Nadezhda Iakovlevna's memoirs would recall the scene with the aging Valery Briusov, who refused to express his gratitude to the American Relief Administration (ARA), the charity organization that had supplied intellectuals and scientists with food packages during the famine years in Soviet Russia: "Briusov considered it to be nationally or personally demeaning and below his dignity to thank ARA for a can of white grease and a bag of flour. Meanwhile the people in line were reserved in their anger at the delay, saying that ARA did not have to feed us at all, and that one's tongue won't dry up from saying a few words of thanks. Mandelstam, for some reason, enjoyed Briusov's stubbornness, which to my mind was totally pointless. He liked people who were rebellious, and he observed this scene with great interest" (NM-2: 91).

Nadezhda Iakovlevna's testimony alludes to the book, "The Hill of Mair," by Mikhail Prishvin, which was published while Mandelstam was still alive. It described the "pointless" rebellion against the ARA yet attributed this rebellion not to Briusov but to Mandelstam himself: "...he raises it as a matter of principle: America provides assistance to our writers, but insists on a signature of "gratitude"—isn't it offensive for a Russian poet to receive help in such a way? Shouldn't this be raised at the Writers Union?" (Prishvin: 265). So whom are we to believe, Prishvin who came up with yet another example of the poet's eccentricity, or the poet's widow, who decided in this cunning way to protect the poet from Prishvin's gibe? It's an open issue.

Thus, every specific recollection about Mandelstam requires a careful critique. My main goal in this book is to try and peel off the emotional, evaluative layers from the existing accounts of the poet's life.

I wish to thank Andrei Ar'ev, Boris Katz, Nikolai Bogomolov, Mikhail Gasparov, and Mikhail Melnichenko for their generous advice and comments on the drafts of this book. A special thanks is in order to Iury Freidin, not only the first editor, but co-author of many of the pages of this book. To be sure, full responsibility for any possible errors is born by the author. Among the most significant biographical sources used, the research of the following authors was especially important: S.S. Averintsev, Clarence Brown, S.V. Vasilenko, Ralf Dutley, A.G. Mets, A.A. Morozov, P.M. Nerler, Omry Ronen, D.M. Segal, R.D. Timenchik, E.A. Toddes, L.S. Fleishman, N.I. Khardzhiev, as well as the monumental memoirs by N.Ia. Mandelstam and E.G. Gershtein.

I would like to dedicate this book to the memory of my mother, Klara Mukhametovna Lekmanova (July 31, 1936—February 11, 2007).

Chapter One

BEFORE THE FIRST "STONE" (1891-1913)

1.

Osip (Iosif) Emil'evich Mandelstam was born on the night of the second (14 New Calendar) into the third (15) of January 1891 in Warsaw. According to family legend, Mandelstam's ancestors originated from Spain, and the founder of the family name was, supposedly, a jeweler at the court of the Duke of Courland, Biron. "The family gave the world famous doctors, physicists, Zionists, assimilationists, translators of the Bible, and specialists in Gogol" (Ronen: 6). "Old timers in Kiev still remember the Professor-Ophthalmologist and social activist with the same family name. In the Leningrad medical world there were my renown contemporaries, also Emil'eviches, two brothers, Morits and Aleksandr Mandelstam. One of the Mandelstams was the head of a department at the University of Helsinki. The other one was a translator and specialist of Arab culture. He worked at the Russian Embassy in Constantinople," wrote in his memoirs Mandelstam's younger brother, Evgeny (E. Mandelstam: 121).

The Jewish-German family name, "Mandelstam," can be translated from the Yiddish as "the trunk of an almond tree," causing the reader of the Bible to recall the budded almond rod of the high priest, Aaron (Numbers 17:1-10) and the prophet Jeremiah's vision: "I said: I see the rod of the almond tree" (Jeremiah 1:11). Mandelstam would frequently play upon the origin of his family name in his poetry:

As the tsar's staff in the sanctuary of prophets,
There bloomed a ceremonial pain.

("There is an unshakeable scale of values," 1914)

CHAPTER ONE

In his open letter to A.G. Gornfeld, published in the newspaper "Vecherniaia Moskva" (Evening Moscow) on 12 December 1928, Mandelstam separates himself as a Russian poet from himself as a Jew: "And now, when all of the apologies have long ago been expressed, — doing away with anything almandine, I, a Russian poet..." (IV: 103). Evgeny Mandelstam remembers how he and his brother would play with their family name in charades: the first two syllables — a sweet, the third — part of a tree (E. Mandelstam: 128).

Mandelstam's father, Emil' (Khatskel') Veniaminovich was born in 1852, if one is to believe the certificate issued by the Dinaburg trade board, or in 1856, if one is to trust the memory of Evgeny Mandelstam, in the borough Zhagory, of the Shavel' district in the Kovno (Kaunas) province. "The fourteen-year-old boy, who was coached to become a rabbi and forbidden to read secular books, escaped to Berlin where he entered the Talmudic high school, a meeting place for equally stubborn, rational boys from remote boroughs aspiring to be geniuses: instead of the Talmud, they read Schiller, and, note, as a totally new book" (II: 362).

Unable to withstand the half-starved, almost pauper-like existence in Berlin, the youth quit his studies in order to search for a job and returned home. At the same time, Emil' Veniaminovich's parents moved to Riga. One of his brothers also lived there, while the second made his home in Warsaw.

On 19 January 1889, in Dinaburg (Dvinsk), Emil' Mandelstam and Flora Osipovna Verblovskaia were married. Mandelstam's financial affairs had improved by this time. Emil' Veniaminovich began producing gloves, and about a month after the birth of his first son, Osip, in the end of February 1891, he received a certificate that he is "worthy master of the glove-making trade along with the additional trade of leather sorter" (E. Mandelstam: 175). The Mandelstam family still has the signet that Mandelstam the elder had used for marking leather.

In 1892, the Mandelstams had a second child, Aleksandr, and then a third, Evgeny, in 1898. By that time, Emil' Veniaminovich moved his family at first just closer to the capital, to Pavlovsk (1894), and then, around 1897, to Petersburg itself.

BEFORE THE FIRST "STONE" (1891-1913)

A couple of decades later, Mandelstam would depict Pavlovsk in his poem "Concert at the Train Station" (1921). Nietzsche's image of stars — "glowing worms" will be found in the beginning lines of the poem next to the quote form Lermontov's poem, "I Walk Alone Down the Road..." ("a star is speaking with a star"), in whom philosopher Vladimir Soloviev saw a "direct forefather" of Nietzscheanism (Soloviev: 275):

Impossible to breathe, the ground swarms with worms,
And not a single star is speaking,
But, God can see, there is music over us,
The train station shakes from singing Aonides
And once again, the steamroller's whistle
Binds the torn violin air.

A huge park. The glass orb of the station.
The iron world is once again bewitched.
Toward the noisy feast in the foggy Elysium
A train-car rolls away ceremoniously.
The peacock's cry and rumble of the piano.
I arrive late. It's scary. It's a dream.

And so I enter the glass forest of the station.
The violin's harmony in disarray and tears.
The wild beginning of the night choir
And smell of roses in rotting hotbeds,
Where a familiar shadow in the migrant crowd
Spent the night under the glass sky.

And so I imagine: the iron world all
In music and foam trembles pauper like.
I rest against the glass entrance.
Where are you going? At the wake of the dear shade
The music sounds for us for the last time.

CHAPTER ONE

Nadezhda Iakovlvena Mandelstam was of the opinion that "familiar" and "dear shade" signified the poet's mother, Flora Osipovna Verblovskaia. Before marriage she lived in Vilnius, where she received a good musical education and became a teacher of music (piano). Flora Osipovna was the relative of the famous literary historian, Semen Afanas'evich Vengerov. Although her native language was Russian, she sometimes spoke German with her husband.

Osip Mandelstam's childhood was not cloudless. "There where among happy generations epics resound in hexameter and chronicles, there is a gaping hole in my life, between myself and the century, a lapse, a ditch full of the noise of time, a place kept for the family and the family archives" (II: 384). It was further complicated by the fact that though the Mandelstam family had abandoned the Jewish milieu and rituals, they were unable to shed the stigma of their Jewishness.

From the second half of the 1900's, Emil' Veniaminovich's business started declining, and by 1917 he was totally bankrupt. Kornei Chukovsky remembered Mandelstam's father's "black hands," which "had become that way from his constant work with leather. These were the hands of a laborer" (quoted by E. Mandelstam: 175). "Our father did not take an active part in our family life," recalls Evgeny Mandelstam—"He would often be morose, reserved, and practically did not deal with the children" (E. Mandelstam: 123).

Decades later, in 1932, the eldest son wrote to his father: "I have become more convinced that there is much in common between us intellectually, which I did not understand when I was a boy" (IV: 148). It took years and years for the relations between father and son to become as close as in happy families would normally exist.

Obscure hints about his parents' constant fighting penetrated into Mandelstam's prose piece, "The Noise of Time." And Emma Gershtein, one of the last to spend a lot of time talking with him, remembers his: "direct and difficult admissions and complaints about a difficult childhood, poor upbringing: he continued being taken to the women's baths for too long, and he would get very worked up when the governess would beat him" (Gershtein: 13).

BEFORE THE FIRST "STONE" (1891-1913)

1895

In addition to this, Mandelstam's mother was constantly and compulsively moving. "The reasons were typically quite unexpected, but they would usually only become known by spring, after yet another move in the fall. Either she did not like what floor the apartment was on, or it was too far for the children to go to school on Mokhovaya, or else the rooms were not sunny enough, the kitchen uncomfortable, and so forth. According to my calculations, by the time up to the February revolution we had changed 17 addresses in Petersburg," wrote the poet's brother, Evgeny, in his memoirs (E. Mandelstam: 125).

The words, "family" and "home" lacked the sweet flavor for Mandelstam as a child that they had for, say, Boris Pasternak and Marina Tsvetaeva. As a child he could not find a clear point of view concerning his own Jewishness: "I was surrounded by Jewish chaos, neither homeland, nor home, nor hearth, but pure chaos, an unfamiliar womblike world, from whence I came forth, and of which I was scared, about which I had some vague ideas, and from which I ran, always ran" (II: 354).

Mandelstam's painful attitude toward his own family and national roots was marked by the fact that he always was clearly aware of how much self-confidence a person was capable of acquiring just from the knowledge that he belonged to a family or ethnic "clan." Mandelstam sang praise to *home* in one of his essays of 1923: "who would dare say that man's abode, the free home of man should not stand upon the earth as the best of its decorations and the most sturdy of all that exist?" (II: 287).

In his childhood and youth, in Mandelstam's consciousness, "Jewish chaos" was in stark contrast to the impeccably organized Empire style of St. Petersburg: "When I was seven or eight years old, this entire massif of St. Petersburg, its granite city blocks, that gentle heart of the city, with its effluents of squares, curling gardens, islands of monuments, caryatids of the Hermitage, the mysterious Millionnaya Street, where there were never any pedestrians and in whose marbles stood one sole bench, and especially the arc of the General Staff, the Senate Square, and the Dutch Petersburg, — all of this I considered to be something sacred and festive" (II: 350).

2.

Even though the Mandelstam family was plagued by financial problems, Osip's mother enrolled him, in September 1899, in the St. Petersburg commercial Tenishev school, where the tuition costs were quite high. Unfortunately, the school never became, in Mandelstam's eyes, the equivalent of Pushkin's Lyceum, despite there being every reason for it. The pedagogical innovations that were being practiced in the Tenishev school could very well have corresponded to the beginnings of the Lyceum of the Aleksandrine era, and such a comparison did cross Mandelstam's mind. In "The Noise of Time" he, perhaps somewhat ironically, did draw a comparison between the Tenishev school — "the most hothouse, the most boiled through Russian school" — and "Pushkin's Lyceum" (II: 375).

By the end of the 1890's Russia was ripe for an impending major radical reform in school education. In order to avoid being under the patronage of the highly conservative Ministry of Education, a group of pedagogues decided to establish a school under the label of a commercial school (which placed it under the jurisdiction of the Ministry of Finances). It was founded with the funding provided by Count Viacheslav Nikolaevich Tenishev.

At first the school was located in an apartment on Zagorodny Prospekt. Later a plot of land was purchased on Mokhovaya street, where in 1900, the architect R. Berzen, built the school facilities — "the most luxurious of the time, with light classrooms, a large school yard for games, a greenhouse, a laboratory for chemistry and physics, and even two theater halls" (Rubakin: 12). The school also had its own small observatory and a pool with fish.

The Tenishev pedagogues considered the harmonious development of the individual as the cornerstone of their program, which was furthered by the overall liberal atmosphere. "There was no punishment, smoking was allowed in the higher classes, however, because it was allowed, hardly anyone smoked" (Kreps: 10). In the Tenishev School there were no grade journals or conduct sheets, the attendance of parents during class was encouraged, attempts were made to approach each child individually. In the school's report for 1901, it was noted that "according to Hippocrates' tempers (physiological temperament), the school children can be categorized as follows:

1) Sanguines	12 people	or 21.43%
2) Cholerics	14 people	or 25%
3) Melancholics	14 people	or 25%
4) and Phlegmatics	16 people	or 28.57%".

We do not have sufficient information to determine into which category Mandelstam fit.

There were many excursions: to the Putilov factory, the Mining Institute, the Botanical Gardens, Lake Seliger and Iversky Monastery, the White Sea, Crimea, and Finland (it is known for certain that Mandelstam took part in one of these excursions, to Great Novgorod).

One can judge about how fondly graduates of the Tenishev School remember their school by the memoirs of A. Rubakin, who was two years ahead of Osip Mandelstam: "I still think about how much this school did for me with great gratitude. Such great pedagogues taught there, such as the artist N.K. Pedenko, V.N. Nikonov, V.A. Gerd, V.V. Gippius, the historians A.Ia. Zaks, I.M. Grevs, the navy officer, mathematician, and students' terror N. Briger, the economist M.I. Tugan-Baranovsky, the physicists Sazonov, A. Dobiash, the geographer E.F. Lesgaft and many others" (Rubakin: 12).

As far as we can surmise from Mandelstam's "Noise of Time," it was difficult for Osip to find a common language with his schoolmates. Granted, Nadezhda Iakovlevna Mandelstam wrote that based on what one of them (V. Zhirmunsky) said, "at the Tenishev school Mandelstam was treated gently and attentively" (NM-2: 32). However, another graduate of the Tenishev school (A. Rubakin) writes that "Osip was a bit of a coward, for which he was famous" and he recalls a not very flattering nickname given to Mandelstam at the school — Proud llama (Rubakin: 13).

"Mandelstam was a smart and capable boy, but at the same time overambitious," the bible teacher, Father Dmitry Gidaspov wrote in one of his reports about the first class students of the school year of 1899/1900 (Mets 2005: 14). "A very capable and unusually diligent boy, truthful, highly impressionable and easy to take offense," were the basic traits of the third-grader Mandelstam's personality according to the Tenishev teacher of geography (Mets 2005: 15).

Why did Mandelstam not feel at ease in Tenishev? Like Vladimir Nabokov, who graduated from Tenishev a few years after Mandelstam, he felt lonely there. But, unlike Nabokov, being a "raznochinets," he had to bear his solitude among his classmates not with ostentatious pride, but with a sense of customary and joyless doom.

Upon graduating from the school, Mandelstam was facing a dilemma. One possibility for him was to become politically active. This way out of his solitude would have resulted in finding like-minded people in the joint task of creating a better future for all mankind, without the threat of losing one's own individuality. The second way out was to write poetry and engage in creative writing. This would have resulted in getting reliable allies and like-minded people with a focus on the past and a reliance on a centuries-old literary tradition: as Mandelstam later put it, "not a single poet was without family or tribe, everyone arrived from afar and had a long way to go" (II: 239).

3.

Mandelstam's first efforts in poetry were colored by as distinct personal influence, as his early interest in politics. The young Mandelstam was initiated into poetry by Vladimir Vasil'evich Gippius, who had taught Russian literature at Tenishev since 1904. Mandelstam was introduced to politics by his classmate Boris Sinani, with whose family the poet became close in the fall of 1906.

Vladimir Gippius was of the same old German family as the poetess, Zinaida Gippius. The decadent Aleksandr Dobrolyubov was one of his classmates and best friends at the sixth St. Petersburg gymnasium. Together with Dobrolyubov and Ivan Konevskoi — "the belligerent young monks of early Symbolism" (II: 388), Gippius was a founder of the decadent movement in Russia. Decades later he would remember: "In religion I became an atheist, aesthetics ruled over religiosity. When it came to politics, I was totally indifferent. Morality was negated in everything, without any compromise" (Lavrov: 565). With some adjustments, these words surprisingly echo the self-characteristics given by the young Osip Mandelstam in a letter to Gippius dated 19 April 1908: "I have no definite feelings toward society, God, and mankind, and that makes me love life, faith, and love all the greater" (IV: 11). One can only surmise what feelings Gippius would have reading these lines, since by the middle of the 1890's he was already feeling like a "repentant decadent." According to his biographer, Gippius saw his teaching at the gymnasium as a "unique experiment in overcoming decadence" (Lavrov: 565).

In the same letter to Gippius, Mandelstam writes with an amazing honesty about his feelings toward his mentor: "For the longest time I have felt especially drawn to you, at the same time I also felt a special distance separating me from you [...] Pardon my being so daring for saying that for me you were what some would call 'friend-enemy'" (IV: 11-12).

In "The Noise of Time" Mandelstam thus mentioned Gippius: "The power of V.V.'s evaluations are still with me now. The great journey taken with him along the patriarchy of Russian literature, from Novikov and Radishchev to Konevets of the early Symbolism remains the only such journey. Later I only *reread* (II: 391). This admission of Mandelstam's makes one treat Gippius' literary tastes more carefully, especially concerning his contemporary literature. In "The Noise of Time" it was mentioned that Gippius was "poisoned by Sologub," "stung by Briusov" and even "in his sleep" he remembered "Sluchevsky's wild poem, 'Execution in Geneva'" (IV: 388). Gippius himself noted in his memoirs of his own personal and aesthetic closeness with the Merezhkovskys. He was aloof to the younger generation of Russian modernists and "not at all excited" about the early Blok ("I did recognize Blok later — in 1908 — as a great poet," he would remember with regret (Lindeberg: 254).

Traces of a determining influence both in the values and tastes of his teacher easily can be found in Mandelstam's verse of 1908-1911.

1910-s

However, that Mandelstam poem, which was first published under the characteristic pseudonym, "Fitil'" [wick] in the first issue of the Tenishev School journal, "Probuzhdennaia Mysl'" [Awoken thought] for 1907, is a typical example of the revolutionary-*narodnik* lyrics of the end of the 19th century in the style of that epoch's idol, Semen Nadson. Such revolutionary political moods were inspired in Osip by his classmate, Boris Sinani, one of the few people whom Mandelstam loved whole-heartedly and unconditionally. "He volunteered to be my teacher," Mandelstam recollected in "The Noise of Time," "and I did not leave him for as long as he was alive, I followed him, in awe of the clarity of his reasoning, his good cheer and presence of spirit"(II: 377).

Through Boris Sinani's family Mandelstam was introduced to the Socialist Revolutionary party circles. Boris' father was a famous psychiatrist and "counselor and confidant of Socialist Revolutionary leaders" ("The Noise of Time," II: 378). "In his personal relations with people, this materialist was totally altruistic. As to ethical issues, in his day-to-day existence they served as nothing more or less than abstract principles," wrote his biographer. "He would despise and make fun of any kind of metaphysics, the mystical, the religious, attributing all of that to either base fear or else even some kind of sick condition of the soul" (Sinani: 184).

Mandelstam became selflessly engrossed in activities that were totally novel for him. Together with Boris Sinani he joined the Socialist Revolutionary youth organization and in 1907 engaged, according to his testimony in the 1934 NKVD investigation, in propaganda at workers' meetings" (Polianovsky: 88). The intense enthusiasm for politics got in the way of Mandelstam's studies. On 18 November 1906 the behavior of the two friends along with that of other classmates was the subject of discussion during one of the meetings of the pedagogical committee of the Tenishev School. Here are some excerpts from the protocol: "[A Ia.] Ostrogorsky : [...] They come to class whenever they feel like it, it may be the second or third lesson, moreover they enter class while it is already in session, without paying any attention to the teacher, often leaving during the last lesson, again, whenever they feel like it." The instructors voiced concern that Mandelstam will not be able to take his final exams and graduate in time. (Mets 2005: 47-48).

On 15 May 1907, Mandelstam nevertheless received his graduation certificate from the Tenishev School. Mandelstam's passion for revolutionary activities peaked in September 1907, when, together with Boris Sinani he travelled to Raivola, in Finland, where they attempted to join the terrorist group of socialist revolutionaries. However, the recent graduates of the Tenishev School were not accepted because they were minors.

By the end of September, Mandelstam's parents, weary of their son's increasingly radical attitudes, decided to send Osip to study in Paris, at the Sorbonne. It was here that the final episode of Mandelstam's revolutionary odyssey culminated, as humorously described in the memoirs of his then friend, Mikhail Karpovich: "In Paris, the summer of 1908, the founder of the terrorist group, Grigory Gershuni, died, and the SR's organized a meeting in his honor. Mandelstam was anxious to go there with me [...] The main speaker of the meeting was B.V. Savinkov. As soon as he began to speak, Mandelstam roused himself, left his seat, and spent the entire speech standing in the aisles. He listened to it in a kind of trance, with half-opened mouth and half-closed eyes, his body thrown back in such a way, that I was afraid he might fall. I must admit that it looked quite funny. I remember how A.O. Fondaminskaia and L.S. Gavronskaia, who were sitting on the opposite side of the aisle, despite the seriousness of the moment could barely keep themselves from laughing when looking at Mandelstam" (Karpovich: 41).

4.

On 3 October 1907, not having yet arrived in France, Mandelstam sent his parents a calming letter: "While en route I feel myself quite well [...] The weather has cleared up, and my head is also almost free from thoughts [presumably — radical revolutionary ones]" (IV: 9).

Having pushed politics aside, poetry had now most definitely moved to the forefront of his life. He was beginning to turn toward modernism and became very interested in Baudelaire and especially Verlaine (PSE: 176).

On 14 September 1907, during the graduation ceremony at the Tenishev School, Mandelstam recited his poem "The Chariot" (it has not been preserved), which the school magazine called "not only the best of what had been written in the school, but in today's literature in general" (Tenishevets: 30).

Having found himself in Paris, free from the care of his parents and teachers for the first time, Mandelstam dedicated himself fully to the "poetic passion" that had taken him over (IV: 10). He moved to the Latin Quarter, across the street from the Sorbonne and enrolled in the literature faculty, but was not very diligent about attending lectures.

Some details from his Parisian life can be found in the memoirs of Mikhail Karpovich, who had first met with the young poet on

24 December 1907, during Christmas Eve celebrations: "…we would engage in discussion either sitting in a café or wandering along Parisian streets. Sometimes we would go to concerts, exhibits, or lectures [...] I remember how he would declaim ecstatically Briusov's 'Approaching Huns.' But he would just as ecstatically recite the lyrical poems of Verlaine, and had even written his own variation of Gaspard Hauser. Once we were with him at a symphonic concert of Richard Strauss' works conducted by the composer himself. We were both, I swear, so astonished by 'Salome's Dance', that Mandelstam immediately wrote his poem about Salome" (Karpovich: 41).

More specific and supplementary details to Karpovich's memoirs concerning Mandelstam's literary tastes of the Parisian period can be found in the already cited letter from Mandelstam to V.V. Gippius dated 14 (27) April 1908. Here mention is made of Lev Tolstoy, Hauptmann, Rozanov, Rodenbach, Sologub, Verlaine, Knut Hamsun, and Valery Briusov. In the latter, Mandelstam "was captivated by the ingenious audacity of negation, pure negation" (IV: 12), which can be seen as presaging Mandelstam's own verse lines written in 1909: "There is nothing to talk about, // There is nothing to learn, // Since, if there is no meaning to life, // Then there is no reason to speak of it." Incidentally, many years later, he would sharply castigate Briusov's "pure negation": "This miserable 'nothingness' will never be repeated in Russian poetry" (I: 230).

As for most young poets of his generation, reading Briusov's writings became a major event in Mandelstam's literary biography. He would even read his favorite Verlaine through the prism of Briusov. When, in 1908, Mandelstam began one of his most important poems with the following lines:

Tell me — in the ease of creative colloquy
Who could have skillfully combined
The rigor of Tiutchev with the playfullness of Verlaine
While imparting his own traits to this fusion?

most likely he was evoking the following lines from Briusov's poem, "Betrayal" (1895):

Oh my dear world: here are Baudelaire, Verlaine,
Here is Tiutchev, — my favorite, faithful books!

In May 1908, Mandelstam returned home from Paris. That summer he spent travelling with his parents in Europe, together they went to France and Switzerland, and at the end of July he would go on his own to Italy.

By the end of the summer, Mandelstam returned to the Russian capital with the firm intention of becoming a student of the St. Petersburg University. Yet Tzar Nicholas II's confirmation of the resolution of the Cabinet of Ministers concerning limiting the number of Jewish students to three percent at Russia's universities rendered such aspirations totally futile.

A few months later, in April 1909, Mandelstam started attending Viacheslav Ivanov's lectures on poetics that Ivanov held for younger poets at his apartment in St. Petersburg (25 Tavricheskaia Street). The apartment had solemnly been dubbed "the tower," and the events themselves just as solemnly, "Pro-Academy." Viacheslav Ivanov's lectures were attended by some 30 people, some regularly, some less so. Among them were Aleksei N. Tolstoy, Elizaveta Dmitrieva (Cherubina de Gabriak), the sisters Adelaida and Evgeniia Gertsyk, as well as Nikolai Gumilev, who was going through the process of freeing himself from Briusov's overwhelming influence. In this circle, at first no one paid much attention to Mandelstam. The transcripts of the lectures did not contain his comments, nor usually even his name. "Mandelstam," was erroneously listed three times out of four as "Mendelson" (Gasparov 1994: 90). Only at the eighth, final session of the "Pro-Academy," which took place on 16 May 1909, "at the end of the lecture and questions from the auditorium and [Ivanov's] answers it was proposed that Mandelstam "read his poems." It was Viacheslav Ivanov who facilitated the publication of the first, fully representative collection of Mandelstam's poems on the pages of the elite St. Petersburg journal, "Apollon."

The younger poet approached the older with respect and love. "Ivanov, in his attire full of old words is like some magnificent

Assyrian king. He is all beauty. It seems to me that if there had not been Ivanov, there would be a great gaping hole in Russian literature." That is how the great Symbolist poet was characterized by Mandelstam as recollected by V.F. Botsianovsky (Timenchik 1988: 187). Even more striking are the direct and indirect declarations of love that are scattered all throughout Mandelstam's letters to Ivanov: "Your seeds have deeply settled in my soul, and I fear as I see the huge shoots" (IV: 13); "...I am ready to travel great distances, if necessary, in order to see you" (IV: 15); "I cannot refrain from sharing with you my lyrical quests and accomplishments. Since I owe everything to you concerning the former, the latter belong to you by right, though it may even have never occurred to you" (IV: 17).

In Viacheslav Ivanov's poetry one can indeed find lines that greatly foretell the young Mandelstam. But perhaps it is more important that for Mandelstam to get Viacheslav Ivanov's blessing, meant, in addition to everything else, becoming a part of Symbolism — the most important and influential modernist poetical school of the early XXth century. Having gotten established in the beginning of the 1890's, Russian Symbolism "consciously aimed to renew poetical means in order to express a renewed perception of the world — a change of great historical epochs [...] Social and civic ideas of previous generations were replaced by the metaphysical themes of Life, Death, and God" (Gasparov 1993: 9-10). The new themes required new artistic means, the main one being the symbol.

In the summer of 1909, when the young poet was living at the datcha in Tsarskoe Selo with his parents, he paid a visit to the poetical antipode of Viacheslav Ivanov, the excellent poet and translator, Innokenty Annensky. "The latter greeted him in a friendly and attentive manner and recommended for him to engage in translation, in order to acquire skills" (NM-2: 88). As some other future Acmeists (Akhmatova, Gumilev, Mikhail Zenkevich) Mandelstam was very much influenced by Annensky. From the author of "The Cypress Chest" might have come his predilection for the ephemeral, short-lived natural and manmade objects. Mandelstam's "toy wolves," "quickliving dragon flies," and "wall of fragile shell" organically fit the list of motifs that originated with Annensky's dandelions, butterflies, and air bubbles. On 3 December 1911, Mandelstam gave a moving speech in memory of Annensky. It is very significant that throughout the rest of his life Mandelstam would never part with the poem "St. Petersburg," by Annensky, which he tore out of the journal, "Apollon," that had just published it.

The first time Mandelstam visited the editorial board of the journal, "Apollon," was at the end of spring or early summer of 1909. According to Sergei Makovsky's memoirs, this visit was almost like a scene out of a Chekhovian vaudeville. A "mama and her boy," "an average young man of about seventeen years of age," pay a visit to the editor who is "bent over manuscripts and proofs." The young man was "clearly timid and clung to his mama as if a child, almost holding her 'by the hand.'" Next the mama bursts into this monologue right out of a vaudeville: "My boy. It is on account of him we are here. We need to know, finally, what to do about him. We are engaged in a trade, we are leather merchants. While he's all about poems and poems! At his age it is high time to be helping one's parents. [...] And so, mister editor, — we are simple folk, not rich, — do us a favor and tell it to us straight: is he talented or not? It will be as you say..." And the heightened finale of the scene: "...I was ready to get rid of the mother and son with the help of a polite formula of an editor's indefinite encouragement, but then I looked up at the young man again, and I saw in his eyes such intense supplication full of suffering that I immediately gave in and took his side: for poetry and against trade in leather.

I said convincingly, even somewhat solemnly:

—Yes, ma'am, your son has talent" (Makovsky 1995: 44-45).

This account of Makovsky's about the "incident" at the "Apollon," as Nadezhda Iakovlevna recalled, "reached us while Mandelstam was alive and he was greatly indignant about it" (NM-2: 34). What was the primary cause of his indignation? The direct speech attributed by Makovsky to his mother, and her description as "a no longer young, fairly plump woman" with "a pale worried face," in which one could barely recognize the real traits of Flora Osipovna. One should not forget that by the time Mandelstam had paid his first visit to the "Apollon," he had already been well received at Viacheslav Ivanov's "tower," and thus Makovsky's belated attempts to present Mandelstam as having just arrived, so to speak, "from the street," and himself as some kind of astute finder of new talent are just not justified.

Around the same time Mandelstam made the acquaintance of Fedor Sologub, who proved to be well disposed toward the beginner poet. The same could not be said of the Merezhkovsky couple. "Zinaida Gippius came out to him and declared that if he will begin to write good poetry, it will become known to her, and then she will talk to him, thus in the meantime there is no need for their meeting" That is how Mandelstam's first talk with Gippius is described in Nadezhda Iakovlevna's memoirs (NM-2: 33). "Someone sent over to me such a young poet, small, dark, stooping, and so timid and bashful that one could barely hear what he was reading and his hands were wet and cold. We had never heard anything about him before, and how he came to see us, I don't remember (maybe he came on his own), I don't have much faith in young poets, his poems were far from being perfect, but at the same time, without a doubt, it did seem to me that they were not typical among the usual dozens of poems one encountered every day." That is how Zinaida Gippius recalled her meeting with Mandelstam (Z. Gippius: 59). Perhaps her version was closer to reality than that of Mandelstam's wife, as can be ascertained from Mikhail Kuzmin's journal entry of 15 February 1909, where Mandelstam is mentioned as "Zinaida's little Yid" (Zinaidin zhidenok) (Kuzmin: 110). It turns out that Gippius not only approved of Mandelstam's poetry, but considered it necessary to share her favorable impressions with her fellow poets. However, Mandelstam was appaled by the patronizing condescension in Merezhkovskys' attitude toward him. In a letter to Maximilian Voloshin, sent at the end of September 1909, he resentfully mentions that when he was "passing through Heidelberg," Dmitry Merezhkovsky "did not want to hear a single line" by him. (IV: 16) In that same letter Mandelstam declares: "Removed from the Russian language milieu more than ever before, I am forced to establish a clear judgment about myself. Those who refuse to give me attention only help me in this" (IV: 16).

"The Symbolists never accepted him," categorically contended Anna Akhmatova in her recollections about Mandelstam (Akhmatova 1989a: 127).

5.

In the German city of Heidelberg resides one of the most famous European universities that at that time "was a kind of Mecca that drew [...] young Russian students" (Nerler 1994a: 13). Mandelstam arrived there in late September—early October of 1909. On 12 November he filed a request for being accepted as a student of the Germanic-Romance department of the Philosophy Faculty and spent two semesters studying Old French with Neumann. Just as in Paris, Mandelstam, however, did not display much zeal toward his studies. His main activity in Heidelberg was writing poetry. From these poems as well as from those written somewhat earlier, one can gather what kind of mood predominated for the fledgling poet.

The most frequent motifs of Mandelstam's poems of 1909 were those of timidity, distrustfulness, fragility, and silence. Following in the steps of Verlaine and Annensky, the early Mandelstam aimed to write "about the sweet and trifling": his "hand" is "hesitant," "his inspirations"—"frightening," and "not much" is capable of inspiring him. The present day and the moment in the poems of that period are preferable to metaphysical eternity. "Do not speak to me of eternity—// It's too big for me," Mandelstam would admit. Already his first poems show his originality both as a person and as a poet. Developing Hans-Christian Andersen's image of transparent eternity made warm by man's breath, Mandelstam wrote in the poem: "I have a body—what should I do with it..." (1909):

My breathing, my warmth has
Already fallen upon eternity's glass.

It was about this very poem that Georgy Ivanov had written most enthusiastically in his memoirs: "I read it as well as a few other 'swaying', foggy poems written by someone not familiar to me, and I got a jolt in my heart: 'Why was this not written by me?'" (G. Ivanov 1994: 88).

The poems written by Mandelstam that had impressed Georgy Ivanov so much were included in the already mentioned debuting selection of his poems published in the ninth issue (July-August) of the journal "Apollon" in 1910. This selection drew many a reader's attention. "Already in my father's library," recollected Leonid Andreev's son, Vadim, "in one of the issues of the journal "Apollon," I read the poem, "I have a body — what should I do with it..." which amazed me with the very unusual turn of the phrase 'I have a body' ('I have a body' was later replaced by 'a body is given to me') and the startling rhythm like a dead surge from which one could not undo oneself: against one's will separate lines would emerge in one's consciousness as though flowers in a thick grass" (Andreev: 141).

Mandelstam was living at the time in Zellendorf, a suburb of Berlin. He returned from Germany to St. Petersburg in the middle of October 1910. On the border with Eastern Prussia Mandelstam was detained due to a lapsed passport. From Dvinsk he travelled without a ticket in the conductor's compartment as he had lost his wallet with his railroad ticket. It is not without cause that Mandelstam's teacher of arithmetic in Tenishev noted in his review about the boy: "his weak side is his absentmindedness" (Mets 2005: 14).

Mandelstam never had the opportunity to travel abroad again.

In 1910, Boris Sinani the younger died from tuberculosis. "As he was dying, Boris was delirious and dreamt of Finland, moving to Raivola, and some kind of rope for packing baggage. Here we played *gorodki* [skittles] and lying in Finnish meadows, he liked to look at the plain sky with the cold startled eyes of Prince Andrei [from Lev Tolstoy's "War and Peace"] (IV: 383). In Mandelstam's poem, "The sail strains its attentive ear..." (1910), which most likely was influenced by the death of Boris Sinani, the looking at the "plain sky," is transferred to the lyrical hero — the poet himself (suffering from poor health as a youth), — through the death of his friend once again being reminded of how fragile and short one's life is:

In 1910, Mandelstam spent March through July in the Finnish spa, Hangö (Hanko). Here, in July, he met a thirty-year-old teacher of mathematics, Sergei Kablukov, who was also an expert in choral music and the secretary of the St. Petersburg Religious-Philosophical Society. Mandelstam would occasionally attend the Society's meetings.

Kablukov, a man of great integrity, was selflessly dedicated to poetry and poets. A good friend of the Merezhkovskys and Viacheslav Ivanov, after the death of Boris Sinani he became a close friend and mentor to Mandelstam. The closer Kablukov got to know Mandelstam, the more attached he became to him, but at the same time, the more strict he was with him. According to N.Ia. Mandelstam, Osip "would inarticulately explain to me that when one is young one needs to have someone older near by. I don't know by how much Kablukov was older, but in any case Mandelstam's father was still alive, and he could not openly admit that he was missing a father" (NM-2: 33). One should cite here an equally significant entry from Kablukov's journal dated 2 October 1911: "I. Mandelstam visited me and I spoke with him about contemporary literature and his personal behavior, which so far expresses itself in idleness and ridiculous wastefulness. I argued that the most important thing was for him to study, i.e. consistently attend lectures at the University" (Kablukov: 245). In this journal entry, where Kablukov describes their first meeting with Mandelstam, one can discern the intonation of the solicitous guardian, which might have irritated Mandelstam slightly. However, Mandelstam continued to gratefully accept Kablukov's guidance well up to the 1917 October revolution.

"He is clearly a gifted and intelligent person, but not educated enough and quite negligent, as well as flippant in relation to the concerns of the "restless world," that is how Kablukov characterized Mandelstam in his diary. "In Hanko I spoke with him daily about poetry, and this carefree attitude of his made me extremely critical of him, which I did not seek to conceal. Nevertheless I came to love him for his sensitivity and refinement of emotional experience and I fully agreed with certain of his opinions about Annensky and Mallarmé, as well as about great poets, about Balmont being a "poet for the masses," the new Nadson, about the significance of Baratynsky and Del'vig" (Kablukov: 241).

At the end of October 1910, Kablukov asked Zinaida Gippius to "take note" of Mandelstam's poetry and to write him "a recommendation to the 'Russkaia Mysl', i.e. to Briusov" (Kablukov: 242). On 26 October, Gippius sent Briusov a letter in which Mandelstam and his poetry were "recommended" in the following way: "A certain neurasthenic Yid, who just a few years ago was still singing loony tunes, but lately has developed significantly, and has quite a few good lines. He came to see me with the request that I recommend his poems to you. I did not let him in [...], and asked him to leave his poems. After reading them I find that they can be recommended to your attention. What you plan to do with them further does not concern me, and it is entirely up to you" (Mandelstam 1990: 359). Briusov was unimpressed by Mandelstam's poems, and they were not published in "Russkaia Mysl.'" Incidentally, seven years later, Zinaida Gippius did include Mandelstam's poems in her anthology, "Eighty eight contemporary poems selected by Z.N. Gippius."

Apparently it was in 1910 that Mandelstam grew particularly fond of Blok's poetry. This somewhat belated enthusiasm parallels the late recognition of Blok's genius by Mandelstam's teacher, Vladimir Gippius. Mandelstam's new found enthusiasm is reflected in his poems of 1910. The personal meetings between the two poets took place in 1911 and were not especially warm on Blok's part. To him Mandelstam appeared to be a mere epigone of Symbolism, albeit an epigone of "the highest sort" (Blok and Bely. Correspondence: 406).

And here is another Mandelstam meeting in 1911 which laid the foundation of a friendship that lasted all of his life. On 14 March, in the Viacheslav Ivanov "tower," Mandelstam was introduced to Gumilev's wife, the young poetess, Anna Akhmatova. "At that time he was quite a thin young man with a lily of the valley in his buttonhole, with his head highly thrown back, glowing eyes, and eyelashes across half his cheek," later reminisced Akhmatova. "The second time I saw him at the Tolstoys on Staro-Nevsky, he did not recognize me, and when Aleksei

Nikolaevich <Tolstoy> began to ask him what was Gumilev's wife like, he showed with his hands what kind of huge hat I had on. I was afraid that something irrevocable would occur, and so I identified myself" (Akhmatova 1989a: 123).

Mandelstam had not befriended Akhmatova and Gumilev right away. He was somewhat wary of the bohemian literary circles. In his journal entry of 6 April 1911 Kablukov noted: "This evening Ios[if] Em[il'evich] Mand[elstam] informed me that "Apollon"'s poetry section has been placed under the sole authority of N. Gumilev, who recently returned from Abyssinia. That has already resulted in the following: Mandelstam's poems scheduled for publication in the April issue of "Apollon" have been, all but one poem, postponed for publication in the May issue, whereas the April issue is going to publish Gumilev's wife's poems < … > , even though they are technically unsophisticated and weak. M[andelstam] notes Gumilev's extreme rudeness and considers taking his poems back and returning the advance […] I had predicted that they would quarrel. This prediction came through quicker than I had expected" (Kablukov: 244-245).

However, in this case Kablukov did not predict accurately. Within just a few months, Gumilev and Akhmatova became Mandelstam's closest friends and literary companions. "Anna Andreevna was not very talkative and would become animated, in essence, only when Mandelstam would read his poetry," noted Georgy Adamovich in his memoirs. "Mandelstam was in awe of her: not only her poems, but herself, her personality, her looks" (Adamovich 1989: 51). "I would frequently witness the discussions between Mandelstam and Akhmatova," Nikolai Punin reminisces, "it was a remarkable conversation that made me both rapturous and envious; they could speak for hours, even though nothing remarkable might have been said, but it was a genuinely poetical dialogue of such intensity that was absolutely inaccessible to me" (Parnis 1991: 28).

The "choleric" Mandelstam and "phlegmatic" Akhmatova complemented each other in the eyes of those who surrounded them. "Around 1930, Anna Akhmatova visited my studio together with the poet, Osip Mandelstam, and his wife Nadia," recollected Aleksandr Tyshler.

"They would look at things completely differently. Anna Andreevna internalized all that she saw with an inherent silence whereas Mandelstam would run around, jump, and break the silence" (Tyshler: 401).

In his book of memoirs, Georgy Ivanov had the following to say about Mandelstam's friendship with Gumilev: "In the pre-revolutionary period he was more influenced by Gumilev than by anyone else. Their literary relations (their day-to-day friendship was not darkened by anything) could be described as love-hate. "I struggle with him as Jacob struggled with God," Mandelstam used to say" (G. Ivanov 1994: 618).

6.

On 14 May 1911, in Vyborg, Osip Mandelstam was baptized at a Methodist Episcopal church by the pastor N.I. Rozen. Getting baptized was a prerequisite for a Jew aspiring to enter a Russian university. On 10 September 1911, he became a student of the Imperial Saint-Petersburg University, at the department of Romance languages of the Historical-Philosophical Faculty. In his memoirs, Evgeny Mandelstam testifies: "...in order to enter the university it was necessary to overcome an obstacle: the grades in his high school certificate were rather mediocre. He did not bother much about his grades, and because there was a quota for Jews, this practically ruined his chances to get accepted in a university. Thus he had to consider getting baptized, which would remove all the limitations, as in Tsarist Russia Jews were subject to persecution primarily as practitioners of a different faith. Our mother was not particularly bothered by the conversion, however for our father, Osip's baptism was a major blow. The procedure for changing one's faith was simple, it merely involved getting one's documents changed and paying a small fee" (E. Mandelstam: 136).

There are, however, two factors that complicate the explanation of the motives that were behind Mandelstam's baptism. First, the theme of Christ surfaces in the poems he wrote well before this, in the years 1908-1911, as well as in his half-admissions strewed about in letters of that period (to Vladimir Gippius and Viacheslav Ivanov). Second,

Osip's preference for the Protestant rather than the more common Orthodox or Catholic church. On the other hand, in the spring of 1911 his decision to become a student at the St. Petersburg University, as opposed to his decision to get baptized, had not fully ripened yet. On 16 May, just two days after his baptism, in conversation with Mikhail Kuzmin, he mentioned his intention to "depart for Rio de Janeiro in a merchant vessel" (Kuzmin: 283). Keen on observing himself with his mystical experiences, Mandelstam enthusiastically indulged himself in his youthful letter to Vladimir Gippius: "Having been raised in a non-religious environment (family and school), I have for a long time longed for religion, both hopelessly and platonically, but at the same time more and more consciously. My first religious experiences occurred at the same time when, as a child, I had a passion for Marxism, and the one was inseparable from the other" (IV: 12).

In Mandelstam's earlier poetry, Christian motifs, as a rule, emerge framed by the uncharacteristic for him motifs of exaltation and personal guilt. Symptomatically, Mandelstam appeared to be as much attracted by Christianity in all its various manifestations as he was wary of entering Christian life too deeply.

But already in 1910 Mandelstam unequivocally, though not yet fully coherently, speaks of God in his poetry as his main "interlocutor" ("The heart is enveloped as if in a cloud"), Sergei Averintsev noted that Mandelstam was baptized not just into Christian faith but also into "Christian culture" (this being Mandelstam's own term that he used in a letter to Vladimir Gippius): "If it was important for him to consider himself a Christian, though without attending any services, nor participating in any community or choosing between any such communities, neither Orthodoxy nor Catholicism, but only Protestantism could make this more or less legitimately possible for him [...] For someone like Mandelstam, who valued keeping a distance from all communities, this was a comfortable position" (Averintsev 1996: 225). Protestantism, the essence of which for the poet consisted in the formula "as modestly and properly as possible," reliably protected Mandelstam from that generous kind of religious exaltation that he imagined existed in Orthodox and even Catholic ceremonies.

CHAPTER ONE

7.

On 13 April 1911, Gumilev recited his new long poem, "The Prodigal Son," at a meeting of the Obshchestvo revnitelei khudozhestvennogo slova [Society of Adherents of the Artistic Word]. This new poem by Gumilev was harshly rebuffed by Viacheslav Ivanov. Journals reported that the maître of Symbolism had suggested to his ex-pupil that he ponder "how freely a poet can treat traditional themes" (Chudovsky: 321). Anna Akhmatova remembers that Ivanov attacked Gumilev "with almost obscene invective": "I remember how we were returning to Tsarskoe Selo totally crushed by what had happened, from then on Nikolai Stepanovich would always see Viacheslav Ivanov as an overt enemy" (Akhmatova 1989: 11).

By the fall of 1911, Gumilev and together with another previously favorite Ivanov's pupil who had now fallen away, Sergei Gorodetsky, founded a poetry circle consisting of young poets. This union was given the pointedly pedestrian title of Tsekh Poetov ("Guild of Poets.")

Gumilev and his colleagues met regularly, several times a month. They would sit in a circle and recite their poems, one after the other. Then the poems that were read would be discussed in the minutest detail. During such discussions Gumilev "demanded supplemental feedback," as he liked to say, i.e. not exclamations, superficial confirmations that something was good or bad, but substantial explanations as to why something was either better or worse than something else. Usually he spoke first, he would speak at great length and provide an extremely detailed analysis, which, for the most part, was completely accurate" (Adamovich 1989: 51).

The first session of the "Guild" took place on 20 October 1911. Mandelstam did not attend it, though by that time he had already returned to Petersburg from Finland, where he had been from March through September. Mandelstam's debut at the "Guild" took place a few weeks later, on 2 December 1911, after which he "already quickly" became "the first fiddle" of the "Guild" (Akhmatova 1989a: 126). What attracted him to the "Guild" was a chance to get an authoritative opinion about his poems. He also enjoyed the overall friendly atmosphere which reigned at the "Guild" sessions. This "Neurasthenic" (as he had been nicknamed by his own mother, Flora Mandelstam), who had not been accepted by any community, for once found a circle of people with whom he could be united as "we" (NM-2: 31). This helped build confidence in the young poet. Having unexpectedly run into him in November 1912 Mikhail Karpovich was struck by the change he observed in his friend: "I found Mandelstam's appearance to have greatly changed: he looked much more important, he had grown Pushkin-like side-whiskers and was already behaving like a mentor. He greeted me without much warmth, in any case there was no longer a trace of the previous effusiveness" (Karpovich: 42).

Returning to the year 1911, one should note that Mandelstam became close with another "Guild" member, the good poet, wonderful man, and great translator, Mikhail Lozinsky, as well as with the less pleasant Georgy Ivanov — at that time — an epigone of Mikhail Kuzmin, and a short time later — that of his older colleagues at the "Guild" (Akhmatova, Mandelstam). Ivanov flaunted his friendship with Mandelstam, "who, in his turn, would parade" in front of others his friendship with Georgy Ivanov, as noted by Riurik Ivnev in his memoirs. "Apparently the one and the other enjoyed "being the source of gossip." They would appear together everywhere" (Ivnev: 41). Osip's friendship with Georgy Ivanov would leave a mark in the poet's writing: one of Mandelstam's poems of 1913 ("We have gone crazy from our frivolous lives") not only contains a portrait of Ivanov but is also clearly stylized in the latter's stylistical manner.

Together with Mikhail Lozinsky and Georgy Ivanov, Mandelstam was actively involved in the composition of the "Guild"'s "Anthology of ancient follies," as well as in composing various kinds of humorous bouts-rimes and acrostics. "We would make each other laugh so hard that we would fall onto the sofa that sang with all of its springs in the "Tuchka" and roar with laughter to the point of fainting, like the girls at the confectioner's in Joyce's 'Ulysses'" (Akhmatova 1989a: 122-123). Nadezhda Iakovlevna comments, "Mandelstam's jokes are based on the absurd. These were a kind of domestic mischief and taunting ditty, only occasionally adressing political themes, and mostly directed at close friends" (NM-2: 133).

Some of the impromptu "Guild" pieces were composed in the Petersburg artistic cabaret, "Brodiachaia Sobaka," [Stray Dog] that opened on New Year's Eve of 1912. Mandelstam, Lozinsky, Georgy Ivanov, and other "Guild" members quickly became the habitués of "the Dog." It was there that Mandelstam entered into an argument with Velimir Khlebnikov on 27 November 1913, which almost resulted in a duel. The author of the "Incantation by Laughter" either expressed himself ambiguously in a poem or said something improper about the acquittal of Mendel Beilis in the famous Kiev trial. According to Nikolai Khardzhiev, going back to Mandelstam himself, "Filonov, Akhmatova, and other frequenters of the basement had objected to one of Khlebnikov's inaccurately stated opinions. Mandelstam was especially harsh in his criticism of Khlebnikov. Khlebnikov, in turn, was disdainful of Mandelstam's poetry. The final part of Khlebnikov's repartee shocked everyone present: "And now Mandelstam should be sent back to his uncle's in Riga…" (Khardzhiev: 334). Khardzhiev quotes Mandelstam's own commentary to Khlebnikov's remark: "— This was totally amazing, because two of my uncles did, in fact, live in Riga. Neither Khlebnikov nor anyone else for that matter had any way of knowing this. I did not correspond with my uncles. Khlebnikov must have guessed this out of the sheer strength of his hate" (Khardzhiev: 334).

In March of 1912, Nikolai Gumilev and Sergei Gorodetsky decided to introduce a new poetic movement to the literary world that has emerged to replace Symbolism — Acmeism, for which purpose the most representative "Guild" members were selected. Almost fifty years later, Anna Akhmatova, prompted by her literary secretary, poet Anatoly Naiman, returned to the question of Acmeism and Symbolism. "Once, to the point," recalls Naiman, "I mentioned that if one were to set aside the organizational motives and principles of the union, then the poetic platform, as well as the program, of the Symbolists was much more grandiose than that of the Acmeists, who became firmly established on the basis of their opposition to Symbolism. Akhmatova pronounced more faintly than ever, and thus more significantly: "Did you think that I did not realize that Symbolism was perhaps the greatest school in poetry?" Perhaps she even said "in art" (Naiman: 21). The most important thing in Akhmatova's assertion is the admission to the difference in scale between two such phenomena in the history of Russian literature, Symbolism on the one hand, and Acmeism (as well as Futurism) — on the other. In the first case, we have the "last greatest school in art," in the other — a small literary circle.

However, this does not, by any means, signify that either Mandelstam or Akhmatova were lesser poets than were Aleksandr Blok and Andrei Bely, or that Acmeism had played a lesser part in their fates than Symbolism had in the fates of either Bely or Blok. Their role was not lesser, but it was different. Incidentally, Mandelstam had agreed to become an Acmeist only in October of 1912, after giving it some thought (perhaps that is why he is the only one among the other six Acmeists who was not mentioned at all in the original Acmeist manifesto written by Gorodetsky). According to Lidiia Ginzburg: "Mandelstam continued to engage in Symbolist heresy even after the "Guild of Poets" had been formed. Only later did he give up. Gumilev would tell his students: one evening, when they were all seeing off Akhmatova to the Tsarskoselsky train station, Mandelstam, pointing at the illuminated dial plate of the clock shop, recited the poem:

No, not the moon, but an illuminated dial
Glares at me, and what am I guilty of
If I sense the milkiness of the faint stars?

And I find offensive Batiushkov's haughtiness;
"What time is it?" they asked him here,
And he replied with the odd response: "Eternity."

These lines were Mandelstam's literary repentance" (Ginzburg: 20-21).

The image of the "milkiness of the stars" in this poem requires some clarification. The older Acmeists, juxtaposing themselves to the Symbolists, hastened to proclaim the priority of the earthly over the heavenly, the domestic over the metaphysical. In Gumilev's version of the Acmeist manifesto written in 1912 and published together with Gorodetsky's version in the first 1913 issue of "Apollon," there is the following categorical comment on the spatial correlation of stars to man living on the dear to the Acmeists' Earth: "...the entire sacred meaning of stars has to do with their being infinitely far from earth, and no advances in aviation will ever bring them closer" (Gumilev: 19).

This statement made by Gumilev echoes the first stanza of the Gorodetsky poem, "Zvezda" [Star]:

I do not wish to read in the eternal
And obscure letters what is held
In the darkness and milky ribbons
By the starry sky.

Although the anti-Symbolist meaning of the quoted Gumilev and Gorodetsky lines in opposition to stars is apparent, the notion of these Acmeist leaders of the distance between the metaphysical stars and the earth is fully in accordance with the canon as set by the Symbolists. Both the Symbolists as well as Gumilev and Gorodetsky believed that the metaphysical stars are *infinitely far* from earthly man. However the Symbolists preferred to write about the metaphysical stars while Gumilev and Gorodetsky wrote about earthly man.

In Mandelstam's first Acmeist poem, "No, not the moon, but an illuminated dial..." everything is different. The poet does not refuse to "read" the infinitely distant "star writing" which holds the "sky" in the "milky ribbons;" just the opposite, he "senses" "the milkiness of the stars." They are, as it is said, "just a kiss away." And the "clock-dial" is preferable to the "moon" not primarily because the moon is a symbol while the clock-dial is a thing, but because the clock-dial is closer than the moon.

That is how the poet brought closer to the Earth the inaccessible metaphysical distance. In his understanding, the main thing about Acmeism is not the juxtaposition between the "starry" and the "earthly," but a "live balance" (a quote from Mandelstam) (I: 180) between the "starry" and the "earthly." In other words, in the poem,

"No, not the moon, but an illuminated dial..." the stars are at home, because the poet's metaphysics is at home as well, it has not been undone, but rather counterpoised through love of the Earth.

It thus becomes clear why in the first quatrain of the Mandelstam poem there appears the half apologizing: "...and what am I guilty of?" as the poet was explaining himself not to the Symbolists but rather to his companions-in-arms, Acmeists. One should, of course, agree with Evgeny Toddes, who claims that Mandelstam's "equilibrium was attained most likely within the boundaries of a given text, rather than was caused by the internal evolution of the poet" (Toddes: 32). And yet drawing on this life saving equilibrium provided Mandelstam with confidence in his own strength and helped him transform himself from a "refined Symbolist into a faithful Acmeist" (Vas. Gippius: 85). So faithful that it could not help but greatly irritate the modernists of the older generation. It is reported in the 21 January 1913 letter of Al. N. Chebotarevskaia to Viacheslav Ivanov: "Mandelstam has been walking around saying: 'From now on not a single line of Sologub, Briusov, Ivanov, or Blok will be published in the "Apollon" — it will soon become the journal of the Acmeists (this remains to be seen)" (LN: 410). The poet was too quick to announce that Sergei Makovsky's journal was about to become a mouthpiece of the Acmeists. Although Makovsky did authorize the publication of the manifestoes of the new literary school written by Gumilev and Gorodetsky in the "Apollon," the program article written by Mandelstam, "The Morning of Acmeism" was not published in this journal.

8.

"The Morning of Acmeism" is permeated with architectural imagery and metaphor. "Acmeism," writes Mandelstam, "is for those who, having been seized with the spirit of construction, do not cowardly refuse their weight, but happily accept it, in order to awaken and apply the architecturally sleeping forces within" (I: 178). The significant parallels between this fragment and Mandelstam's poem of 1912,

"Notre Dame," have already been noted by scholars. The source of the imagery in Mandelstam's "Notre Dame" lies in the introduction that Valery Briusov wrote to the book of poems by the "Guild" member, Nikolai Kliuev, "The Chiming of the Pines": "How beautiful are the gigantic, Gothic cathedrals, built over centuries according to a single, deeply thought out plan. Massive columns arose there where the artist's drafts intended, heavy stones piled up one on top of the other were arranged into light arches, all of which, in its entirety, to this day amazes us with the perfection, elegance, and proportionality of all its parts. But how beautiful is the wild forest, growing all over, along glades, slopes, and ravines. Nothing is foreseen or arranged ahead of time, every step one faces the unpredictable, either a fanciful stump, or a long fallen trunk covered with moss, or an accidental, small meadow, all of which has the power and the beauty of independent life" (Briusov: 376).

For both Mandelstam and Briusov, the "heavy stones" form "light arches." Each refers to an "unfathomable forest" juxtaposed with that which is constructed according to a "deeply thought out plan" of the architectural building. However, Mandelstam's forest emerges as a part of the overall architectural design. In nature, according to the optimistic concept of Mandelstam the Acmeist, nothing exists "randomly," everything is subordinate to a "secret plan" of the Architect-Creator. This made it possible for the poet to feel liberated from the frightening sense of chaos of life around him and to begin one of his poems with the lines where nature could be on a par with architecture:

Nature — is Rome, and mirrored there.
We see its grandeur, civic forms parade:
a sky-blue circus in the clear air,
fields a forum, trees a colonnade.

(1914) translated by A.S. Kline

Thus one should not be surprised that Mandelstam chose for his debut book of poems the "architectural" heading, "Stone," that replaced the initial, "natural" variant — "Seashell." The word "stone" and its contextual synonyms are found eleven times in Mandelstam's book.

The key to the understanding of the meaning of the heading can be found in the second quatrain of the fourteenth poem:

Become lace, stone,
And a spider web:
Pierce with a fine needle
The empty breast of the sky.

This stanza, which echoes one of the fragments of Proust's novel, "Swann's Way" ("...the bell tower...pierced the blue sky with its sharp steeple..." (Proust: 92)) and harks back to the line "On the needles of the lace tower" from the poem by Sergei Gorodetsky, "I have grown numb and do not dare..." (1906), reveals not only the architectural, constructive function of Mandelstam's "stone," but its "lace" and "decorative" foundation. N. Gumilev also noted the lace pattern of the composition in his review of Mandelstam's first poetry book (Gumilev: 131).

The poems of Mandelstam's first book are linked one to the other through key motifs, in the same way as filaments of wool are linked in knots, creating lace out of separate threads in the same way that Mandelstam's consciousness as a child did to the objects of his father's study: "While my father's home study did not bear any semblance to the granite heaven of my elegant outings [...], and the mixture of its furnishings, the choice of objects were all linked in my consciousness into a tightly knit combination" (II: 354-355).

"Stone" was published end of March 1913, and was only thirty pages in length. "This collection is too sparing even for a debut," noted Sergei Gorodetsky (Mandelstam 1991: 214), and this quality of being "sparing" can be explained first of all by the overall tendency that the post-Symbolists had of economy and compression. It is no wonder that the Acmeist Vladimir Narbut, whose book of poetry, "Hallelujah" (1912) consisted of even less poems than the first "Stone," disparagingly spoke of "two hefty volumes" of Viacheslav Ivanov's "Cor Ardens" (Narbut: 122). The Cubo-Futurist, Aleksei Kruchenykh, had the following to say about the Symbolists' collections: "I cannot stand endless productions and huge volumes — it is impossible to read them at one sitting and one cannot get from them a unified impression. Let the edition be small, but without lies; it's all one's own, belonging to the book, up to the last ink spot. The editions of Gryphon, Scorpio, Musagetes…large white pages…a grey stamp…making one want to wrap some herring in it…and a cold blood runs through these books."

One should also note Mandelstam's restrained financial circumstances. The first "Stone" was published at his own expense. Evgeny Mandelstam writes: "The publication of 'Stone' was a 'family' affair — the money for the publication of the book was provided by father. The circulation was a mere 600 copies. I remember the day when Osip took me with him to the typography on Mokhovaya and we received the freshly printed publications. He took one pack and I the other. Our common objective was getting the books circulated, as in St. Petersburg the booksellers did not buy poetry books, they only sold them on commission. After giving it much thought, we submitted the whole edition under commission to the large bookstore, Popov-Iasnyi, on the corner of Nevsky and Fontanka, where now there is a pharmacy.

From time to time my brother would send me over to find out how many copies had been sold, and when I informed him that 42 had already been sold, it was cause for great celebration at home. On the scale of the times in the conditions of the book market, such sales were the first acknowledgement of the poet by his readers" (E. Mandelstam: 136).

Chapter Two

BETWEEN "STONE" (1913) AND "TRISTIA" (1922)

1.

There were five reviews published of Mandelstam's "Stone" (1913), all of them favorable. Nikolai Gumilev reviewed the first section of the book as follows: "In these poems though one finds the weariness, pessimism, and disappointment typical of all young poets, for whom they merely give rise to useless efforts of the pen, in O. Mandelstam they become crystallized into a poetical idea-image: into Music with a big M" (Gumilev: 217). "O. Mandelstam Has Given Up on His Fancy for Symbolism Forever" (Gumilev: 217). Such was the conclusion and prognosis drawn by the head of the "Guild of Poets" at the end of his review.

However, this prognosis proved to be rash: in the middle of 1913, Mandelstam attempted to not only "give up" on his fancy for Symbolism, but for Acmeism as well. By this time, an alliance between Mikhail Zenkevich, Vladimir Narbut and Mandelstam with the Cubo-Futurists from the group, "Hylaea" (V. Khlebnikov, V. Maiakovsky, A. Kruchenykh, B. Livshits, and the Burliuk brothers) was about to take shape. Mandelstam became so close with Benedikt Livshits that Livshits even called the Acmeist poet his "comrade-in-arms" in his memoirs (Livshits: 516). Mikhail Zenkevich recalled: "The Futurists agreed to include me, Narbut, and Mandelstam. They agreed to form an alliance. At the time the go-between was the brother of [David] Burliuk—Nikolai Burliuk, [a member of the "Guild of Poets"] and it was here [at the K.I. Chukovsky lecture on Futurism in November 1913] that they had the first joint performance. Mandelstam presented theory and not just poetry, he was also involved in the preparation of this evening. He came to me and said: 'I was there...' That is, what he said: 'I saw them. They are so bohemian, you know. We will go to the performance...I have rewritten my talk for it' [...] They went to Chukovsky's lecture...Then Maiakovsky gave a talk, and so did Mandelstam" (these oral recollections of Zenkevich are quoted in: Lekmanov 2000: 569).

In the end, however, the alliance between the three Acmeist apostates with the Cubo-Futurists never materialized. Perhaps it was because the Acmeists themselves were too different as poets. When Zenkevich proposed in a letter to Narbut to publish together with Mandelstam a collection of poetry of the three, the former replied: "Concerning publishing a collection—I totally agree, but we need two, yours and mine. We can do this together (it would be good to include the poems of some recently joined Cubist). Mandelstam is not exactly the poet of choice for this. Better Maiakovsky or Kruchenykh, or someone else rather than the refined (such as Mandel is, in essence) aesthete" (Narbut Letters). Georgy Ivanov recalls how Mandelstam was talked out of joining the Hylaea group by Benedikt Livshits, himself a Cubo-Futurist (G. Ivanov 1994: 619).

In his memoir book, "The One-and-a-Half-Eyed Archer," Livshits portrayed Mandelstam in the St. Petersburg circle of modernist poets. He described the salon of a "woman of unusual beauty," the artist, Anna Mikhailovna Zel'manova-Chudovskaia, "where the author of the thin, green "Stone," with his thinly growing side-whiskers—a tribute to the fashion of 1830s—the fashion he liked because of his obessession with Chaadaev, proposed to "discuss ancient Rome" and to "hear the Apostolic credo" (Livshits: 521).

More will be said about the "Stone's" author's interest in Catholic Rome and Chaadaev later; in the meantime, a few words should be said about Mandelstam's interest in Anna Zel'manova-Chudovskaia.

The theme of love was conspicuously absent from the first version of Mandelstam's "Stone," except for one poem, in which the reader can discern a barely perceptible hint of the presence of a woman:

The snow-covered bee hive is getting slower,
A crystal-like window is getting more transparent,
And the turquoise veil
Is carelessly thrown on a chair.

  ("The snow-covered bee hive is getting slower …," 1910)

In the ten earlier poems which were not included in the first edition of "Stone," but which might have been read as love poetry, the heroine is difficult to recognize. She either only appears for a short moment ("You slipped out in a light shawl") or else doesn't appear at all, despite the main hero's expectations:

The place has emptied. The evening lasts,
Pining from your absence.
The drink on the table steams,
Longing for your lips.

In such charmed steps of an
Anchorite you will not draw near;
Nor trace the pattern on glass
With your sleeping lips…

  ("The place has emptied. The evening lasts," 1909)

Frequently, as if trying to keep his loved one within the framework of the poem, the poet addresses her directly ("More tender than the tenderest // Your face"; "You have passed through the cloud of fog"). It comes as no surprise that no one really knows or will ever know the real names of all the "you's."

It is with the name of Anna Zel'manova-Chudovskaia, "a woman of unusual beauty" (Livshits), that Mandelstam begins his "Don Juan list," which was later meticulously put together by Anna Akhmatova: "The first one that I can remember was Anna Mikhailovna Zel'manova-Chudovskaia, the beautiful artist. She did a portrait of him on a navy blue background, with his head thrown back (1914, on Alekseevskaia street). He did not write Anna Mikhailovna any poems, he regretted this himself, as he did not yet know how to write love poetry" (Akhmatova

1989a: 127). And yet one of his poems from 1914, "Invitation to the Moon," was apparently dedicated to none other than Anna Zel'manova. The second part of her hyphenated name (Zel'manova-*Chudovskaia* <*chudo* means 'mircale' in Russian>) begs for comparison with the first half of the compound image "miraculous-dovecote" from "Invitation to the Moon" (these "dovecotes are called "*blue* houses" because *dove* in Russian (*golub'*) is linked to, or homonymous with, blue (*goluboi*):

> *On the moon it's half dark*
> *And houses are tidier;*
> *On the moon the houses*
> *Are genuine dovecotes;*
> *They are blue houses—*
> *Miraculous dovecotes.*

The poem can definitely be considered a distinct, though timid, sketch of Mandelstam's future "love lyrics." The "dear Princess" depicted in the poem sharply differs from the heroines of Mandelstam's earlier lyrics. The poet is calling the "dear Princess" not just anywhere, but to the moon; taking a perceptible step toward a real love letter, Mandelstam, however, immediately steps backwards, as he chooses for his poem a deliberately infantile subject and manner.

The infantilism of the manner and tone of "Invitation to the Moon" is striking. Its style can be compared to that of an animated cartoon. Especially considering the fact that a whole set of motifs from "Invitation to the Moon" echo the motifs of the well-known movie by George Melies, "A Journey to the Moon" (1902), in which animation was used for the first time.

2.

On 19 July 1914, Russia found itself drawn into the World War. Mandelstam's friends Nikolai Gumilev and Benedikt Livshits joined the Army as volunteers. Anna Akhmatova, in her "war" poems, dealt, for the first time, with the theme that will become critical for her post-revolutionary poetry: the theme of Christian self-sacrifice for the sake of the salvation of the beloved Homeland. Whereas Viacheslav Ivanov branded Russia's opponents as "an impertinent tribe parodying Rome in the hastily constructed scaffolding of an extemporized empire without filial memory" (V. Ivanov: 106). Mandelstam did not qualify for the draft due to his cardiac asthenia. Nevertheless, in December of 1914 he left for Warsaw where, with the help of the "Guild of Poets" member D.V. Kuzmin-Karavaev, who had been assigned as the plenipotentiary of the sanitary train, Mandestam hoped to become a medical orderly (perhaps he had been inspired by the December 1914 issue of "Novyi Zhurnal dlia vsekh" [New Journal for Everyone] that had published the "Notes of a volunteer orderly" of another member of the "Guild," Nikolai Bruni). On 25 December 1914, Sergei Kablukov wrote in his journal: "On the 19th he showed up unexpectedly, in order to announce his decision and to say goodbye. I began by mercilessly and harshly raking him over the coals, as there is no other way to deal with hysterics. But his "hysterics" ended up being very stubborn. It was hopeless to think that he would not be let into Warsaw, though one thought that maybe he, smart as he was, would be able to realize that he was no orderly, and would return to his usual occupation, and return, hopefully, healthy and unharmed. As he prepared to leave on the 21st of December, he called me on the phone to say goodbye and to ask for financial help. Perhaps it was cruel of me, but I categorically refused" (Kablukov: 249). Kablukov had predicted everything accurately: already by 5 January 1915 Mandelstam had returned to St. Petersburg (according to some not very reliable sources, in Warsaw the despairing poet had attempted suicide). The remaining two years of the world war he worked for the Union of Cities, an organization that provided support for the army.

In the first months of the war, Mandelstam abundantly used the political rhetoric in the spirit of his favorite 19th century poet, Fedor Tiutchev. In his first war poem, "Europa," he attempted to show the map of combat action as if from the bird's eye view, inviting the reader to take a look at the fanciful contours of Spain and Italy, and to admire the delicate pale green color of swampy Poland:

CHAPTER TWO

Primordial land of the conquerors,
Europe in rags and tatters of the Holy Union;
The heel of Spain, the medusa of Italy,
And tender Poland without a king.

In Mandelstam's poem with the Tiutchev title, "Encyclica" (written on the occasion of the peace-loving epistle from Pope Benedict XV to all of the people at war), the Catholic, "Roman" theme comes to the fore:

There is a type of freedom, inhabited
By spirit — destiny of the chosen.
With his eagle eye and marvelous hearing
The Roman priest remains intact.

Even the dove fears not
the Church's thunderous speech;
In the apostolic harmony: Roma! —
It merely makes the heart merry.

I repeat this name
Under the eternal cupola of heaven,
Even though he who speaks to me of Rome
Has disappeared in the sacred twilight!

In the last quatrain of this poem, apparently the reference is to Chaadaev, who "according to the Russian person's right" has set foot "onto the sacred soil of tradition, with which he was not connected through succession" (as Mandelstam wrote in his article, "Petr Chaadaev," 1914) (I: 199). Following Mikhail Gershenzon, Mandelstam considered the author of "Philosophical Letters" to be the only representative in Russia of Roman "Catholic universalism" (PSE: 177). Chaadaev had a special appeal to Mandelstam because of his aspirations throughout his whole life to transform the chaos inherent in Russian man into an architecturally structured cosmos: "Russia in the eyes of Chaadaev still totally belonged to the unorganized world," wrote Mandelstam. "He himself was one bone and one flesh of that Russia and he viewed himself as raw material. The results were surprising. The idea organized his entire personality, not just his mind, structured it architecturally and completely subordinated it to itself, and as a prize for this absolute subjugation, gave it absolute freedom" (I: 195).

There is no slightest doubt that this statement on Chaadaev alluded to Mandelstam's own credo during the Acmeist period of his life. What is especially significant is that in Mandelstam's poem, "Posokh" [Staff] (1914), one can easily find numerous echoes in the essay, "Petr Chaadaev," which proves that the lyrical "I" of "Staff" is Chaadaev. However the reader who is not familiar with the essay would be tempted to identify the lyrical hero of the poem with Mandelstam himself.

Another close "interlocutor" of Mandelstam's at this time was Pushkin. As testified by Anna Akhmatova (Akhmatova 1989a: 133), "Mandelstam spoke of Pushkin in a somewhat uncanny, impertinent way." Sometimes Mandelstam would engage in a direct argument with his great predecessor. As, for example, when Pushkin, irritated while reading P.A. Viazemsky's essay, "About V.A. Ozerov's Life and Writing," crossed out the sentence where it said that Ozerov's tragedies had become "the new dawn of Russian theatre" (Pushkin: 378). At the end of his poem, "There is an Unshakeable Scale of Values..." (1914), Mandelstam demonstratively sided with Viazemsky's statement: "And for me the phenomenon of Ozerov — // Is the final beam of a tragic dawn." Nadezhda Pavlovich describes a touching scene from a later period (Feburary 1921): "St. Isaac's Cathedral was functioning at the time, and there was a church there. And Mandelstam proposed that we go there and hold a memorial service for Pushkin. He passed out candles. I will never forget his comportment, up to the occasion, while giving the candles out" (Osip and Nadezhda: 122).

3.

Mandelstam's great interest in Catholic Rome preceded his immersion in Roman Antiquity, of which he had studied the literature and culture at the Petersburg University. Mandelstam was not an exemplary student: he dealt with the university program in spurts, as a rule, they corresponded with the due dates, often retaking examinations and being forced to rewrite term papers.

In the summer of 1912, as Mandelstam was preparing for his exams in Greek, he availed himself of the assistance of a young philologist, Konstantin Vasil'evich Mochulsky. "He would come to class incredibly late, completely amazed by the mysteries of Greek grammar that had been revealed to him," Mochulsky would recollect many years later. "He would wave his arms, run around the room and declaim in a singsong voice the declensions and conjugations. Reading Homer would turn into a magical event; adverbs, enclitics, pronouns would pursue him in his sleep, and he would enter into enigmatic personal relations with them." "Mandelstam never mastered Greek, but he guessed it," noted Mochulsky (Mochulsky: 65-66).

On 25 July 1913, by a resolution of the Governing Body of the Imperial St. Petersburg University, Mandelstam was expelled from the university for not having paid for the spring semester of 1913. In August he paid the arrears, and in September-October took finals in Latin, Logic, and the work of Clément Marot.

In the end, he did not complete his studies at the University. On 18 May 1917 he received a university certificate № 1879 signed by the dean of the History Faculty, Fedor Braun: "Six out of eight semesters have been completed, no state examinations were passed, and a full curriculum was not completed" (quoted as per: IV: 439). This prompted some biographers and literary critics to sympathetically discuss Mandelstam's "inability to pass even a single university exam" (Khodasevich 1997: 280).

One of the most striking episodes of Mandelstam's university career was his failure to pass an exam in Latin authors, attempted in the end of September 1915.

Veniamin Kaverin reports in his memoir book: "Iu. N. Tynianov told me about how Mandelstam, being a student of the St. Petersburg University, took an exam in Classical Literature. Professor Tsereteli, exceedingly courteous and wearing a cylinder, which was quite rare in those times, asked Mandelstam to tell him about Aeschylus. Mandelstam thought a minute and said:

"Aeschylus was religious."

Then he was silent. There was a long pause, and finally the professor, in a considerate way, without a trace of irony, continued to examine:

"You have told us a lot, mister student," he said. "Aeschylus was religious, and this fact, strictly speaking, does not require any proof. But perhaps you would be so kind as to tell us what Aeschylus wrote, comedies or tragedies? Where did he live and what was his position in ancient literature?

Mandelstam was silent again, and then said:

"He wrote 'Orestes.'"

"Wonderful," said Tsereteli. "He did indeed write Orestes. But perhaps, mister student, you would be so kind as to tell us what is 'Orestes?' Is it a separate piece or a sequence of several tragedies?

There was a long silence. Mandelstam looked up proudly and silently observed the professor. He did not say anything else. Tsereteli let him go. With an independent demeanor and looking straight ahead of him, Mandelstam left the auditorium" (Kaverin: 300-301).

Through this rendition of Tynianov's anecdote, Kaverin adds strength to his own explanations about Mandelstam's behavior: "...the setting of the exam, the role of student, the atmosphere, seemingly typical but totally foreign to Mandelstam. He lived in his own separate world that did not resemble any other, which was infinitely distant from any exams, from the fact that he was required to answer questions, as if trying to convince a professor that he knows about the life of Aeschylus and his works. His pride was hurt by the fact that Tsereteli, apparently, doubted him. Of course, life made him realize that he too was a part of reality. If only because it treated him harshly. But this incident was significantly symptomatic" (Kaverin: 301). It is interesting that for Kaverin, knowing Aeschylus' works is a sort of metaphor, if not outright obligatory condition, for knowledge of life. Mandelstam's failing the exam was interpreted by the memoirist as the eccentric poet's refusal to face cruel contemporary reality.

Now let's take a look at Kablukov's journal. His journal entry was based on what Mandelstam told him, immediately after the ill-fated incident: "I.E. Mandelstam visited, having failed his exam in Latin authors from Malein on 29 September.

Malein insists on knowledge of Catullus and Tibullus, Mandelstam had only studied Catullus. He refused to translate Tibullus, for which reason he was sent away from the exam. Moreover his borrowed Catullus with excellent commentaries was stolen" (Kablukov: 251).

Comparing the objective depiction of Mandelstam's exam in Kablukov's journal entry with that of Kaverin's version, we get the opportunity to observe how reality gets transformed into legend. In his memoirs, Kaverin preferred the great Hellenist, Grigory Tsereteli to the great Latinist, Aleksandr Malein (most likely because next to the eccentric poet, the memoirist wanted to depict the eccentric professor; and Tsereteli did have such a reputation, while Malein did not). Kaverin opted for Aeschylus most likely because Mandelstam does mention Aeschylus in his poetry, but does not mention either Catullus or Tibullus. And finally and most importantly, Kaverin chose to depict a quite common situation as an extraordinary one: a student who had studied for the first question but not for the second is portrayed as a meditative egocentric, paying the price for his inability to get along with life.

Incidentally, Mandelstam did complete his exam in Latin literature with a grade of "satisfactory" on 18 October 1916.

4.

On 14 April 1915, the great Russian composer, Aleksandr Nikolaevich Skriabin, died. "For people of the "Apollon" circle," notes R.D. Timenchik, "Skriabin's music was more than music, it was both invocative and prophetic of the fate of a whole generation. The day that Mandelstam found out about Skriabin's death he supposedly literally threw himself at Blok, with whom he was barely acquainted, in order to speak with him about Skriabin" (Katz, Timenchik: 54).

As the son of a music teacher, Mandelstam throughout his entire life never abandoned musicosophy (the term coined by Boris Katz), i.e. the attempt to "understand music" (Katz: 42). Of course, one should also consider the opinion of the faultfinding companion of Mandelstam's later years, Boris Kuzin, who believed that "music was not...the [poet's] natural element" (Kuzin: 216). However, the futurist composer, Artur Lur'e (Lourie), who knew Mandelstam very well, held a different opinon. In his memoirs he wrote: "It often seemed to me that for poets, even for the most original, contact with sounding, rather than imagined, music, is not a requirement, and their mention of music is usually of an abstract, metaphysical nature. But Mandelstam was quite the exception: live music for him was a requirement. Music fed his poetic consciousness" (Lur'e: 196). "In music, O[sip] was as if at home, and this was an extremely rare quality," confirmed Anna Akhmatova (Akhmatova 1989a: 122). On 18 November 1915, Mandelstam together with Kablukov attended the concert of the conductor, S.A. Kusevitsky, held in memoriam of Skriabin.

On 30 December, the poet gave Kablukov the gift of a second edition of "Stone," brought out by the Acmeist publishing house "Giperborei" [Hyperborean] (the cover of this edition has year 1916 on it). "...its appearance was poor: the paper was thin and slack, poor quality laid paper, weak typeset, more than enough typos, some quite jarring," Kablukov wrote in his journal disappointedly (Kablukov: 251).

When the second "Stone" was published, there were close to twenty reviews of it in the metropolitan and local press, for the most part they were reservedly approving. Among the most benevolent reviews, those by Gumilev and Voloshin especially stood out. The most malevolent was the review by Nikolai Lerner published in the newspaper *Rech'*: "Albeit Mr. Mandelstam has a gift, it is ordinary and insignificant, and the heavy, poorly polished, and bland "Stone" brought to the altar of the Russian muse will soon be lost in the heap of just as many diligent, but poor sacrifices" (Mandelstam 1990: 229). Twenty years later, giving a copy of the second edition of "Stone" to S.B. Rudakov, Mandelstam autographed it as follows: "This book was the cause of much grief for my late mother, who had read the review in "Rech'" by N.O. Lerner" (Rudakov: 184). Many reviewers characterized the poetry of the author of "Stone" as the most representative sample of Acmeism, even though by this time Acmeism had pretty much run its course.

On 16 April 1914, the day after a regular meeting with Nikolai Gumilev, Sergei Gorodetsky sent him an extensive letter in which he accused him of a "slant away from Acmeism," which Gumilev does not consider a school. In his reply, an offended Gumilev insists: "...the decision about my departure from Acmeism or the "Guild of Poets" is purely mine, and your any initiative in this direction would only be considered a treachery [...] I was always honest with you and, believe me, I won't latch onto our union if it is destined to end." Subsequently, the relations between the two doyens of Acmeism were, to a certain extend, re-established. "But clearly the fracture was too deep, and it was impossible to return to the former ways," comments Akhmatova (Akhmatova 1989: 7).

Mandelstam's relation with Gorodetsky had strained even earlier. On 21 October 1913, a "Guild" session took place at the apartment of Nikolai Bruni, during which the author of "Stone" had been temporarily voted as the spokesman of the group (in lieu of the absent Gorodetsky). "Suddenly Gorodetsky appeared. There were angry exchanges, during which Mandelstam and Gorodetsky were rude with one another, and they parted enemies" (M. Dolinov's letter to B. Sadovskoy quoted in: Timenchik 1998: 421). The comfortable and homey atmosphere of the friendly Acmeist circle was irreparably tarnished. In the winter 1913-1914 Akhmatova and Mandelstam presented Gorodetsky and Gumilev with a request to disband the "Guild of Poets" (Akhmatova 1989: 7).

One of the most significant reviews of "Stone" was written by Voloshin (see: Mandelstam 1990: 238-239). It combined the discussion of Mandelstam"s "Stone" with the discussion of another recently published collection — "Poems," by Sophia Parnok. Such combination turned out to be later ironically prophetic. In the early part of 1916 Mandelstam was to supplant Parnok from Marina Tsvetaeva's heart and poetry. Mandelstam first met Marina and her sister Anastasia in the summer of 1915 in Koktebel, and then again in Petrograd in the first part of January, 1916. It was this second meeting that gave a spur for a stormy, albeit short-lived love affair between Osip and Marina.

His inscription of a copy of the second edition of "Stone" presented to her reads: "To Marina Tsvetaeva — stone-amulet. Osip Mandelstam. St. Petersburg, 10 January 1916" (Mandelstam 1990: 280). Ten days later, on 20 January, Mandelstam came to Moscow to see Marina again. This was his first visit ever to Russia's second capital. Both in Mandelstam's and Tsvetaeva's verse of this period the theme of love and Moscow are intricately interwoven with one another. Both in the short-lived union and poetic dialogue, Tsvetaeva took the "lead" role, whereas Mandelstam — that of the "led." The motifs from Tsvetaeva's Moscow poems addressed to Mandelstam were taken up and developed in Mandelstam's poems addressed to Tsvetaeva. Up until June 1916, Mandelstam visited Moscow so regularly that it provoked M.R. Segalova to joke in a letter to Sergei Kablukov (who was trying to find the poet a position in one of the Moscow banks): "If he is going to travel so often from Moscow to Petersburg and back, shouldn't he get a position in both places? Or is he already working for the Nikolaevsky railroad? Not a person, but an airplane" (Kablukov: 255).

Kablukov was very much distressed by the moods that had possessed his friend. "Clearly some woman had entered his life," he wrote in his journal. "I find the way religion and eroticism got connected in his soul to be rather blasphemous. He himself confirms this and admits that sex became especially dangerous for him after he abandoned Jewry. He claims to understand that he is on a dangerous path and to know all the perils of his situation, but he is incapable of leaving this path, nor is he able to cease composing poetry during this erotic folly" (Kablukov: 256). One can imagine how shocked Kablukov would be to discover the "blasphemous" gift from Tsvetaeva to Mandelstam, namely, a ring, "silver, with a seal — Adam and Eve under the tree of good and evil" (the description is from Tsvetaeva's notebook, see: Tsvetaeva 2001: 90).

In the first days of June, 1916, Mandelstam came from Petrograd to visit Tsvetaeva at Aleksandrovskaia Sloboda near Moscow. Marina described his visit with some humor in her letter to Elizaveta Efron, dated 12 June 1916: "...he begged me to allow him to come right away and barely agreed to wait until the next day. He arrived the following morning. It being a gorgeous day, we of course immediately offered to take him for a walk, but he of course refused, lied down on the couch and barely spoke. A little while later I got bored, and I resolutely took him to the cemetery [...] The day passed in his complaints about his fate, with our consolations and praises, in food, and in literary news. By evening and night time, around midnight, he grew silent, lay down on the deerskins and became unpleasant [...] At one a.m. we walked him almost right up to the train station. He left haughtily" (Tsvetaeva. Vol. 6: 90-92). Echoes of the visit to Aleksandrov can be heard in the last of the poems addressed by Mandelstam to Tsvetaeva ("Not believing in the miracle of resurrection...").

In the summer of 1916, Osip and his brother Aleksandr were staying at Voloshin's house in Koktebel, in the Crimea, where the poet Vladislav Khodasevich was also among the guests. If one is to believe the latter, there was not much warmth on behalf of local society toward Mandelstam. "Mandelstam. Fed up with him. He is insolent. Smoked all of my cigarettes. A low self-esteem. The laughing stock of all of Koktebel'," wrote Khodasevich to his friend on 18 July (Kupchenko 1987: 191). Around the 20th of July, Osip and Aleksandr Mandelstam received a telegram from their father notifying them that their mother, Flora Osipovna, had had a terrible stroke. On the 26th of July, never coming to, the poet's mother passed away. The two older brothers made it just in time for the funeral. The memorial service took place in the chapel for burial services of the Jewish Preobrazhensky cemetery. The description of this service can be found in the enigmatic poem written by Mandelstam inspired by his impressions from his mother's burial:

This night was irreparable,
Though there it is still light!
By the gates of Jerusalem
A black sun has risen. < ... >

And over my mother rang
Voices of the Israelis,
I woke in my cradle,
Bathed in the rays of the black sun.

"With his mother's death begins the disintegration of the Mandelstam family," wrote the poet's younger brother Evgeny. "Each of us had suffered through his own deep grief. We immediately felt an emptiness and disorderliness. We were tormented by a sense of guilt before our mother for her young death, by our own egoism and lack of attention. Mother's death left its trace on the spiritual constitution of each of the sons. It especially affected the most reactive one of us all, Osip [...] The older Osip got, the more guilt he felt before mother. In time, Osip came to finally understand how much he owed to her and how much she had done for him" (E. Mandelstam: 141). Nina Balmont-Bruni describes in her memoirs a somewhat funny and touching trait the brothers shared: "…the brothers had loved their mother very much, and whenever they needed money, they would send each other a telegram with the words: "In the name of our late mother, send (or: asking for) a hundred." And Osip Emil'evich said: 'No one ever refused, though we did not take advantage of it either'" (Osip and Nadezhda: 74).

Mandelstam spent New Year's 1917 at Kablukov's, having fallen in love once again, with the Georgian Princess, Salomeia Nikolaevna Andronikashvili (Andronikova). "She <…> did everything with style: smoked with style, sat with her legs in the large armchair with style, held a cup of tea with style, and even in her manner of slightly stooping and leaning her head forward, when she was speaking while standing, there was something sweet and feminine" (from V. Karacharova's story, "The Sorcerer's Student," where Andronikova has served as the prototype for the heroine, as determined by R.D. Timenchik) (Kofeinia: 11). Mandelstam had dedicated a few poems to Andronikova, including the famous "Solominka" [Straw stalk] (1916).

5.

Mandelstam was in Petrograd during the February revolution. Ten years later, in his tale, "The Egyptian Stamp" (1927), he will disdainfully call the automobiles of the provisional government "mad" (II: 473), the government itself — "lemonade" (II: 473), and the state — fallen asleep, "like a perch" (II: 478). But without a doubt this is a retrospective assessment. Initially Mandelstam greeted February of 1917 with enthusiasm. E.A. Toddes notes fairly that Mandelstam's moods at the time are reflected in his decision in the spring of 1917 to publish his recently written poem, "Palace Square" (Toddes: 35). This poem ends with the sinister emblem of the imperial black-yellow colors:

Only there, where the firmament is light,
The black-yellow shred grows angry —
As if the air is full of the streaming
Bile of the double-headed eagle!

Four years earlier Mandelstam had written an enigmatic octet about the same Palace Square, in the third line of which there was a caricature of Paul I combined with one of Aleksandr I, and in the fourth line, Aleksandr I and Aleksandr II were combined through their common names into a unified image of the emperor, tormented by the ominous Beast from the Apocalypse (the use of the formula "on stone and blood" in the sixth line was supposed to remind the reader of the temple constructed on the spot of Aleksandr II's assasination):

The mobs now sleep! The square gapes with an arch,
The bronze door drips with moonlight.
Here the harlequin pined for bright fame,
And Aleksandr was tortured by the Beast.

The chiming clock and shadows of monarchs...
Russia, you are on stone and blood,
To take part in your iron retribution,
Bless me at least with gravity!

This makes one think of Mandelstam's comment on Auguste Barbier, who was capable "in one line, in one apt expression to determine the essence of a major historical event" (II: 305).

And yet, until October 1917, Mandelstam, for the most part, considered himself to be more of a private person rather than a poet-citizen. By the end of May 1917, he once again left the capital for Crimea. Much later, in his poem "My connection to the sovereign world is merely that of a child…" (1931), the reason for Mandelstam's departure from Petrograd was explained as follows:

Sensing the upcoming executions,
I chose to escape to the nereids on the Black Sea,
 away from the roar of mutiny,
And from the beauties of the time, those gentle
European ones that made me suffer such grief and confusion!

There were plenty of beauties among those who were part of Mandelstam's circle in Crimea during the summer and fall of 1917, in Alushta. These included Anna Mikhailovna Zel'manova, Salomeia Nikolaevna Andronikova, and the poetess, Anna Dmitrievna Radlova, whose poetry had been praised by Mikhail Kuzmin and parodied by Mandelstam ("The legend concerning his falling for Anna Radlova has not been substantiated," Akhmatova, who hated Radlova, found it necessary to note this in her "Pages from a journal") (Akhmatova 1989a: 128). On 3 August, on Andronikova's nameday, the group of poets and philologists performed a comic play, "The Coffee House of Broken Hearts," in which Mandelstam participated as the poet, don Jose d'Amande, the French calque of his last name, Mandelstam. In the play, this character's lines consisted of paraphrases of Mandelstam's poems. What is interesting is that apparently no one in this circle, including Zel'manova and Andronikova, were aware of Mandelstam's love poetry. This explains d'Amande's statement in his monologue that alluded to the heading of Mandelstam's first book:

Never wrote I any love poetry.
My fireproof stone strophes
Made no mention of the heart.

CHAPTER TWO

A few days after Salomeia Andronikova's namesday, Mandelstam went to visit another datcha in Alushta, where the artist, Sergei Iur'evich Sudeikin, was living with his beautiful wife, Vera Arturovna (later Mme Stravinsky). This visit was described in Sudeikin's journal: "A white, two storied house with white columns surrounded by vineyards, cypress, and the aroma of the wild fields [...] Here we will be village recluses, we will work and nap in the silence of the village hills. That is the way it was. Heaven on earth. And then Osip Mandelstam showed up [...] We were so glad to see him [...] We took him to the vineyards: "There is nothing else that we can show you, and nothing to treat you with except for tea and honey. There is no bread." But the discussion was lively, non-political, about art, literature, and painting. A witty, lively, and charming talker. We enjoyed his visit" (Kofeinia: 19).

In early October, in Feodosia, Mandelstam briefly crosses paths with the Tsvetaeva sisters. Marina had asked Anastasia and others travelling with them: "Please do not leave us alone" (Kupchenko 1987: 193).

Mandelstam returned to Petrograd on 11 October 1917, i.e. right on the eve of the October upheaval, the "mutinous events" which echo in the poet's heart with pain and fear. Much later, during his interrogation in May of 1934, he confessed: "I perceive the October revolution extremely negatively. I see the Soviet government as a government of occupiers and this was expressed in my poem "Kerensky," published in the newspaper "Volya naroda." [The Will of People] In this poem I relapse to the Social Revolutionaries: I praise Kerensky, calling him Peter's fledgeling, whereas I view Lenin as an ephemeral historical figure" (Polianovsky: 88-89).

Together with Akhmatova at the end of 1917 and beginning of 1918 Mandelstam took part in the concerts organized by the Political Red Cross, whose proceeds were to assist the members of the provisional government imprisoned in the Peter Paul fortress. "Mandelstam met the revolution as a mature and quite famous poet, albeit in closed circles," wrote Akhmatova. "His soul was full of the events that had taken place. Mandelstam was one of the first to start writing poems on civic themes. The revolution was for him a great cataclysm <...>" (Akhmatova 1989a: 130).

The frequent meetings between Mandelstam and Akhmatova during the first post-revolutionary months were cut off due to a sudden crisis. From Akhmatova's memoirs: "After some wavering I decided to say in these notes what I had to explain to Osip, that we should not meet so often as it might give people cause to misinterpret our relations. After this, approximately March [1918] Mandelstam disappeared [...] He unexpectedly took great offence with me" (Akhmatova 1989a: 131). In the journals of Pavel Luknitsky there is a harder version of what happened: "There was a time when O. Mandelstam actively showed his interest in her. [A. A.]: "I found him physically repellent, I couldn't stand it, for example, when he kissed my hand" (Luknitsky: 115). To be fair, it should be noted that in Nadezhda Mandelstam's "Second Book," the emphasis is completely different: "Mandelstam called this "Akhmatova's tricks" and laughed that she was obsessed with thinking that everyone was in love with her" (NM-2: 256).

In April 1918, Mandelstam took a job as clerk (and head of the press bureau) of the committee responsible for relocation of Petrograd government offices to Moscow. Soviet employment was not just a compromise with the new authorities, justified by the need to earn one's daily bread. Speaking of this moment, Mandelstam said when interrogated in 1934: "I made a sharp turn toward Soviet activities and people" (Polianovsky: 89). The formula, "made a turn" is evocative of Mandelstam's poem, "Let's glorify, oh brothers, the twilight of freedom...," written in May 1918 (scholars still disagree as to whether or not he meant dawn or dusk):

> *Let's glorify, oh brothers, the twilight of freedom,*
> *The great twilight year!*
> *Into the boiling waters of the night*
> *A fierce forest of snares is lowered.*
> *You are ascending the deaf waters —*
> *Oh sun, the judge, the people!*
> . . . .
> *So let us try: the huge, clumsy*
> *Squeaky turning of the wheel.* < ... >

Mandelstam turned away from the scorn and loathing of the new order toward the acknowledgement of the historical truth and inevitability of all that had occurred. "The October revolution could not help but affect my work, as it took away my "biography," the sense of personal significance," wrote Mandelstam in 1928. (II: 496).

On 1 June 1918, Mandelstam, on Lunacharsky's recommendation, went to serve in the People's Commissariat for Education as head of the subdivision of the artistic development of students in the department of secondary school reforms, his earnings were 600 rubles. When the commissariat moved to Moscow, Mandelstam also relocated to the new old capital. From the memoirs of Mandelstam's co-worker, Petr Kuznetsov: "The work was boring, clerical. The most interesting part was traveling to conduct inventories of libraries that remained in the confiscated manors" (Osip and Nadezhda: 77).

In Moscow the poet briefly relapsed to his previous political passion for socialist revolutionaries, though he had renounced the terrorist methods of their struggle long ago. "Any type of terror was unacceptable for Mandelstam," Nadezhda Iakovlevna testified. "Mandelstam met with the assassin of Uritsky, the younger poet Leonid Kannegiser before the revolution in the "Stray Dog." When I asked about him Mandelstam answered reservedly and added: "Who gave him the right to judge?" (NM-2: 24) (Kannegiser was quoted as saying: "By taking money from me, Mandelstam does me a great honor" (Sokolova: 77)).

The poet lodged at the hotel "Metropol," which was where Soviet officials of different ranks resided. In 1923, Mandelstam would recollect nostalgically in his essay, "A Cold Summer:" "When out of the dusty hole of the "Metropol," an international hotel, where under a glass tent I wandered through the corridors of the streets of an internal city, rarely stopping before a mirrored ambush or resting on a peaceful lawn with rattan furniture, I would exit out onto the square, and still blind, gulping the sunlight, my eyes would be struck by the majestic reality of the Revolution and the great aria for a powerful voice would resound over the horns and sirens of the automobiles" (II: 307).

In Moscow, Osip Emil'evich became, if not friends, then close acquaintances with the left socialist revolutionaries (SR); this was the only party that had agreed then to enter the coalition with the Bolsheviks in the Soviet government. He began to actively publish in left SR press, whose staff would even call the author of "Twilight of Freedom" "their poet." In one such publication, the newspaper, "Rannee utro" [Early Morning], Mandelstam submitted for publication his "enigmatic" as Akhmatova called it (Akhmatova 1989a: 131), poem "Telephone" (Moscow, June 1918), apparently about the suicide of a state official. (This is hinted at by the reference to a "high austere cabinet" of the suicide), secondly this "high austere cabinet" was not far from the Theater Square, which explains Mandelstam's use of theatrical imagery in the poem. It is possible that the cabinet of the suicide is in the hotel "Metropol," which would lead one to believe that Mandelstam had met the future suicide there and was maybe even his neighbor. Thirdly, it is not often that one finds in the early Mandelstam such an "exact" date of a poem ("June 1918"), which makes one think that it had been written under the fresh impression of a recent suicide. Furthermore, why would Mandelstam want to publish this mysterious and not "newspaperish" poem in the "Rannee utro"? Could it be that the newspaper itself was contemplating responding in such a way to the the suicide of the person who was the hero of the poem?

The only mention of a suicide of a state official in the "Rannee utro" newspaper in May or June of 1918 appeared under the heading, "The Suicide of a Commissar," in the 28 May issue: "In the house № 8 of Ermolaev lane, R.L. Chirkunov, commissar for the relocation of troops, committed suicide by shooting himself in his temple out of a revolver in his apartment. The motives for the suicide remain unknown." Perhaps Chirkunov was Mandelstam's co-worker in the committee responsible for relocation of Petrograd government offices. Whatever the case, the poem was not printed on the newspaper pages and remained unpublished for several decades. Incidentally a certain Chirkunov (the name that sounds very similar to that of the suicide) belonged to the inner circle of the notorious SR activist and Chekist, Iakov Bliumkin.

In early July of 1918, Mandelstam entered into a serious conflict with Bliumkin, another of his neighbors at the "Metropol." The circumstances of this conflict are recounted in Georgy Ivanov's half-fictional memoirs and in the depositions given by the head of the Cheka, Felix Dzerzhinsky, concerning the case of the murder of the German envoy Mirbach by Bliumkin. Odd as it may seem, the Dzerzhinsky version appears to be more reliable, it is quoted as follows: "A few days before the assassination attempt, maybe a week, I received some information from [Fedor] Raskol'nikov [husband of the poetess, Larisa Reisner] and Mandelstam (who works in Petrograd for Lunacharsky) that this guy [Bliumkin] goes around saying things such as: the lives of these people are in my hands, I can sign a paper — and in a few days a human life is gone [...] When Mandelstam, incensed, protested, Bliumkin began to threaten him, that if he says anything about him to anyone, he will retaliate with all his might" (VChK: 154). Georgy Ivanov claims that the poet even grabbed from Bliumkin a pack of "shooting orders" and tore them up (G. Ivanov 1994: 95). However one should take such information with a grain of salt: it is doubtful that Bliumkin had such a pack of orders, as his position in the Cheka did not have any direct connection with shooting executions.

Fleeing from Bliumkin, Mandelstam hastily left Moscow. "In the beginning of July I fell ill with hysteria," that is how he explained his reasons for suddenly leaving the capital without getting the permission from his superiors in the Narkompros (Nerler 1989: 276). In the next seven months the poet commuted between Petrograd and Moscow. Later he would recollect that his depression was caused by the political circumstances of those days (Polianovsky: 89). During a chance meeting in Petrograd with an acquaintance (Sergei Rittenberg), Mandelstam quoted some lines of his favorite poet Verlaine and significantly added: "Did you know that Verlaine wrote this while in prison?" (Timenchik 2005: 475).

In the middle of February 1919, on the eve of the repressions launched by the government against the left SR's, Mandelstam together with his brother, Aleksandr, departed for Kharkov. Here he was assigned a position with the lofty title: Head of the Poetry Section of the All-Ukrainian Literary Committee under the Council for Arts of the Provisional Worker-Peasant Government of Ukraine.

6.

Mandelstam ended up being in Kharkov at the same time as Georgy Shengeli and Riurik Ivnev. In Ivnev's memoirs one finds a description evocative of Mandelstam's moods of that time: "Something incredible was going on with Mandelstam, as if someone had substituted the Petersburg Mandelstam. The revolution went into his head the way strong wine goes to the head of a person who had never drunk before. I never met a person who, like Osip Mandelstam, managed to at the same time accept and reject the revolution" (Ivnev: 43).

At the end of March and early April of 1919, the poet, accompanied by his brother Aleksandr and the same Ivnev, moved to the capital of Ukraine. A young poet, Iury Terapiano, saw Mandelstam there in the bohemian café, "Khlam" (meaning 'trash' in Russian; the playful abbreviation for "Artists, Men of Letters, Actors, and Musicians"), which Mandelstam frequented during his stay in Kiev: "Not tall, about 35 years old, reddish hair with a bald spot, shaved, he was writing something sitting at a table, rocking on his chair, paying no mind to the cup of coffee that had been served to him" (Terapiano: 110).

On 1 May 1919, while celebrating the birthday of the critic and poet, Aleksandr Deich, at the "Khlam," Mandelstam met the young artist, Nadezhda Iakovlevna Khazina, who was to become his wife. The entry in A. Deich's journal reads: "O[sip] Mand[elstam] unexpectedly entered and immediately advanced in our direction. Being nearsighted, I did not recognize him right away, but he introduced himself: "Osip Mandelstam greets wonderful Kiev ladies (he bowed toward Nadia Kh[azina]), and wonderful Kiev gents (a general bow toward everyone)." A lively discussion followed. [...] He was asked to recite some of his poetry—and he willingly complied. Reading with closed eyes, he floated with the rhythms...As he opened his eyes, he looked only at Nadia Kh." (Deich: 146). A little bit later, on 23 May, Deich recorded another encounter with Mandelstam in a caffe house: "A couple clearly in love appears—Nadia Kh. and O.M. She is carrying a bouquet of water lilies, clearly fresh from the Dnepr" (Deich: 146).

CHAPTER TWO

Nadezhda Mandelstam. 1923

Nadezhda Iakovlevna herself wrote in her "Second Book": "On the very first evening that he appeared in the "Khlam" we immediately and carelessly became intimate. We consider our date the first of May 1919, although afterwards we ended up living apart for a year and a half. During that period we did not feel bound together, but already then we shared two common characteristics that remained with us for the rest of our lives: lightness and the feeling of doom [...] We rode a boat down the Dnepr, he knew how to steer well and was an excellent, effortless, rower, however he kept asking: "Where is the Old Man?" That is how everyone called the whirlpool where swimmers frequently drowned" (NM-2: 21; 269).

As opposed to those women who at various times would attract Mandelstam with their beauty, Nadezhda Iakovlevna was not known for her strikingly good looks. According to Akhmatova, "Nadiusha was what the French would call laide mais charmant [ugly, but charming]" (Akhmatova 1989a: 132). According to Olga Vaksel', "She was very ugly, tubercular, with straight yellow hair and legs like that of a dachshund" (Poliakova: 171). The portrait drawn by Maria Gonta: "His young wife, sweet, pink, and smiling" (Gonta: 538). From the memoirs of Semen Lipkin: "Nadezhda Iakovlevna never took part in our discussions, she would sit with a book in the corner, occasionally lifting her bright blue, sad and smiling eyes. I confess that back then I did not see anything special in her; to me she seemed to be the mere wife of a poet, moreover an ugly one. Only her thick reddish hair was lovely. And the color of her face was always young, freshly mat" (Lipkin: 307). From the journals of V.N. Gorbacheva: "His wife's face was long and thoughtful, it reminded one of the face of a hungry lioness" (Gorbacheva: 210).

When the first cloudless months of mutual love were past, after which one usually expects some cooling and almost always the complication of relations, Mandelstam, on the contrary, fully came to terms with the significance and appropriateness of his choice. Now, up to his final arrest, the poet would never be so fatally lonesome — Mandelstam had found a woman whom he could address with the words "my 'you'" (NM-2: 145). On 5 December 1919 Mandelstam wrote to Nadezhda Khazina from Feodosia: "I beg of God that you will hear what I have to say: my dear child, I can't go on without you, nor do I want to, you are my joy, my dearest one, and that is for me clear as God's day. You have become so dear to me, that I am always talking with you, calling you, complaining to you" (IV: 25-26).

The Mandelstam brothers ended up in Feodosia when in late August or early September they were travelling in the same traincar with actors moving from Kiev to Kharkov, and then later, in mid-September, from Kharkov to Crimea, overflowing with troops. This is where the Russian white volunteer army was being grouped, that had been commanded by Baron Petr Wrangel since April 1920. In Crimea, Osip and Aleksandr Mandelstam spent some depressing winter months. "The worst circumstances were those of O.E. Mandelstam," reported the Simferopol newspaper "Krymsky vestnik" on 5 September 1920, "who was the least capable of adapting himself to hardship and had become worn and famished to the last degree" (Mandelstam 1990b: 402).

Together with the stage director, Nikolai Evreinov, who had recently arrived to Feodosia from the Caucasus, Mandelstam took part in a reading that had been organized by the Feodosia Literary-Artistic circle (FLAK). The poet often went to the local café, "Fontanchik," where in the summer of 1920 he was first seen by the beginner writer, Emilii Mindlin: "He walked with his head held high, red-faced from the sun, in a skullcap and a black jacket, all sharp angles and very quick in his movements" (Mindlin: 81).

From March up to July 1920, Mandelstam lived in Koktebel' at Maksimilian Voloshin's. The first part of August was marked by an argument between the two poets, which had been depicted in great detail by many memoirists, some taking Mandelstam's side, others—Voloshin's. But in order to avoid taking sides, let us limit ourselves to fully quoting two documents describing the events at the time. The first document is a note from Voloshin to the Commander of the Port of Feodosia, Aleksandr Aleksandrovich Novinsky, dated approximately 2 August. The second was a letter from Mandelstam to Voloshin dated 7 August.

Voloshin's letter:

> Dear Aleksandr Aleksandrovich, I have two requests for you: first, please get me, as you yourself proposed, some medications [...] And the second request is as follows: Aleksandr Mandelstam, urged by his brother, stole from [the poetess] Maya [Kudasheva] a copy of "Stone," and moreover impertinently admitted it to Maya herself: "If you want to, you can say that my brother doesn't want M[aksimilian] A[leksandrovich] to have his poems any longer because they have quarrelled."
>
> Moreover, the book does not belong to me, it belongs to Pra [—Voloshin's mother]. I found out about this, unfortunately, too late, as he had already gone to get Osip as they are headed for Batum. So if you could do me a favor: without your help they will not be able to go to Batum, therefore, issue them an ultimatum that the book gets returned, and only then they can leave, otherwise not. Mandelstam has already robbed my library for

quite a while, which he himself admitted: in the past he had stolen my Dante in Italian and French. I only found this out this year. But I really like "Stone" very much, and it is still here, within reach. Please save it.

M. Voloshin

P.S. I just found out that Mandelstam gave the stolen book to Lub[ov'] Mikh[ailovna] Erenburg, who is returning it to me, thus my second request, naturally, is moot [...]

(Kupchenko 1991: 178-79).

Letter from Mandelstam to Voloshin:

> Dear Sir!
>
> With great pleasure I have become convinced that you, under a thick layer of spiritual fat, which many naively perceive as sophisticated aesthetic culture, are in fact concealing the hopeless cretinism and boorishness of a Koktebel Bulgarian. You allow yourself to write our mutual friends that I have been stealing from your library for "quite a while," and have, incidentally, "stolen" your Dante, and even "admitted to it," plus that I stole from you my own book through my brother.
>
> I sincerely regret that you are beyond reach and that I do not have the opportunity to personally call you a vile creature and a slanderer.
>
> One needs to be a total idiot to assume that I am even interested in whether or not you own a copy of my book. I only today remembered that you do.
>
> From all of your abominable, manic delirium, the only thing that is true is that because of me you lost a Dante: unfortunately three years ago I did lose one of your books.
>
> But what is even more unfortunate is to have been at all acquainted with you.

O. Mandelstam (IV: 26-27)

Literally a few days after leaving Feodosia, Mandelstam was arrested by Wrangel's counter-intelligence. The reasons for this arrest remain unknown. One can only be sure of the fact that Voloshin's letter to Novinsky did not play any role here, the guarantee being the P.S. to the letter. Apparently the Whites were suspicious of Mandelstam's friendly contacts with local Bolsheviks, he even stayed with one of them, I.Z. Kamensky, in Feodosia (according to some sources, he supposedly agreed to bring from Crimea to Batum some clandestine correspondence). Mandelstam was released thanks to the assistance of the Colonel of Counter-Intelligence in Feodosia, who was at the same time a poet and friend of Mandelstam's, Aleksandr Viktorovich Tsygal'sky. "Tsygal'sky was created in order to take care of someone and especially watch over their sleep" (from Mandelstam's essay, "Royal Robes of the Law") (II: 399).

Even the offended Voloshin lent a hand in assisting getting the poet released. Under the pressure of their mutual friends, he wrote a letter to the head of the political investigation, Apostolov: "I was told that Mandelstam is being accused of serving the Bolsheviks. Rest assured that Mandesltam is not capable of any kind of service, nor of having any political beliefs, this is something he never went through in his life" (Kupchenko 1991: 181).

After his release, the poet together with his brother departed on a barge from Feodosia to Batum. "For five days the Azov eggshell floated along the warm, salty Pont, for five days we crawled on all fours across the deck for boiled water, for five days fierce Dagestanis looked our way sideways" (from Mandelstam's essay, "The Return") (II: 313). In Batum, Osip Emil'evich was immediately arrested by the local authorities who were loyal to the Whites. The reason was the lack of a Georgian visa in Mandelstam's passport. This time Manelstam was rescued from custody with the help of his escort, Chigua, who at his own peril and risk delivered the arrested poet to the civil governor of Batum, and thanks to the mediation of the Georgian poets, Titsian Tabidze and Nikolaz Mitsishvili. From the memoirs of Nikolaz Mitsishvili: "A short, lean Jew enters, bald and without teeth, in dirty, wrinkled clothes and slippers with holes. Looking authentically biblical" (Mitsishvili: 164). From the memoirs of Titsian Tabidze's wife Nina: when Titsian was "shown Mandelstam, at first he did not believe that this poet, this aesthete, was sitting on a rock all overgrown and dirty. Titian for a while did not believe that this was indeed Mandelstam, and even began to ask him questions that only he could answer. Such as: "What poem of yours was published in such and such a year, and in such and such journal?" To which the poet responded and even recited the poem by heart" (N. Tabidze: 41). From the memoirs of the poet Kolau Nadiradze: "...he gave the oppressive impression of a worn out, exhausted, and famished person who had gone through a number of horrible minutes, hours, or even days and weeks."

On 19 September, at the Batum Society of Workers of the Arts (ODI) (Obshchestvo deiatelei iskusstva), an evening dedicated to Mandelstam was organized upon the initiative of a former "Guild of Poets" member, Nikolai Makridin. From a newspaper account of the evening: "The poet O. Mandelstam gave a poetry reading in two parts [...] His manner of reading is quite unusual [...] Logical stress, meaning of the words, and the instrumentation of the verse have all been sacrificed to rhythm. Of course, in this lies the uniqueness, but at the same time a significant loss of beauty in one's poetry. The overflowing audience of the studio listened to the poet very attentively and showered him with much applause" (Timenchik 2000: 149).

From Batum, Osip and Aleksandr Mandelstam headed for Tiflis [Tbilisi], where they were being hosted by Titsian Tabidze and Paolo Iashvili. In Tiflis the poet met with his old acquaintance, Il'ia Erenburg, who vividly described some of the details of this meeting in his memoirs. "Paolo put us up in an old, dirty hotel [...] Osip Emil'evich refused to sleep on the bed, he was afraid of bedbugs and germs; so he slept on a high table. At dawn, I saw his profile above me; he slept on his back in a stately manner" (Erenburg 1966: 321). On 26 September a joint reading of Mandelstam, Erenburg, and the Petrograd actor, N. Khodotov, was held at the Tiflis Conservatory.

In early October, the Mandelstam brothers together with the Erenburg couple returned from Tiflis to Moscow. They traveled as diplomatic couriers in an armored train. In the Moscow Press House Mandelstam met face to face with Bliumkin, who attacked the poet with curses and threats. Fearing additional conflicts with Bliumkin, Mandelstam left Moscow for Petrograd in the middle of October 1920. He soon received a "lopsided room with seven corners" (Odoevtseva: 132) in the legendary House of the Arts.

7.

The portrait of Mandelstam as a resident of the House of the Arts has been included in the numerous memoirs and belles-lettres about the literary life of Petrograd in the early twenties. It is then that many of his contemporaries began thinking of Mandelstam as a "walking anecdote" (Odoevtseva: 144) — "an eccentric with bulging red ears" (Gollerbakh: 105), "resembling Don Quixote" (Minchkovsky: 106), "crazy and incredibly amusing" (Onoshkovich-Iatsyna: 398). One could only guess how much spiritual pain such a reputation caused Mandelstam. "Such an attitude allowed for a certain unceremoniousness in relations," wrote Emma Gershtein. "Of course he knew that his unique intellect and poetical genius deserved respectful admiration. This disharmony was the cause of much constant suffering for Osip Mandelstam" (Gershtein: 12). "For some reason, everyone more or less closely acquainted with Mandelstam called him 'Os'ka,'" wrote Nikolai Punin indignantly (Parnis 1991a: 190).

On the other hand, it was during this time period that the author of "Stone" acquired the status of a brilliant poet in the eyes of the wider public, and not just with his fellow Acmeist poets. On 22 October 1920, Mandelstam read his new poems at the Poets' Club on Liteiny prospect. These poems were the first to be acknowledged for their quality by Aleksandr Blok. Nadezhda Pavlovich recalls: "At first glance, Mandelstam's face did not surprise one. Thin with irregular lines of the face... And then he began reading, singsong and slightly rocking rhythmically. Blok and I were sitting next to each other. Suddenly he quietly touched my sleeve and with his eyes led me to look at Osip Emil'evich's face. I had never seen a face change so much from inspiration or self-abandonment" (Pavlovich: 234). Blok himself

Olga Arbenina-Gil'debrandt. 1920-s
Photograph by Moisei Nappel'baum

wrote the following entry in his diary: "The hit of the evening was Mandelstam, who came here after having been in Wrangel's prison. He has grown much. At first it is unbearable to listen to the typical Gumilev type of singsong. Eventually you get used to it, the 'yid' disappears, and only the genuine artist is seen. His poems emerge out of dreams, very unusual ones, the kind that exist only in the realms of art. Gumilev has determined his way: from the irrational to the rational (directly opposite to my way). His [poem] 'Venice'" (Grishunin: 155). The characteristic of "person-artist," "the genuine artist" in Blok's language was practically the highest praise possible.

The poems that Mandelstam read at the Poets' Club also amazed the young actress of the Aleksandrinsky Theater, Olga Nikolaevna Arbenina-Gil'debrandt: "I did not like his previous poems ("Stone"), they seemed to me to be motionless and dry [...] When his first reading took place (in the House of Literature), I was overwhelmed! The poems touched upon my favorite themes: Greece and the sea! "Odysseus ...full of space and time" ...It was stupendous. I also very much liked 'Venice'" (Arbenina: 549).

"I dealt with him as if he were a close girlfriend, who understands everything. About religion, flirting, books, and about food," Arbenina wrote further. "He liked children and seemed to see a child in me. And also, strange as it may seem, something like a princess, this kind of deference was very much to my liking. I never noticed any kind of mockery, irritation, or reprimands, he was "ready" for everything [...] When speaking of the past, M. spoke primarily of his infatuations. Zel'manova, M. Tsvetaeva, Salomeia. He noted which poems were written for whom. About Naden'ka [...] very tenderly, but more like about a younger sister. He told about how they had hidden (from the greens?) in Kiev" (Arbenina: 549-550). Incidentally, it should be noted that Akhmatova's name is not to be found in Arbenina's list.

Arbenina's idyllic description reflected only one side of the relations between Osip Emil'evich and Olga Nikolaevna. The other side, known only by the poet, was reflected in Mandelstam's poem "Equally with others..." (1920), dedicated to her. In this poem love is depicted as suffering, torture, but the suffering is unavoidable, and the torture — desired. In the end of November 1920, Mandelstam wrote yet another poem that was inspired by his meetings with Arbenina:

> *We shall meet again in Petersburg,*
> *as though there we'd buried the sun,*
> *and for the first time, speak the word*
> *the sacred, the meaningless one.*
> *In black velvet of the Soviet night,*
> *in the velvet of earth's emptiness,*
> *flowers still flower everlasting, bright,*
> *women sing, beloved eyes are blessed.*
>
> (Translated by A.S. Kline)

The House of the Arts served as a heaven for Mandelstam up to the beginning of March 1921. A year later he self-mockingly admitted: "We lived in wretched luxury of the House of the Arts, in the Eliseev house, the one that faces Morskaia, Nevsky, and Moika, poets, artists, scholars, all lived as a strange family, deranged over rations, wild and sleepy. There was no reason for the government to feed us, and we did not do anything" (II: 246). This period included intense relations between Mandelstam and Gumilev, Mandelstam's none too eager participation in Gumilev's revived "Guild of Poets," as well as some joint poetry readings. "Memories of Osip's stay in Petersburg in 1920, other than the incredible poems dedicated to Arbenina, include the live, faded, like Napoleon's banners, posters of that time, advertizing the poetry readings, where Mandelstam's name was listed next to that of Gumilev and Blok" (Akhmatova 1989a: 128-129).

In March 1921 Mandelstam left Petrograd for Kiev. From Nadezhda Iakovlevna's "Second Book": "We were apart from Mandelstam for a year and a half, during which time we practically did not have any news of each other. All communication between the cities was down. Those who departed would forget those left behind, because to see each other again seemed almost impossible. It was by chance that it ended up different for us. Mandelstam returned to Moscow with the Erenburgs. He went to Petersburg, and when saying goodbye, asked Liuba [Erenburg] to find out where I was. In January, Liuba wrote him that I was still in Kiev and she gave him my new address as by that time we had been evicted. In March he came to get me—Liuba even now calls herself our matchmaker. Mandelstam came into the empty apartment out of which my parents had again been evicted, this was the second such eviction. The minute he entered, a crowd of female prisoners were brought in under convoy to wash the floors, as the apartment was to be assigned to some big-wig. We did not pay any attention to either the female prisoners nor the soldiers, and we spent two more hours in the room that no longer belonged to me. The prisoners swore, the soldiers cursed, but we did not leave. He read me a whole heap of poems and said that now he will most likely take me away. Then we went to the apartment below, where rooms were assigned for my parents. Two to three weeks later we headed north together. From then on we never parted" (NM-2: 28).

The Mandelstams spent the entire year roaming throughout the country: Kiev, Moscow, Kiev again, Petrograd, Rostov, Kislovodsk, Baku, Tiflis, Batum, Novorossiisk, again Rostov, Khar'kov, again Kiev, again Petrograd, again Moscow. One is to assume that Osip Emil'evich and Nadezhda Iakovlevna were not so much guided by the desire for a change of place as they were by the urge to latch onto life, find their place in the cardinally changing world. "I want to live in a real home. I am no longer young. I am tired of living in rooms," the thirty-two-year-old Mandelstam wrote to his brother, Evgeny, on 11 December 1922 (IV: 30).

Mandelstam's previous circle of acquaintances and friends was perhaps not quite falling apart, but in any case was changing beyond recognition. Georgy Ivanov, Vladislav Khodasevich and Marina Tsvetaeva left the country and came by to say goodbye to Mandelstam before departure. The following is how Nadezhda Mandelstam recalled Marina Tsvetaeva's farewell vist: "Due to our indifference toward each other, preconceived notions, and bad tempers, neither of us was able to say a single human word or, as they used to say, break the ice" (NM-2: 466). Tsvetaeva, by the same token, in one of her letters of that time had characterized Nadezhda Iakovlevna not only as the "recent" but as the "jealous" wife (Tsvetaeva. Vol. 6: 579).

Early April 1921, Vadim Shershenevich, as a result of some insignificant quarrel with Mandelstam at an evening at the Kamerny theater, "got fired up and slapped his face" (Shershenevich: 638). The next day, the imagist poet was challenged to a duel, but Shershenevich backed out of the duel.

In June 1921, the Mandelstams went to Rostov. Here, a poetry reading was organized for Mandelstam. It was described in the memoirs of N.O. Gratsianskaia:

"Osip Emil'evich appeared on the stage in a white shirt with a turn-down collar. He wore dark trousers held up by a narrow belt.

Lifting himself up somewhat onto his toes, he began to recite his poetry. His voice was monotonous, his poetry was exquisitely good...

Rows of listeners sat still. < ... > Whereas Mandelstam kept reading and reading, and it was a genuine pleasure to listen to him."

From Rostov through Kislovodsk the Mandelstams made their way to Baku, where both Osip Emil'evich and Nadezhda Iakovlevna were depressed by their meeting with Sergei Gorodetsky. "He stayed sitting for a long time and kept on like a buffoon, but in such a way that he appeared to me to be completely senile" (NM-2: 39). Mandelstam though for some time continued to try and renew his more or less friendly relations with Gorodetsky. "Despite everything, I insist that Gorodetsky remained true to himself. I recognize in him the old Gorodetsky from the Guild days and Acmeism, and I await with great love and clearly see the future Gorodetsky" (II: 550). With such generous words Mandelstam greeted his former comrade-in-arms that same year of 1921.

In June 1921, Mandelstam visited Viacheslav Ivanovich Ivanov, who had settled in Baku a while ago, and who had praised Mandelstam's new poems as "technically very strong." Moisei Altman's diary entry conveys Mandelstam's profound disappointment from his conversation with Ivanov: "I thought all the while, when we were walking to your place, V[yacheslav] I[vanovich], that you would tell me about what is going on, and here you are telling me that you know, understand, or see absolutely nothing. I call this sacred cataracts" (Altman: 69).

Finally and most importantly, August 1921 was marked by two tragic events that symbolized the end of the epoch of the flourishing of Russian modernist poetry. On 7 August Aleksandr Blok died. Then on 25 August his rival in poetry Nikolai Gumilev, accused of taking part in anti-Soviet conspiracy, was executed by shooting. "Time will be, rather, already has been, their judge," later wrote Akhmatova, "but how terrible to have this literary enmity end with the simultaneous death of each of them" (Akhmatova 1989: 7).

Mandelstam immediately commented upon Blok's death: he read a lecture about the author of the "Twelve" in the Batum Central Union, later he would repeat the lecture with some variations elsewhere. "Recently in the literary life of Kharkov as well as in my personal life a joyful event occurred," wrote L. Landsberg to M. Voloshin on 3 March 1922. "Mandelstam, who was on his way from Tiflis to Kiev (later Moscow-Petrograd), spent a week here. He arrived unexpectedly at one of the literary evenings, and he delivered an impromptu lecture about Blok, which was unique to him, a bit awkward but graceful, one of his surprising aphorisms. A reading was arranged for him that drew the best of Kharkov's public [...] There were few new poems (am sending you practically all there was). He had been writing many articles, feuilletons, correspondence, and earning a good living. Touchingly tender with his wife, in general he has become better—softer and more tolerant" (Mets 2006: 138).

In Tiflis, Mandelstam found out about Gumilev's execution from Boris Legran, the Russian Federation's representative in the then independent republic of Georgia. The poetic response to the death of his close friend was the poem, "I washed myself at night outside..." (1921) with its central image of salt on the axe. Gumilev's death dashed any hope for the revival of Acmeism. That is why at the end of December 1922, Osip Emil'evich angrily responded to the Moscow poetess, Susanna Uksha's invitation to head a newly formed group with an Acmeist precept and orientation: "There are no Muscovite Acmeists, there were and are no longer Petersburg Acmeists, farewell" (Bogomolov: 587). He was somewhat softer in a letter to Lev Gornung written in 1923: "Acmeism in 1923 is not the same as that of 1913. To be correct, there is no Acmeism. It merely wanted to be the "judgment" over poetry. It is the judgment over poetry and not poetry itself" (IV: 33).

In the beginning of 1923, Gumilev's posthumous book, "Letters about Russian Poetry," was published. Valery Briusov published a review of this book under a rather ambivalent title "An Acmeist's Judgment." In his quoted letter to Gornung, Mandelstam borrowed Briusov's metaphor, defining Acmeism as "judgment over poetry, and not of poetry itself."

At the end of February and early March of 1922, in Kiev, Mandelstam and Nadezhda Iakovlevna were married. In March of that same year, the Mandelstams moved to Moscow. In April they were assigned a room at the writers' dormitory, in the left wing of the Hertzen House (Tverskoy Bul'var, 25). "...the room is practically without furniture, occasional food in the cafeteria, bread and cheese spread out on paper, and out of the only window of the first floor of the wing — dense greenery of the garden in front of the Empire style Moscow house with columns in front" — that is how Valentin Kataev described the Mandelstams' life style of that time (Kataev: 80).

At the Hertzen House Mandelstam was visited a few times by Velimir Khlebnikov. Osip Emil'evich and Nadezhda Iakovlevna would help him in every way they could. "Khlebnikov was hungry, whereas with our food rations of the second category we felt as though we were wealthy" (NM-2: 98). In an attempt to to help the homeless Khlebnikov Mandelstam took him to the book store of the Writers' Union to introduce him to N.A. Berdiaev and the critic, V. L'vov-Rogachevsky who worked there. The critic has asked Khlebnikov:

"Are you a member of the writers' organization?"

"I think not..."

Mandelstam told L'vov-Rogachevsky that there is a room available in the left wing of the Hertzen House. The critic replied:

"We have some talented writers who also need rooms."

Mandelstam passionately claimed that Khlebnikov was the most significant poet of the epoch.

Khlebnikov listened, smiling.

Mandelstam's passionate speech was unsuccessful, the room was assigned to D. Blagoi" (Khardzhiev: 335).

Despite almost total paralysis of book publishing and trade during the Civil War, Mandelstam made efforts to bring out his second poetry collection. On 5 November 1920 he signed a contract with the owner of the private publishing house "Petropolis," Ia. N. Blokh, for the publication of the collection "New Stone." This publication did not materialize. On 11 May 1922, Mandelstam concluded an agreement with Gosizdat (the State Publishing House), committing himself to preparing for publication an original book of poems, "Aonides" (another version of the title, "Blind Swallow"). No book was published under such a title. However, in August 1922 "Petropolis" transferred by that time to Berlin managed to bring out the new book of poetry by Osip Mandelstam under the title suggested by Mikhail Kuzmin — "Tristia."

Chapter Three

BETWEEN "TRISTIA" (1922) AND "POEMS" (1928)

1.

Although there were much fewer reviews of "Tristia" published than there had been of "Stone" (1915), practically everyone who wrote about Mandelstam's second book gave it high marks. Even the malicious Sergei Bobrov, who had called Mandelstam's earlier verse "snobbish chatter" (Bobrov: 259), resorted to much different words for "Tristia": "Where did Mandelstam get this bewitchingly fresh voice? ... Where is this tramway ticket simplicity, real, from the streets, and chilly from? Where is this heat, passion, and slightly morbid but real grief from, with freshness bursting through?" (Bobrov: 259). Il'ia Erenburg, on the contrary, found in the metaphor of architecture a connective link between the poems in "Tristia" and the poems from "Stone": "In the epoch of constructivism, Mandelstam is one of the few real builders" (Erenburg 1922: 19). Vladislav Khodasevich saw in this new book by Mandelstam "a noble example of pure metaphorism" (Khodasevich 1922: 11). Nikolai Punin, on the other hand, who warmly greeted the arrival of "Tristia," could not help but resist pointing to Mandelstam's "retrograde" style in comparison with the new, revolutionary, more radical trends in art (Punin 1922: 3).

Mandelstam himself, however, met the appearance of "Tristia" without much enthusiasm. He was greately disappointed by the financial aspects of the "Petropolis" publication. When giving a copy of the book to one of his friends, Mandelstam inscribed it as follows: "To dear David Isaakovich Vygodsky, with the request that you remember that this book was published against my will and without my consent" (Mandelstam 1990a: 452-453). There still exists a copy of "Tristia" with an even harsher inscription by Mandelstam: "This book has been prepared without my consent and against my will by illiterate people out of a bunch of randomly selected pages" (Mandelstam 1990a: 453).

The author's own version of collected new poems was submitted by Mandelstam for publication to the Moscow newly established publishing house, "Krug," on 25 November 1922. It was titled "The Second Book" and was dedicated to "N.Kh." — Nadezhda Khazina. "The Second Book" appeared in book stores by the end of May 1923, two months before the third and final publication of a supplemented edition of "Stone."

In Valery Briusov's review of "The Second Book" which was included into his survey of contemporary Soviet poetry (his final extensive statement in print), he expressed his two fundamental criticisms of Mandelstam. The first one had, by this time, become practically cliché: Mandelstam is a "skillful master" but he "has nothing to say." The second criticism was fated to become cliché for the subsequent years: Mandelstam's poems are "out of touch" — "upon reading "The Second Book" by O. Mandelstam, which is also his "Sorrows" ["Tristia"], the question arises, what century was the book written in? Sometimes the present shines through, with references to "the current century," the great war in Europe is hinted at, there is mention of "battleships" even "breeches" — attributes of the contemporary world, as neither the ancient Greeks nor Romans wore them. But these glimpses fade behind the clouds of various Heracles, Trezen, Persephone, Pierides, and Lethean chills, and so forth and so on" (Briusov: 641).

Despite the somewhat inappropriate mockery over the adjacency of "breeches" with "Persephone" in Mandelstam's book, the experienced critic, nevertheless, was right in noting Mandelstam's desire to combine in his poems the contemporary world with classical antiquity. Briusov uncovered perhaps the most important theme of Mandelstam's poetry of the period in question: Hamlet's theme of the torn connection of "the times and generations," the connections which need to be re-established, even at the cost of one's own life:

BETWEEN "TRISTIA" (1922) AND "POEMS" (1928)

1923

The question as to whether or not it was possible to enter the new era with baggage from the previous culture was not only Mandelstam's concern in the early twenties. The uniqueness of Mandelstam's approach consisted of the attempt to establish the links between the epochs and generations through the affirmation of historical continuity between new Russian poetry and the old, pre-revolutionary, as well as with the cultural tradition of classical antiquity. In his articles of that period, his main concern is the development, before the reader, of a complex hierarchy of literary correspondences that have emerged from the end of the century to the contemporary period. "What has occurred can be called the splicing of the spinal columns of two poetical systems, two poetical epochs" (II: 238). He said in 1923: "Contemporary Russian poetry did not fall out of the sky, it was predicted by all of the previous poetry of our country" (II: 298).

CHAPTER THREE

This very same theme is touched upon in Mandelstam's enigmatic "Ode to Slate" (1923), prompted by Derzhavin's poem "Reka vremen v svoem stremlen'e..." [The River of Time in its Flowing...] scratched "upon a slate board" "on the threshold of the nineteenth century" (II: 265). The theme of the clash of two poetical epochs introduced in the "Ode to Slate" echoes Lermontov's famous poem "Vykhozhu odin ia na dorogu" [I Set Out Alone Down the Road...].

In his articles of the early 20's, Mandelstam attempted to cardinally reevaluate Acmeism's legacy and hierarchy of values, which had initially been created with his direct participation.

In his articles of the early 1920's, Mandelstam had nothing but words of the highest praise not only for Annensky, but for many other Russian Symbolists, though they would frequently get tempered with caustic invectives and hints (note, for example, the analogy between Viacheslav Ivanov and the character from Dostoevsky's "Possessed" Stepan Verkhovensky). At the same time, those poets who previously were closest to Mandelstam's circle were treated with reproach and mockery. Thus, in his article, "Literary Moscow" (1922), Marina Tsvetaeva's poems about Russia were criticized for "lack[ing] taste and [being] historically hypocritical" (II: 258). In his "Storm and Onslaught," Akhmatova was accused of "vulgarizing" "Annensky's methods" (II: 293).

Mandelstam was much more benevolent when it came to those poets of his generation who were close to Futurism, first of all, toward Boris Pasternak. According to Georgy Adamovich, Mandelstam raved over Pasternak's early poem "In the posad, where not a single foot..." (1914), (Adamovich 1996: 111) (from this poem he would subsequently borrow an exotic toponym Zamost'e ("beyond the bridge") for his poem "Batiushkov"). In the fall and winter of 1922-1923, Mandelstam wrote three articles one after another, in which he expressed great enthusiasm for Pasternak's book, "My Sister, My Life" (1922).

The two poets's first encounter happened most likely in the spring of 1922, after the Mandelstams had settled in Moscow. Mandelstam's and Pasternak's personal and creative lives had many similarities. Iury Tynianov had stressed this "semblance of closeness" between them (Tynianov: 187). In both cases, their mothers were professional pianists. Their wives were both artists. Both experienced the death of Skriabin as a personal tragedy. Both poets were castigated for masking an internal emptiness with technical sophistication.

Despite the "semblance of closeness" and high opinion of each other's work, the two poets never became close friends. There was a certain degree of guardedness in Pasternak's treatment of Mandelstam that stemmed from differences in their literary genealogies and artistic principles. Semen Lipkin recalls, "I cannot swear, I admit, I might be wrong, but somehow I have the impression that Pasternak was somewhat cool toward him; as far as I know, they did not see each other often, although at one time they were neighbors at the Hertzen House. Once I found Mandelstam to be in a bad mood. Eventually it turned out that it was Pasternak's birthday, but the Mandelstams had not been invited" (Lipkin: 308). Lipkin's testimony echoes that of Akhmatova: "[Mandelstam] said about Pasternak: 'I have thought about him so much that I am tired', and 'I am convinced that he never read a single line of mine'" (Akhmatova 1989a: 122). We will later find that Akhmatova's judgment of the relations between Pasternak and Mandelstam doesn't reflect the whole picture.

At the end of May 1923, Mandelstam's broken off friendship with Akhmatova got a new lease on life. Osip Emil'evich and Nadezhda Iakovlevna went to Petrograd, where Mandelstam's wife met Anna Andreevna. From N.Ia. Mandelstam's memoirs: "She would often tell me that her friendship with Mandelstam was restored thanks to me. I would be glad if that were the case, however I believe that this happened thanks to her, she displayed a sincere desire to be friends and to avoid any future ruptures. For this she was ready to do anything, the first of which was to become friends with me. In this too she took the lead, and I am very grateful for this" (NM-2: 459).

By this time Mandelstam came to realize that his hopes for stronger status in Soviet literary life had been futile. "I have been barred from everything but translation," O.M. would complain," says Nadezhda Iakovlevna (NM-2: 163). From 1923 on, translations, and primarily translations of prose works, would become Mandelstam's main source of income. The tough conditions of the book market during the NEP period pushed Mandelstam toward thinking of writing prose. It was in Crimea, at Gaspra, where the Mandelstams arrived early August of 1923 to stay at the resort facility owned and administered by the TsEKUBU (Central Commission for the Improvement of the Life Style of Scholars) that the poet started working on his first big piece of prose. It was supposed to be a book about his childhood and youth. The book was commissioned by the editor of the Journal "Rossiia" Isai Lezhnev. "He would dictate to me, on the terrace, 'The Noise of Time', rather, that which would later become 'The Noise of Time'," Nadezhda Iakovlevna would recollect. "He would dictate in pieces, approximately a chapter at a time. Before a session of dictation he would often go for a walk alone, sometimes an hour or two. He would return all tense, mean, and demand that I quickly sharpen the pencils and begin writing down. He would dictate the first phrases so quickly, as if he remembered them by heart, that I would barely be able to write it all down. Then the speed would slow down [...] When there was already a pile of paper, he would ask me to read it out loud: 'But without any expression...' He wanted me to read as if I were a tenth-grade school girl, before a teacher had the chance to teach her how to raise and drop her voice 'with a tear'" (NM-2: 203-204).

In the summer of 1923, Mandelstam entered into a direct clash with his peers in writing for the first time. This clash would become the prologue to many years of ongoing conflict with other members of the Soviet literary establishment. In the end of August, one of the leaders of the All-Russian Union of Writers, the literary critic and art historian, Abram Efros, arrived in Gaspra. He informed Mandelstam that while he was gone, he had incurred a "censure" from the directorate of the Union for his uncomradely action: while living in the Hertzen House, Mandelstam had tried to reason with his neighbors who were constantly making noise in the communal kitchen, while they, in turn, complained to the higher-ups. Incensed by the "censure," Mandelstam sent the directorate a hostile letter in which he announced not only his refusal to return to the writers' dormitory, but also his withdrawal from the Union.

On their way back home from Gaspra, Osip Emil'evich and Nadezhda Iakovlevna made a stop in Kiev. They arrived in Moscow in the first part of October. Here the Mandelstams initially lived at Evgeny Khazin's, Nadezhda's brother, on Savelievsky Lane near Ostozhenka Street. In the end of October they moved to a rented room on Bol'shaya Yakimanka. N.Ia. Mandelstam thus described this dwelling in her memoirs: "We lived in a large square room, which used to be the living room, with a cold tiled wood stove as well as a small cast iron stove that would cool by morning. Firewood was sold on the embankment, the rations had exhausted themselves, we barely survived, having to waste lots of money on cabbies < … >" (NM-2: 209). In an attempt to get some rest from their homelessness in Moscow, at the end of December 1924, the Mandelstams went for a brief visit to Kiev, to Nadezhda Iakovlevna's parents. They spent New Year's in Kiev, and this is where Mandelstam wrote his poem, "1 January 1924" in which he reiterated his faithfulness to "a marvelous oath to the fourth estate" — the social class consisting of those who were not of noble birth and who had become enfranchised by the 1917 revolution. Before the end of the month, back in Moscow, Osip and Nadezhda Mandelstam would join the endless line of people who came to see the coffin with Lenin's corpse on the eve of the funeral. They stood in line together with Boris Pasternak.

1924 was primarily filled with the composition of "The Noise of Time." The book marked a profound reevaluation by Mandelstam of the past, differing significantly from his earlier essays written just a couple of years before. As opposed to his attempt there to "glue together" various pages of history, to stress their continuity, he now brands the epoch of the 1890s as a totally fruitless one, as "placid backwater," "deep provincialism" (II: 347). Perhaps that is why very soon, just a year later Mandelstam will admit to Anna Akhmatova and Pavel Luknitsky that he is "ashamed of the contents" of "The Noise of Time" (Luknitsky: 117).

In the end of July, the Mandelstams became residents of Leningrad. They moved to the very center of the city, on Bol'shaya

CHAPTER THREE

Morskaia, where they rented two rooms in a private apartment. Mandelstam received there an additional source of income: upon Samuil Marshak's suggestion, he began to write children's poetry. Even though later, Nadezhda Iakovlevna would complain that Marshak's edit of Mandelstam's children's books "Two Tramways" and "Balloons" "greatly ruined" them, it should be noted that Mandelstam's poems for children were to a large degree modeled after Marshak's own poetry for this constituency (Gasparov 1987: 103). Some poems utilized the new form of verse invented by Andrei Bely and Vladimir Maiakovsky's — the so-called "ladder":

>   — And the water pipeline
>   Where
>   Does
>   It
>   Get Water?

Others would imitate the infantile manner of Innokenty Annensky. Compare, for example:

> — Oh, blue balloons
> On a white thread,
> I will sell you, balloons,
> And won't make a loss!
> . . . .
> Huff and puffing, the ripe balloons bristle —
> Lilac, red, and blue...
>
>   (Mandelstam, "Balloons")

> Buy some balloons, sirs!
> . . . .
> Children's balloons,
> Red, lilac. Very cheap!
>
>   (Annensky, "Children's Balloons")

When, in September, Pasternak went to Leningrad for a short visit, he met with Mandelstam several times. In a letter sent to Osip Emil'evich on 19 September, already from Moscow, Boris Leonidovich regretted that he did not get a chance to hear Mandelstam's new prose book "The Noise of Time."

2.

It was in the middle of January 1925 that Olga Aleksandrovna Vaksel' first appeared on Morskaia. Olga Vaksel' or Lutik, as she was called by family, first met Mandelstam at Voloshin's house in Koktebel'. In the fall of 1920, she attended the young poets' circle that was directed by Gumilev. Later she would try herself out in different fields: she had some episodic parts in the movies, worked as a model for fur trade auctions, served as proofreader, and a timekeeper at a construction site. "A dazzling beauty," said Akhmatova of her (Smol'evsky: 163).

The story of the brief but stormy relations between Olga and the Mandelstam couple is told by Vaksel' herself in her own Notes as well as by Nadezhda Iakovlevna in "The Second Book." Predictably, these two versions offer completely different explanations of Olga's and Mandelstam's behavior.

Olga Vaksel's version: "He took me to meet his wife (they were living on Morskaia); I liked her, and I would spend all of my spare time with them [...] Everything would have been fine had there not been tension between the spouses. He began to be more interested in me than she was. She would take turns being jealous of me toward him, then of him toward me. I was, of course, totally on her side, I had no need of her husband for anything. I respected him as a poet, but as a person he was quite weak and deceitful. Rather, he was a poet in life, but greatly unlucky [...] In order to speak with me about his love, in other words, of his love for me for his sake and the need for him to love Nadiusha for her own sake, he would use every opportunity to see me again and again. He would get so tangled up in contradictions

CHAPTER THREE

Olga Vaksel

and would so desperately latch on to what remained of common sense, that it was pitiful to look at [...]

I told him of my intention not to visit them anymore; he was inconsolable, he cried, got on his knees, and begged me to take pity on him, for the hundredth time insisting that he cannot live without me, and so forth. Soon I left and never went to visit them again. But a few days later Osip came to our place, and repeated all of this in my room, much to my mother's consternation, as she knew both him and Nadiusha, whom he brought here when visiting. I barely was able to talk him into calming down and leaving" (Poliakova: 172-173).

Nadezhda Iakovlevna's version: "Olga started coming over every day [...] and was leading Mandelstam away right under my very nose. And he suddenly quit looking at me, did not come near, did not speak about anything but everyday stuff, wrote poems, but did not show them to me [...] This was his only infatuation throughout our entire life together, and that was when I found out what tearing asunder was all about. Olga was aiming to tear us asunder, and life hung as if on a hair [...]

Her mother was in charge of everything, a domineering and energetic woman, she managed her daughter's affairs as well. She asked Mandelstam to come over, and also would come over herself for discussion, she attempted to clarify and formulate her daughter's demands in my presence [...] I realized that I needed to find a refuge [...] and pretty quickly I found a person who invited me over [...] My note concerning my leaving [him] for T. [the artist Vladimir Tatlin] was in Mandelstam's hands—he read it and threw it into the fireplace. Then he made me connect him with Olga on phone. He wanted to part with her in front of me, so that I would not have any doubts, though I would have believed him without any primitive signs of proof. He parted with Olga rudely and harshly: I won't come over, I am staying with Nadia, we will never see each other again, never..." (NM-2: 216-220).

3.

The parting with Olga Vaksel' took place in the middle of March 1925. "In the spring of 1925 Mandelstam had his first heart attack, he began to be short of breath. I don't know whether or not Olga Vaksel' was to blame," comments Nadezhda Iakovlevna (NM-2: 227). On 25 March, Osip Emil'evich and Nadezhda Iakovlevna who also fell very sick left Leningrad and moved to Detskoe (Tsarskoe) Selo, to the Zaitsev boarding house. Anna Akhmatova also moved into this boarding house shortly for medical treatment. As N.Ia. Mandelstam recalled, "Our real friendship with Akhmatova began on the terrace of the boarding house, where we would lie all wrapped in short sheepskin coats, breathing the medicinal air of the Tsarskoe Selo. It indeed was medicinal, as we both survived" (NM-2: 230-231).

In the middle of April, the publishing house "Vremya" brought out "The Noise of Time"—Mandelstam would get irritated and laugh at the tautological combination on the cover between the title of the book and the name of the publishing house [Time]. The few reviews of "The Noise of Time" that appeared in the Soviet press generally echoed Briusov's familiar carping. On the one hand: "Sparingly mincing his epithets, Mandelstam, a genuine master, uses only full-weight words" (Fish: 5); "Mandelstam turned out to be a magnificent prose writer, a master of the refined, rich, and accurate style" (Lezhnev: 151). On the other hand: "The book is just a document of the world-view of the literary movement of 'Acmeism', an autobiography of 'Acmeism'" (Fish: 5); "...there is much in the book by Mandelstam that is not contemporary; it is not contemporary not because it speaks of the past, but because one senses an indoor, a bookish attitude to life" (Lezhnev: 152).

A very high assessment of Mandelstam's prose was given by Boris Pasternak. On 16 August 1925, he wrote to Mandelstam: "The Noise of Time" provided me with the kind of rare pleasure that I had not experienced in a long time. The fullness of the sound of this book, which managed to happily express much that is elusive, and that had been completely wiped away from memory, kept absorbing me and carried me along so resolutely and nicely, that I enjoyed reading and rereading it wherever I was. I reread it as soon as I had moved to my datcha, in the woods, i.e. in conditions that are a killer and expose any art that is not perfect. Why have you not written a large novel? You have already managed to do so — you just need to write it down. That my impressions about your prose are not unique or unusual I know from experience; others feel about your prose the same way, including, inter alia, [Sergei] Bobrov" (Pasternak 1992: 171-172).

In striking contrast to Pasternak's enthusiasm was Marina Tsvetaeva's wrathful judgment, which she included in her letter of 18 March 1926 from London to D.A. Shakhovskoy: "I am sitting and tearing into pieces that base book by Mandelstam, 'The Sound of Time'" (Tsvetaeva. Vol. 6: 385). She was primarily indignant about the Crimean chapters of the book, which, she believed, defamed the White Army. But most likely Mandelstam's mean irony concerning his earlier days was not to Marina Tsvetaeva's liking as well, with her idolatry of her childhood. Let us compare a phrase from a letter from Tsvetaeva to L.O. Pasternak dated 5 February 1928 in which she addresses the kinship of her and Boris Pasternak's early cultural milieus: "We are close because of common Germanic roots, somewhere deep in our childhood, 'O Tannenbaum, Tannenbaum' — and everything that grew out of it" (Tsvetaeva. Vol. 6: 256) with Mandelstam's sarcastic description of a lesson of German language at the Tenishev school: "During our lessons of German language we would sing 'O Tannenbaum, Tannenbaum!' under the direction of the Freulein. Milky landscapes of the Alps with milking cows and tiled houses adorned the setting" (II: 368). As a whole, though, the émigré critics accepted Mandelstam's prose enthusiastically. The poet himself wrote about this with some exaggerated irony in a letter to his wife on 11 November 1925: "'The Noise of Time' provoked a 'stir' of delight and enthusiasm in the foreign press, for which I congratulate you" (IV: 48).

On 24 April 1925, after their stay in the Tsarskoe Selo boarding house, the Mandelstams returned to Leningrad, and in the second half of May made a short trip to Kiev. Here Mandelstam was amazed by the Jewish theater productions and especially by the performance of the great artist Solomon Mikhoels. In June the couple stayed in a boarding house in Luga, and then again in the Detskoe Selo. In September, doctors diagnosed Nadezhda Iakovlevna with tuberculosis of the mesenterial glands, and recommended that she urgently change climates. She went to Yalta.

Mandelstam wrote his wife almost every day. These letters are a combination of touching, tender muttering ("I love you, Nadichka, and kiss your forehead and lips") (IV: 45) with detailed reports about his financial successes and failures ("In the newspaper they promised to pay me 60 rubles tomorrow") (IV: 45). In order to pay for Nadezhda Iakovlevna's medical bills, Mandelstam worked tirelessly on the translations commissioned by publishing houses.

Practically in every letter that Mandelstam wrote to his wife from this period onward one finds numerous distinct references to his Christianity. Apparently choice of faith by that time was no longer an issue for Mandelstam. He was neither Orthodox, nor Catholic, nor Protestant, but of an all-encompassing Christian faith "under the cover of the humble worldly forms" (as S.S. Averintsev writes of the early Akhmatova) (Averintsev 1996: 222).

In the middle of November 1925, Mandelstam joined Nadezhda Iakovlevna in Yalta. He returned to Leningrad in early February 1926. There was an attempt made by Il'ia Gruzdev and Konstantin Fedin to include a book of poetry by Mandelstam into the State Publishing House's plan. Nothing, however, came of this attempt: there were no new poems written by Mandelstam and the publishing house was not willing to reissue the old ones. The memoirists recall Mandelstam rushing about Leningrad in search of earnings. During that year, Mandelstam had written 18 reviews of foreign books; his translations were published in 10 anthologies of prose and poetry by publishing houses in Moscow, Kiev, and Leningrad. Two small books of poetry written by Mandelstam for children, "Kitchen" and "Balloons" were also published. Until Nadezhda Iakovlevna came back from Yalta, Mandelstam was living at his brother Evgeny's on the 8th line of the Vasil'evsky Island. From June through the middle of September 1926, Osip Emil'evich and Nadezhda Iakovlevna lived in Detskoe Selo, where they rented furnished rooms. Next door to them Benedikt Livshits with his wife and son took rooms.

The whole of the following year, 1927, was marked by Mandelstam's attempts to overcome his creative crisis. His first step in this direction was to engage in a summing up of his previous work. Overwhelmed with endless translations and book reviews, Osip Emil'evich tried to find time to prepare for publication three volumes of his original writings — poetry, prose, as well as literary criticism. It should be stressed that poets of that time took the preparation of their poetry collections very seriously. The author would first create a *bunch* of poems that would merit, in his view, a new publication. He would then give thought to the internal logic and order in which the poems should be placed to underscore the unity of his creative evolution.

The second step in Mandelstam's return to his true calling was his new project in prose — the tale, "Egyptian Stamp." On 21 April 1927, he signed a contract with the publishing house, "Priboi," for the publication of a novel, "The Adventures of Valentin Garkov" as the future "Egyptian Stamp" was initially called.

Mandelstam started writing the "Egyptian Stamp" in the summer of 1927 in the Detskoe Selo and completed it in February of 1928. It became one of the most difficult and challenging prose texts for contemporary readers. "I am not afraid of disconnectedness or ruptures," said the author (II: 482). Responding to one reader's laments about her inability to understand the "Egyptian Stamp," Mandelstam explained, "I was thinking in omitted links..." (Gershtein: 19). Such structure forces the reader to guess and restore the missing parts and complete for the author the words, phrases and passages that he had concealed. Indeed, such technique is reminiscent of early 20th century modernist poetry, and "The Egyptian Stamp," along with some prose pieces of Boris Pasternak, has since been regarded by critics as a most characteristic specimen of "poet's prose."

The protagonist of the tale is Parnok, who, according to Mikhail Gasparov, "was Mandelstam himself minus his most important part — his creative work" (Gasparov 1995: 40). The fear of poetic numbness that was tormenting Mandelstam was overcome in "Egyptian Stamp" through the creation of a double of the author deprived of the ability to speak. Another striking feature of the tale is the absence of any plot. Mandelstam's general fear of life without plot was to be overcome by the creation of a text without plot. "It is difficult to imagine that our life is a tale without plot or characters, made out of emptiness and glass and the hot babble of mere digressions, from influenza delirium," wrote Mandelstam in the "Egyptian Stamp" (II: 493). This helps us understand better a strange exclamation of the author in the tale: "Dear God! Do not make me resemble Parnok! Give me the strength to be able to distinguish myself from him" (II: 481).

The first publication of the "Egyptian Stamp" occurred in the May 1928 issue of the journal "Zvezda," [Star]. The author kept working on the text till the very last moment: "...he would ask that his manuscript be returned three times, so that he could add more new corrections," a member of the "Zvezda" editorial board, Veniamin Kaverin, recollects (Kaverin: 303).

CHAPTER THREE

It is doubtful that three books by Mandelstam would have been brought out at the same time by state publishing houses, were it not for the behind-the-scenes support of one of the most intelligent and influential party leaders of that time, Nikolai Ivanovich Bukharin. On 10 August 1927, he, presumably upon Mandelstam's own request, appealed to the chairman of the governing board of the State publishing house (Gosizdat, or GIZ in abbreviated form), Artemii Khalatov: "You most likely know the poet O.E. Mandelstam, one of our best writers. They will not publish him in GIZ. I am deeply convinced that this is wrong. It is true, by no means is he a poet for the "masses." And yet he does have and should have his own significant place in our literature. I am writing this letter to you *privati,* as I believe you understand my intentions. I would ask of you to either speak a "few minutes" with O.E. Mandelstam or else to somehow provide him with your enlightened assistance. Yours, N. Bukharin" (Galushkin: 13). Already on 18 August 1927, Mandelstam signed a contract with the Leningrad branch of Gosizdat for the publication of the volume of his collected poems. A contract with the publishing house, "Academia," for the publication of his third original book in this year, a collection of articles "About Poetry" was signed earlier — in February 1927. The advance payments for these contracts allowed Osip Emil'evich and Nadezhda Iakovlevna to travel in October to Sukhum, Armavir, and Yalta. They returned to Detskoe Selo in December 1927.

4.

David Vygodsky whom Mandelstam visited on 9 February 1928, entered into his journal the following day these impressions of their meeting: "Yesterday evening Mandelstam. Unbearable, unpleasant, but one of the few, perhaps the only (besides Andrei Bely) real one, with a genuine spiritual passion and genuine depth. Wild, restless. Equally horrified by that which he knows, and that which is not given to know. After him everyone else is so small, talkative, and pedestrian" (Mandelstam 1990: 355).

Soon thereafter, on 5 March 1928, Mandelstam took part in an evening dedicated to the memory of Fedor Sologub that was organized by the Union of Writers. Pavel Luknitsky described in his journal Mandelstam's persistent efforts to get the organizers of the event to invite Vladimir Piast to take part in the evening. This was by far not the first time that Mandelstam was sticking up for someone who was even less well-adjusted to life than him. In April 1922, as we remember, the poet attempted to get living quarters assigned in Moscow for Velimir Khlebnikov. In the case with Piast, the situation was further aggravated by the fact that he, like Mandelstam himself, was considered to be the eccentric-poet. It was even worse for Piast than for Mandelstam, since Mandelstam was believed to be just half crazy, while Piast was considered to be crazy. Back in the early 1910's, when Mandelstam's and Piast's literary reputations had not yet fully taken shape, the elder poet was the only one among all of the Russian Symbolists who recognized Mandelstam's talent without reservation and he took upon himself the role of promoter of the younger poet. There were perplexed newspaper reports and testimonies of contemporaries about Piast's public talk on 7 December 1913. Ivan Evdokimov wrote in his diary: "I returned from Piast's lecture […] his excessive praise of O. Mandelstam seemed definitely for me a sacrilege. Piast persistently contrasted Mandelstam to A. Blok, and it was obvious that Piast considered Mandelstam to be a much greater poet than A. Blok" (LN: 426). This is particularly poignant given the fact that Piast was one of Blok's closest friends. Much later, Piast would portray Mandelstam with great love in his memoir book, "Meetings" (1929), which he presented to Mandelstam with a somewhat enigmatic dedicatory inscription: "To my co-author, Osip Mandesltam, from the author, with love" (Freidin 1991: 236). (The book cited many of Mandelstam's unpublished comic poems, which is perhaps what emboldened Piast to call him his co-author). One can furnish more examples to prove that Mandelstam had all the reasons to see in Piast a co-brother in misfortune. Thus it comes as no surprise that the author of "Egyptian Stamp" consistently took an active part in the fate of his older companion (Piast, by the way, became one of the prototypes of Parnok; the other prototype of the protagonist of "Egyptian Stamp" was the poet and dance theoretician, Valentin Parnakh, the brother of Sophia Parnok).

However the group of the members of the board of "Society of Mutual Credit" who in April 1928 were sentenced to be shot were not known by Mandelstam personally at all. Nevertheless, he deemed it necessary to intercede on their behalf. On 18 May, he sent Bukharin a copy of his recently released book of collected poems, with the inscription stating that everything in this book voices protest against the impending execution. Shortly thereafter the author of the book received from Bukharin a telegram notifying him of the commuted sentence.

Chapter Four

BEFORE THE ARREST (1928-1934)

When speaking about Mandelstam's 1928 "Poems," Soviet critics favored, to the point of setting one's teeth on edge, two clichés — "master" and "out of tune with the times <uncontemporary>." A substantially new sound however took over the majority of the reviews, replacing "friendly" reproaches with quite ominous overtones. Thus, in one of the reviews (A. Manfred), Mandelstam was called "a bourgeois poet through and through," a representative of the "upper," "most aggressive" bourgeoisie (Manfred: 22). It is worth mentioning that Mandelstam's poetry book as well as his collection of his articles, "About Poetry," were bowdlerized by censors.

But even greater misfortune lay ahead. In the middle of September 1928, the publishing house, "Zemlia i fabrika" [The Land and the Factory] (ZIF) brought out a novel by the Belgian author Charles de Coster "The Legend of Thyl Ulenspiegel." Mandelstam was erroneously listed as the translator on the title page, whereas he had in fact edited two previous translations, one by Arkadii Gornfeld and another by Vasily Kariakin. Mandelstam's task was to combine these two translations into one. Neither Gornfeld nor Kariakin knew anything about the publisher's plans and received no advance payment.

As soon as Mandelstam learned about the publisher's blunder, he rushed to let Gornfeld know about it. He interrupted his trip to Crimea and announced that he would vouch his entire earnings from the publication for the fee due to Gornfeld (IV: 101). Gornfeld, who was stricken with paralysis, found the behavior of ZIF to be appalling while that of Mandelstam — flippant. Even Mandelstam's close friends reproved him. "Osip was wrong!" Anna Akhmatova commented on Mandelstam's behavior in a later conversation (Gershtein: 416).

"...he is at fault," thus Boris Pasternak wrote about Mandelstam in the "Gornfeld case" to Marina Tsvetaeva.

In October 1928, Gornfeld wrote to his relative in Simferopol': "...'Ulenspiegel' was published in the supposed translation of O. Mandelstam (the poet), but in fact stolen from me and another translator. Mandelstam — a talented but dissolute person, smart, a pig, a petty swindler — keeps bombarding me with telegrams, begging me of mercy (I could make him appear in the docks as defendant), but I am continuing to be stern and would like to punish the publishing house ('The Land and Factory') for his swinishness" (Musatov: 295-296).

Upon Mandelstam's initiative, in the 13 November 1928, issue of the Leningrad "Krasnaia Gazeta" [the Red Paper], a short letter to the editor was published, signed by A.G. Venediktov, member of the board of "Zemlia i fabrika": "In the title page of "The Legend of Thyl Ulenspiegel" published by ZIF, an error had occurred. It was printed as follows: "translation from the French by O. Mandelstam" whereas, it should have stated as follows: "the translation from the French was modified and edited by O. Mandelstam."

It comes as no surprise that Gornfeld was not appeased by such "apologies." On 28 November, he published his letter to the editor of the same "Krasnaia Gazeta," under the biting title of "Translators' Trash." In this note, Gornfeld rightly pointed out that Mandelstam did not work with the original text of the "Legend of Thyl Ulenspiegel," rather he practically mechanically combined two translations "with their different styles and different vocabularies": "Where Gornfeld wrote: "When North kisses with the West," Kariakin erred and instead of North wrote "East;" a perplexed Mandelstam proposes the following compromise: "A combination of North-West with East." Such a compromise especially makes no sense, as it is later explained that in this allegory, North represents Holland, and West — Belgium, which is located not North-West but South-East of Holland" (Musatov: 296-297).

The letter from Gornfeld ended with a metaphor that insulted Mandelstam: "When wandering at some second-hand market I see a coat, though remade, but taken out of my vestibule yesterday, I have the right to announce: 'Hark, this coat was stolen'" (Musatov: 296). On 12 December 1928, Mandelstam appealed to Gornfeld through the newspaper, "Vecherniaia Moskva" (the Mandelstams had moved back to Moscow in the beginning of December). He did not so much discuss the translator's specific reproaches, as he heatedly disputed the fairness of Gornfeld's "clothing" metaphor: "...it doesn't matter whether or not I corrected the old translations and made them better or worse or if I created a new text along their lines. Can't Gornfeld have any consideration for the peace of mind and moral virtues of the writer who traveled 2000 verst [1 versta = 1.6 km] to resolve this, to iron out this ridiculous, vexatious negligence (the poet's own and that of the publishing house). Did he really want us to be standing, for the pleasure of the petty bourgeoisie, like two hucksters clutching each other's hair? [...] How could he even sink as low as that phrase about the "fur coat"? The two mistakes, mine — that I should have insisted on the publishing house coming to an agreement with the translators in a timely manner, and Gornfeld's — that he distorted my entire writer's demeanor in the press, are incomparable" (IV: 103).

Gornfeld, in his turn, considered himself to have been "guiltlessly reviled" (from a letter to A.R. Palei, dated 18 December 1929) (Gornfeld: 176). On 2 January 1929, he sent a venomous reply to Mandelstam to "Vecherniaia Moskva," however the editors did not publish it. At this point the irritated translator started circulating the typescript copies of his letter. "He dares speak of the spirit of the original, he who has not seen the original with his own eyes. He dares discuss the quality of my translation, he who had misappropriated it [...] I don't want anything from him: neither his apology, his visits, his worries. He should, however, learn from the writer and "older contemporary," that in those cases when one has to do with the reader's interest and social morality, we shouldn't care about anyone's peace of mind" (Musatov: 300).

Meanwhile, the translator Kariakin issued a hysterical statement to the Directorate of the All-Russian Writers Union. In particular, he mentioned that he plans to "seek the defense of his aggrieved interests before the Soviet Court" (Musatov: 301). And indeed, he did take it to court, but in June of 1929 the action over the case of "Thyl Ulenspiegel" was thrown out of court.

The paradoxicality of Osip Mandelstam's behavior in this difficult situation is puzzling. Instead of coming to terms with the conditions, repenting, and hiding his head in the sand, the poet switched to an active offensive on all fronts, in every way possible underscoring his dissent and his incompatibility with the people around him.

"I am alone. *Ich bin arm* [I am poor—German]. Everything is irreparable. Severance <Breaking off relations> is a treasure, it must be preserved, not squandered," Mandelstam wrote to his wife in March 1930 (IV: 136). In another letter he compared the case of "Thyl Ulenspiegel" to "the Dreyfuss case" (IV: 134).

From the end of December 1928 until March 1929 the Mandelstams lived in Kiev. Isaak Babel had hooked Mandelstam up with a local film studio, giving him the opportunity to earn some money. In Kiev, Nadezhda Iakovlevna had her appendix removed, the operation was performed by the surgeon, Vera Gedroits, who, just as Mandelstam, had, in her time, attended the "Guild of Poets." "Things were very tight," Mandelstam wrote in a letter to his father, sent in the middle of February. "There was practically no money. Nadia's parents are totally helpless and poor. Their apartment is cold and neglected. They have no connections. The mother is a very bad housewife. I had to fight for every cup of broth that I took to the hospital. I had a permanent pass to the clinic, and since a separate room was provided, I would spend entire days there, even occasionally nights, thereby substituting for the nurse and orderly. The worse thing was preparing Nadia for her return home, getting the wood stove going, getting the rooms heated, providing something for the household, for a maid" (IV: 111).

The poet returned to Moscow early April 1929, and immediately entered into battle: on 7 April, the newspaper "Izvestia" ran a huge article by Mandelstam, "Potoki khaltury" (Currents of Hackwork), that was aimed against defective translation practices. Among the measures that the author recommends in the article is to call for "an all union conference on issues of foreign literature" and the creation of "an institute of foreign literature with a permanent department of translation theory and practice." This was greeted by the sour reaction of his fellow writers: "Osip Mandelstam writes *pro domo mea* [in his defense — latin], without mentioning, however, the case with the novel by De Coster," was a caustic remark in a letter by R.V. Ivanov-Razumnik to A.G. Gornfeld) (Musatov: 305).

On the same day, when the "Currents of Hackwork" was published in Moscow, the first session of the arbitration tribunal took place in Leningrad over the "Mayne Reid case": the new director of ZIF, Il'ia Ionov, accused Mandelstam and Benedikt Livshits of using French translations rather than the English originals when translating Mayne Reid's novels. Mandelstam and Livshits asserted that they were right.

The anti-Mandelstam campaign culminated in the publication in the "Literaturnaia Gazeta" (The Literary Gazette) on 7 May 1929 of a satirical article, "O skromnom plagiate i razviaznoi khalture" [About Shy Plagiarism and Unbridled Hackwork]." The author of this article was the journalist David Zaslavsky, to whom Soviet authorities liked to entrust the most loathsome assignments. Gornfeld commented on Zaslavsky's article "he is now a rascal worse than Mandelstam" (Musatov: 308). The first section of the article recounted a story about a minor Kiev writer who had received a prize of 150 rubles for a story that had been written by another writer. In the second part, Mandelstam, the author of "Currents of Hackwork," judges Mandelstam, the editor of "The Legend of Thyl Ulenspiegel" and passes a resolution: "Let's grab him by the collar, he who poisons literary wells, dirties public toilets, and present him to Mandelstam to administer justice and mete out punishment. And what would O. Mandelstam do with him is difficult to imagine!" (Musatov: 307).

In the 13 May issue of "Literaturnaia Gazeta" appeared Mandelstam's own letter to the editor, as well as a petition in his defense signed by fifteen famous Soviet writers (K. Zelinsky, Vsevolod Ivanov, N. Aduev, B. Pil'niak, M. Kozakov, I. Selvinsky, A. Fadeev, B. Pasternak, V. Kataev, K. Fedin, Iu. Olesha, M. Zoshchenko, L. Leonov, L. Averbakh, E. Bagritsky) that reads: "Zaslavsky, through the use of a range of outrageous devices attempts to cast aspersions on the writer's good name" (Musatov: 307-308). Zaslavsky replied with a new "Letter to the Editor" published in the "Literaturnaia Gazeta" on 20 May. At the same time, the case was turned over to the grievance committee of FOSP (Federation of Association of Soviet Writers), which denounced Zaslavsky's article and refused to treat Mandelstam's actions as plagiarism yet declared that Mandelstam was morally responsible. The decision was worded with the participation of Boris Pasternak, who wrote to N. Tikhonov on June 14, 1929: "Mandelstam will become a total enigma for me if he fails to learn lofty lessons from the misfortune that befell him lately" (Pasternak 1992: 277). Mandelstam, nevertheless, was infuriated with FOSP's decision.

A few weeks before that, on 18 June, P.N. Luknitsky saw Mandelstam and made the following entry in his journal: "O.E. is in a terrible condition, he hates everyone around him, is extremely angry, pennyless as well as without any opportunity to earn money, he is literally starving. He is living (separately from N.Ia.) in a TsEKUBU dormitory, for which he is unable to pay, his debt is escalating, he will be evicted if not today, then tomorrow. He is covered with a bristle of a beard, he is nervous, quick-tempered, and irritable. He is incapable of speaking about anything else but this incident. He considers all writers to be enemies. He insists that he has left literature for good and will not write a single line again, he has torn all of the contracts that he had in place with publishing houses. He said that Bukharin is trying to get him set up somewhere as a secretary, but most likely nothing will come of it. He wanted to go to Yerevan, where he was promised a possible "civil servant" position (Luknitsky: 142).

It was Bukharin that tried to arrange Mandelstam's trip to Yerevan. On 14 June 1929 he wrote to the Chairman of the Armenian government: "One of our major poets, O. Mandelstam, would like to get a culture-related job in Armenia (for example, in the history of Armenian art, literature, in particular, or something of that sort). He is a very educated man and you would benefit greatly from him. All he needs is to be left alone for a while and given the opportunity to work. He could write something about Armenia. He is ready to learn Armenian and so forth. Please respond by telegraph to your legation in Moscow" (Mandelstam 1990b: 422). Soon there was an affirmative reply from Yerevan, it was signed by the People's Commissar of Education, A. Mravian. However, after A.A. Mravian's sudden death on 23 November 1929, the trip was indefinitely postponed.

In the summer of 1929, Mandelstam went together with Nadezhda Iakovlevna to Yalta. Upon his return to the capital end of August, he went to work for the newspaper, "Moskovsky Komsomolets," where he directed the poetry section and edited the weekly "Literaturnaia stranitsa" [Literary Page].

2.

Mandelstam worked for the "Moskovsky Komsomolets" for four months. "The editorial office was trustful and friendly toward Mandelstam [...] He was asked to supply the editorial office and its staff with 'culture'," recalls Nadezhda Iakovlevna (NM-2: 539). A regular job demanded from the poet maximum concentration and self-discipline. The young staff and guests of the "Moskovsky Komsomolets" remembered his reticence and tactfullness: "Externally he appeared to be calm. We even thought that he was somewhat haughty, as he held his head high!" (S. Poliakova "<...> a quiet, even voice, the ordinary appearance of a provincial teacher, an intelligent face without a smile, doleful eyes" (Kochin: 319); "<...> a friendly smile on a rose face, clean, elegant, his eyes emitting attentiveness and kindness" (A. Glukhov-Shchurinsky: 20). Aleksandr Tvardovsky, who once brought his poems to the literary section of the "Moskovsky Komsomolets," recalls otherwise: "An irritated person on thin legs, like a grass-hopper, kept yelling something at me excitedly, I quietly left with my poems" (Lakshin: 128).

During the day, the "calm" Mandelstam headed the poetry section of the "Moskovsky Komsomolets;" at night, a frantic Mandelstam would dictate to his wife his "Fourth Prose," in which he squared accounts for the "Thyl Ulenspiegel" story as well as satirized the Komsomol and its newpaper (III: 168-169).

CHAPTER FOUR

For the first time in Mandelstam's life the ominous shadow of I.V. Stalin seemed to hang over the pages of "The Fourth Prose." In the fifth section, speaking about the children of Soviet writers, he indignantly says that "their fathers have entered into a forward contract with the pockmarked devil three generations in advance" (III: 171). As is well known, Stalin became pockmarked after he had come down with smallpox. He was called "pockmarked" by his comrades in the revolutionary underground. And in the final, sixteenth section referring to a circulation of political jokes in Moscow, Mandelstam says: "Lenin and Trotsky are walking around arm in arm, as if nothing happened. One has a bucket, the other a fishing pole from Constantinople in his hand" (III: 179). The implication is not only the Russian idiomatic expression *"smatyvat' udochki"* [take to one's heels], hinting at Lev Trotsky's deportation from the Soviet Union to Turkey on 1 February 1929 as well as at a specific joke. It was quoted in the book of a UPI correspondent in the USSR, Eugene Lyons, published in New York in 1935: "Trotsky, who was in exile in Turkey was fishing. A newspaper boy decided to play a practical joke on him:

"A sensation! Stalin has died!"
But Trotsky did not even lift an eyebrow:
"Young man," he said to the newspaper boy, "that can't be true, if Stalin had died, I would already be in Moscow."
The next day, the newspaper boy tried again, but this time he yelled:
"A sensation! Lenin is alive!"
But Trotsky still was not to be fooled.
"If Lenin were still alive, he would be here, next to me, right now" (Lyons: 328).

In February 1930, the commission for inspection of the staff of the editorial board of the "Moskovsky komsomolets" gave the worker Mandelstam the following characteristic: "Can be used as a specialist, but under supervision." Out of protest, Mandelstam quit the newspaper.

For a while he led a group of worker-correspondents at the office of the newspaper "Vecherniaia Moskva." In the stifling atmosphere of the Moscow and Leningrad literary world it was impossible for him to even dream of returning to poetry writing. But a miracle did happen: Nikolai Bukharin was able to arrange a trip for Mandelstam to the Transcaucasia. In March, the Mandelsatms left the hateful "Hertzen House," where they had to live once again since January 1930, and took off on a long awaited journey.

During two months, from the end of March through May, the Mandelstams rested at the governmental datcha in Sukhum, from where they would take excursions to the Novyi Afon, Gudauta, and Tkvarcheli. In Sukhum, on 14 April 1930, Mandelstam was struck by the "oceanic piece of news about the death of Maiakovsky. Like a mountain of water the spine is stricken by tourniquets, <this news> hindered one's breathing and left a salty taste in one's mouth" (from drafts for "Travels to Armenia") (III: 381).

Both poets had entered literature (Mandelstam—a bit earlier, Maiakovsky—a bit later) during the epoch of the crisis of Symbolism when beginning poets no longer chose to join this movement. Some joined Futurism, others—Acmeism.

Maiakovsky quickly began to be perceived by the public as the Futurist № 2—less radical and less prone to theorizing than Khlebnikov, but by no means less talented. Mandelstam—not exactly as quickly—came to be seen as the Acmeist № 2—whose place follows that of Gumilev and is next to Akhmatova. Despite their participation in the opposing, even hostile literary movements, and despite his critical attitude toward Maiakovsky's works of the post-revolutionary, Soviet period, Mandelstam saw in Maiakovsky "the whetstone of our poetry" (Lipkin: 309). One of the contemporaries recorded Mandelstam's hyperbolic assessment: "Maiakovsky is a giant, we are not even worthy of kissing his knees" (Sokolova: 90).

When Mandelstam went to the Caucasus, and thus disappeared from the sight of his colleagues in Moscow and Leningrad, rumor had it that the author of "Tristia" had committed suicide like Maiakovsky (Chukovsky-2: 7, entry of 22 April of 1930).

CHAPTER FOUR

Boris Kuzin
1930-s

Boris Pasternak

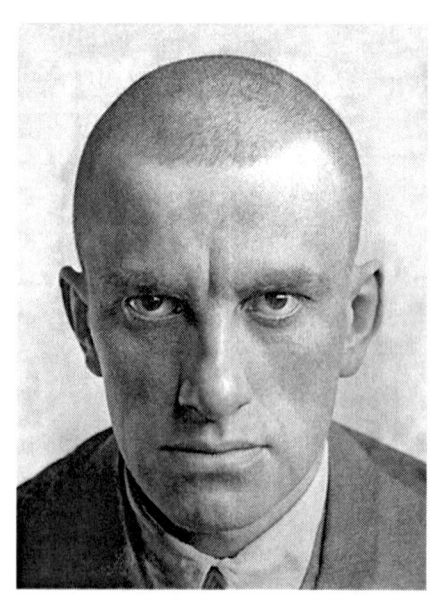

Vladimir Maiakovsky

In May-June 1930 the Mandelstams were living in Tiflis, and then they moved to Yerevan. There Mandelstam met the young biologist, Boris Sergeevich Kuzin. As Emma Gershtein recalls, "He was not a Darwinist, but a Lamarquist. [...] [He] knew foreign languages, constantly reread Goethe in German [...] worked at the Zoological museum of the University" (Gershtein: 22-23). A warm relationship grew out of their first encounter. "Our close friendship came into being not just quickly, but as if instantly," Kuzin recollected. "I was immediately pulled into all of their plans and misfortunes. From the first to the last days of our association, every meeting of ours consisted of a mixture of conversations on the loftiest of themes, discussions concerning the various ways of getting out of impossible situations, the acceptance of impracticable decisions (or if practicable, then incapable of being implemented), and jokes and laughter in the midst of the most grim conditions" (Kuzin: 165). "…the encounter was fate for all three of us. Without it, Osia would often say, he might not have resumed writing poetry," Nadezhda Iakovlevna wrote to Boris Sergeevich soon after Mandelstam's death (Kuzin: 639). And here is how Mandelstam characterized Kuzin: "It is perhaps to him and only to him that I owe what I brought to literature in the so called "mature Mandelstam" period" (Kuzin: 150).

From 1 until 15 July 1930, the Mandelstams were on holiday in the house of rest at Lake Sevan. From the recollections of Anaida Khudaverdyan: "Since it was difficult for him to endure the extreme heat of Yerevan, it was proposed that he stay at the Lake Sevan. That is how the Mandelstams ended up at this house of rest. The Mandelstams did not have any children of their own, but they very much liked children and wanted to have some. The wife yearned for a son [...] While Osip Mandelstam sat at the table to work, she would leave the room quietly on tiptoe, shutting the door after her, and would lead away the children who were playing under the window, so that they 'would not get in the way of the man writing his poetry'" (Khudaverdian: 78). The last phrase leads one to assume that it was on Sevan that Mandelstam started writing poetry again after a five-year pause. Though most likely it happened a bit later. In any case, when Kuzin returned to Yerevan, Osip Emil'evich did not read to him any new poems. "The last days in Yerevan took place in the midst of endless conversations and plans for the future," Boris Kuzin would recollect. "To go back to Moscow and try and achieve something new, some kind of arrangement there, or to stay in Armenia? It is difficult to count how many times the decision changed. But by the day of my departure it was finally decided. The only possible decision was to stay here. Only in the setting of the ancient Armenian culture, through the penetration into the life, history, and art of Armenia (this included, of course, the complete mastery of the Armenian language) could put an end to creative lethargy. Returning to Moscow was absolutely out of the question" (Kuzin: 165).

Even though in the end the Mandelstams did not remain in Armenia, their stay there exerted an enormous impact on the poet. "In the thirty-first year from the birth of this century // I returned, no — rather was by force // Returned into the Buddhist Moscow. // But before that I still had the chance to see // The magnificent Ararat covered by a biblical tablecloth // And I spent two hundred days in the country of the Sabbath, // That which is called Armenia," — he wrote in one of his poems written in 1931.

The advent of new poems was a result of Mandelstam's withdrawal from the literary world and the rejection of his previous interests in literary matters. In the rush of renunciation of "literary interests," Mandelstam was almost ready to reject the Russian language in exchange for the Armenian (in the poem dedicated to Kuzin, "On German Speech," he admitted to the desire of "ruining myself, in contradiction," "to exit our native tongue // For all that I am grateful to it in perpetuity"). It is symptomatic that when writing his "Journey to Armenia" in April 1931, Mandelstam discussed extensively and in great detail biology and art, but almost avoided any talk of literature. The only exception was a paragraph on Maiakovsky's death, which Mandelstam chose not to include in the final version of his "Journey to Armenia," perhaps because he did not want to compete with Boris Pasternak, who had just published his "Safe Conduct."

3.

In the middle of October 1930, the Mandelstams moved from Yerevan to Tiflis. They returned to Moscow in November. In December they tried to secure themselves in Leningrad, but failed to find a place to live there. The secretary of the Leningrad branch of the Writers Union, the poet Nikolai Tikhonov, refused to help them. Nadezhda Iakovlevna recalls: "When I found out about the rejection [...], I asked Tikhonov whether or not O.M. needs to get permission from the writers' organization to reside in Leningrad, say in a private room. Tikhonov stubbornly replied: 'Mandelstam will not live in Leningrad'" (NM-1: 280-281).

In an attempt to somehow improve their housing situation, the Mandelstams appealed to the head of the Soviet government, V.M. Molotov, in writing. The letter signed by Nadezhda Iakovlevna read: "Mandelstam was not able to get work in Armenia because he does not know the Armenian language, and after several months of rest, we ended up having to return to the north. In Transcaucasia Mandelstam fully recovered from his illness, but upon returning to the north, to more difficult living conditions, he will undoubtedly quickly ruin his health, and everything will return to how it was [...] The main problem is that Mandelstam is unable to survive purely by his literary work — his poems and prose. As a brief and oligophyllous author, his output is quite scarce... After a heavy life crisis, after undergoing illness, Mandelstam, an old and weary man, has found himself back to square one [...] And in order to save him, normal living conditions need to be provided to him, he should be given calm brain work [...] The second issue is that of the housing problem. All these years we never had enough funds to buy an apartment [...] It is impossible to get living quarters in any city. Mandelstam has become homeless all across the entire USSR" (Grigor'ev, Petrova: 181).

No help came to the poet from above. The couple spent their last days in Leningrad separately. Osip Emil'evich, at his brother Evgeny's, and Nadezhda Iakovlevna at her sister's, "in a closet behind the kitchen." They returned to Moscow in the middle of January

1931. Nadezhda Iakovlevna temporarily moved in with her brother on Strastnoy boulevard. Osip Emil'evich lodged with his brother, Aleksandr, on Starosadsky Lane.

The despair over the unsettled domestic situation somehow coexisted in the poet with his enthusiasm over the resumption of writing poems. Nadezhda Iakovlevna nostalgically wrote of these days: "We were mobile and would walk a lot. Everything that we saw would end up in the poems: a Chinese laundry where we had our linen washed, an open-air bazaar where we would thumb through books, not buying any for lack of funds and living quarters, a street photographer who took a picture of me, Mandelstam and Shura's [Aleksandr's] wife, a Turkish drum and the jet of water from a trailer tank for street washing. The return to poetry led to a feeling of unity with the world, people, crowds on the streets... It was a blissful feeling, and we lived miraculously" (NM-2: 548).

Mandelstam's poems written in 1931 provide a kind of response to all those critics that for years had reproached the poet for his aloofness and a lack of contact with the present. "You think that I am with the XIXth century? No, I am not with the XXth, but not with the XIX either!" the poet wrote to one of his younger acquintances (Feinberg: 70). In his poem, "Enough sulking. Let's push the paper into the table..." (7 June 1931), he affirms his inseverable connection to the present: "Let me bet that I am not yet dead, // And like a jockey, I bet my head, // That I can still get up to mischief // On a trotting racing lane. // I keep in mind that it's thirty one // A wonderful year blooming in the May Day tree..."

A prominent place among Mandelstam's texts of 1931 is held by the famous poem, "For the Future Ages' Resounding Glory," written from 17 through 28 March. In one of the episodes of "The Journey to Armenia," (which he began working on in April of the same year) Mandelstam compares himself with "the boy Mowgli from Kipling's Jungle Book" (III: 195). In the poem, "For the Future Ages' Resounding Glory," playing with the key phrase of Kipling's tale ("We are of one blood, you and I"), he, like Mowgli, renounces his "wolfish" past for the sake of the "human" present:

For the future ages' resounding glory,
for their noble race of human beings,
I was deprived of my cup at the feast,
my own honour, and joyous things.

Our wolfish era runs at my shoulder,
but there's no wolf's blood in me,
better to crush me like a hat deeper
into a Siberian fur's hot sleeve —

. . . . .

Take me into the night, where the Yenisey
flows, where pines reach the starlight,
because there's no wolf's blood in me,
and only an equal shall take my life.

Translation by A.S. Kline

The first ones to hear the poem, "For the Future Ages' Resounding Glory," were the distinguished actor-reader Vladimir Iakhontov and his wife Liliia (Elikonida) Popova, with whom the Mandelstams were especially close in 1931. "... like an animal at bay he was ready to burst into tears, and he indeed did burst into tears, falling on the couch, as soon as he had read it to us (most likely the first time, to the first ones) — "Our wolfish era runs at my shoulder, but there's no wolf's blood in me," — Iakhontov wrote in his journal (Iakhontov: 139).

Mandelstam still had nowhere to live. He and his wife led a nomad's life in Moscow and moved from one set of compassionate friends to others. "From January 1931 until January 1932, i.e. throughout the year, the homeless man without any residence was left out in the streets. During this time, hundreds of apartments and rooms were distributed, improving the living conditions of other writers," Mandelstam sadly lamented in a letter to the high party functionary, the editor I.M. Gronsky (IV: 146). In January 1932, the Mandelstams finally were assigned a small, ten meter boxroom in the Hertzen House. Pretty soon they were able to move to a slightly larger room in the same wing. However, Mandelstam described his living conditions in a written complaint to Gronsky as follows: "I was provided with lodging in a damp wing unfit for living, without a kitchen, with a drinking faucet in a rotting toilet, mould on the walls, boarded partitions, an icy-cold floor" (IV: 146). "I noticed that Mandelstam constantly tried to hold himself in such a way as to cover his back," Nikolai Tikhonov thus described one of his meetings with Mandelstam at that time. "It was somehow unclear why he was constantly pressing [with his back] against the wall. But his wife said: 'Don't pay any attention to him. He can't turn around because he split the seat of his pants and there is such a gaping hole that he has to cover it with a newspaper" (Tikhonov: 18).

Yet at the same time, the first half of 1932 can be said to be a period of relative stability, albeit short, in the anxious lives of Osip Emil'evich and Nadezhda Iakovlevna. It was around this time that Mandelstam started sharing with select listeners his new prose about Armenia. One of them was a famous revolutionary writer and journalist Viktor Serge (Kibal'chich), who recalls Mandelstam as follows: "A Jew, not tall, with a face full of condensed sorrow and anxious as well as contemplative hazel eyes. Mandelstam, who is highly respected in the literary world, lived poorly and with difficulty [...] Having completed reading, Mandelstam asked us: "Do you believe it will be possible to get this published?" (Timenchik 2005: 386). As it turned out, in the atmosphere of the liberalization of cultural life, after the disbandment of the Russian Association of Proletarian Writers in April 1932, such a miracle became possible. "The Journey to Armenia" was printed in the May 1933, issue of the Leningrad journal "Zvezda" (Star).

Mandelstam's financial situation was gradually improving. In the spring of 1932, Bukharin obtained for the 41-year-old Mandelstam a lifelong personal monthly pension in the amount of 200 rubles for "outstanding services in Russian literature" (the pension payments ceased after the end of Mandelstam's exile in Voronezh in 1937). With the help of Mikhail Zenkevich, it was possible to publish two poems by Mandelstam in the April issue of "Novyi Mir," the most respectable and inflential Soviet literary journal edited by Ivan Gronsky, and later four more in the June issue (the last publication of Mandelstam's poetry in his lifetime took place in November 1932, in the "Literaturnaia Gazeta"). On 8 September, Mandelstam signed a contract with the State publishing house of literature (GIKhL) for the publication of his book "Poems" (the publication never saw the light of day). In the 21 April 1932 issue of the newspaper, "Za kommunisticheskoe prosveshchenie" [For Communist Enlightenment], Mandelstam's article, "The Issue of Darwin's Scientific Style" was published. An old close friend of the Mandelstams, Aleksandr Osipovich Morgulis, worked on the editorial staff in this newspaper. "Osip Emil'evich tenderly loved my husband," Morgulis' widow recalled in her memoirs and added that the poet had great trust in her husband's literary taste (Khantsyn: 68). Morgulis was able to arrange for Nadezhda Iakovlevna to work as an editor at the same newspaper.

Another partner of Mandelstam's in both joyful and serious conversations was his neighbor at the Hertzen House, a talented peasant poet, Sergei Klychkov. From the memoirs of B.S. Kuzin: "Once during some argument with Mandelstam, he [Klychkov] said to him: "Nevertheless, O.E., your brains are Jewish." To which Mandelstam immediately countered: "That's entirely possible. But my poems are Russian." — "That is correct. Indeed that is correct!" Klychkov admitted with the greatest sincerity (Kuzin: 174).

In those years, Klychkov was struggling to extricate himself from an incident that was very similar in circumstances to that of Mandelstam's with the "Legend of Thyl Ulenspiegel." In the 7th and 8th issues of "Novyi Mir" for 1932, Klychkov published a long epic poem, "Madur-Vaza the Conqueror," which was a free adaptation of "Yangaal-Maa," a text by M. Plotnikov based on Mansi oral folk tales. Klychkov was accused of plagiarism. The case of "Plotnikov vs. Klychkov" was closed only in 1933. The commission of the Soviet Writers Union Organizing committee removed the charges of plagiarism faced by Klychkov and, at the same time, resolved to provide Plotnikov with material compensation for the publication of the Klychkov poem in "Novyi Mir." Mandelstam significantly dedicated to Klychkov the third part of his recently written "Poems about Russian Poetry" (27 July 1932).

Mandelstam's relative improvement in his financial situation allowed him to once again provide some assistance to his older friend, Vladimir Piast, who at the time was languishing in exile in the faraway Arkhangelsk. Yet, as before, he showed no indulgence to the majority of his fellow writers.

Must one be surprised over the fact that whenever opportunity presented itself, others would get even with Mandelstam? His neighbor at the Hertzen House, Amir Sargidzhan (Borodin), who had once borrowed 75 rubles from Mandelstam, kept evading him to avoid paying back the debt. Once when Osip Emil'evich reminded Sargidzhan about the debt Sargidzhan turned to his fists in response, going after not only Mandelstam but Nadezhda Iakovlevna as well. On 13 September 1932 a community court session was held over the "case of Mandelstam vs. Sargidzhan." An old friend of Mandelstam's, Aleksei Tolstoy, served as chairman in court. Prior to the session he was instructed how to conduct it: he should show lenience toward the younger poet who was a member of the party. (Volkenshtein: 55-56). Mandelstam was furious as he realized that the court actually sided with Sargidzhan and failed to condemn his violent behavior. All of Mandelstam's hate was focused personally on Aleksei Tolstoy, as testified by Emma Gershtein (Gershtein: 39).

4.

The more Mandelstam felt appalled by the Soviet literary establishment the more acutely he felt a blood kinship with poets that had already gone. Here one should note, first of all, two poets: Velimir Khlebnikov and Konstantin Batiushkov. In the June issue of "Novyi Mir" for 1932, Mandelstam published his poem, "Lamarck," which reflected Mandelstam's interest in the teaching and ideas of the great French naturalist, Jean-Baptiste Lamarck, whom Boris Kuzin also admired very much. A close analysis of the text convinces one, however, that Mandelstam sneaked into the poem a number of allusions to Velimir Khlebnikov. As was often the case, Mandelstam combined two in one portrait: through the character of the genius biologist, Lamarck, shines through the portrait of the genius poet, Khlebnikov, whose work exerted a profound influence on Mandelstam during the 1930's. "In Khlebnikov there is everything!" he told Khardzhiev in 1938 (Khardzhiev: 336).

A reproduction of the self-portrait of the other poet, a great representative of the "Golden Age" of Russian poetry, Konstantin Batiushkov decorated Mandelstam's room in the Hertzen House. "He would speak about Batiushkov with the passion of a discoverer," as S.I. Lipkin recalled, "he would disagree with certain critical notes made by Pushkin in the margins of Batiushkov's poetry" (Lipkin: 306). Apparently Mandelstam felt that he was the direct successor of Batiushkov's line in Russian literature. This notion was enhanced by Iury Tynianov's well-known article "Promezhutok" ["Interval"] (1924) that compared Batiushkov's and Mandelstam's poetry. Ten years later Tynianov would write to Kornei Chukovsky about Mandelstam: "Even his tastes were like those of Batiushkov" (Tynianov: 480). Mandelstam's paradoxical definition of Batiushkov's writing as "the notebook of the unborn Pushkin" (III: 401) should be interpreted not as "the notebook of the *yet* unborn Pushkin," but as "the notebook of the *never* born Pushkin" since Batiushkov never found his own "Pushkin." Perhaps this is a slight exaggeration, but one could safely assume that Mandelstam, in the end, played exactly the role of that "unborn" genius poet of his time, who was able to fully realize the "outlines" that were contained in the highly promising "notebook" of Batiushkov's poetry and prose. In his poem "Batiushkov" (1932), Mandelstam would address the early 19th century Russian poet as if he were Mandelstam's contemporary, as if he were alive. This poem, incidentally was published in the same issue of "Novyi Mir" as was "Lamarck."

The Mandelstams spent November 1932 in the sanatorium of TsEKUBU "Uzkoe" near Moscow. On November 10, Mandelstam went to Moscow for a day, as the editorial board of "Literaturnaya Gazeta" had organized his poetry evening. "When he began to read in that strange, purely 'poetical' manner totally opposite of that of the 'actor's', though perhaps more conventional, it made my heart contract for some reason," the dramatist, A. Gladkov, who attended the reading, reported in his diary (Gladkov: 321). Nikolai Khardzhiev conveyed his impressions to Eikhenbaum in a letter: "It was a majestic spectacle, the grey-bearded patriarch shamanized for two and a half hours. He read all of his poems (of the past two years) in chronological order! These were such scary invocations that many got frightened. Even Pasternak, who mumbled: "I envy you your freedom. For me you are the new Khlebnikov, just as alien. I need unfreedom" (Eikhenbaum: 532). Khardzhiev's description of Mandelstam as a "grey-bearded patriarch" not only echoes that of Mandelstam's portrait of Lamarck, ("Awkward, bashful patriarch"), but also the first line of Mandelstam's poem of 1931, "Still a long way off from being a patriarch...", which surely was read at the literary evening at the "Literaturnaya Gazeta." The now-bearded Mandelstam was perceived as a living classic, a symbol of the departing, "Petersburg" era of Russian culture. "By this time Mandelstam had greatly changed, heavier, hair grey, he breathed with difficulty and gave the impression of being an old man (he was 42), but his eyes still sparkled as previously," recalles Anna Akhmatova (Akhmatova 1989a: 136).

Two Mandelstam evenings were organized in late February and in early March in Leningrad. One of those present entered into his journal: "Mandelstam — bald, with a grey beard. The Leningraders are dumbfounded. They are used to seeing him shaved here. His beard gave [Nikolai] Tikhonov the right to say at one of the subsequent evenings concerning the difficult path of the poet:

"You see, even Mandelstam, buried in his work, grew a beard, this is what it means to work, to write real poetry!"

Mandelstam did not read the way he used to. He used to practically sing his verse. Now he chants them hastily in a mellow bass voice, monotonously, without expression, swallowing the end of the line, though with the same persistence of persuasion. One minute he rises on tiptoe, the next he is rhythmically beating a new rhythm with his foot. He reads quietly..." (Basalaev: 108).

At the evening held at the House of the Press, someone passed him a provocative note: "Are you the same Mandelstam who used to be an Acmeist?" He replied: "I am the same Mandelstam who was, is, and will be the friend of his friends, comrade-in-arms of his comrades-in-arms, and a contemporary of Akhmatova." Then — thunder, a squall, a thunderstorm of applause" (Tager: 239).

On 14 March 1933, the evening of Mandelstam's poetry was organized at the Moscow Polytechnic Museum. It became a significant event. Mandelstam was "greeted with applause. The applause was fervent and lasted a long-long time, as if they could not be sated. < ... > Applauding, they were amazed and rejoicing over the fact that here, in this auditorium, there were gathered so many great admirers of Mandelstam's poetry." One such admirer was B.M. Eikhenbaum, who opened the Mandelstam evening with a lengthy lecture about his poetry. Eikhenbaum's presentation aimed to destroy the stereotypes of how Mandelstam was perceived by Soviet literary criticism. "Lately in the lobbies I hear it said that 'Mandelstam is a true master', Do not forget that mastership is a term that has to do with a trade. [The Soviet poet Semen] Kirsanov — he is a master. But Mandelstam is not a master, oh no!" "'Mastership'," concluded Eikhenbaum, "bears the relation to something of a museum value" (Eikhenbaum: 449).

Mandelstam's last public poetry reading of his life took place on 3 April 1933 at the Moscow Club of Artists. The day after, Boris Kuzin was arrested. Osip Emil'evich immediately turned to Marietta Shaginian, who had connections in the upper echelons, with the appeal to assist with Kuzin's release. The request was drafted as an attachment to Mandelstam's "Journey to Armenia," in which Kuzin appeared as a character: "From the attached manuscript you will get a better sense than from conversations with me as to why it was inevitable that this person would have been denied external freedom, and, by the same token, why this freedom must inevitably be returned to him [...] I have been deprived of my interlocutor, my second self, a person whom I had time and opportunity to convince that there is entelechy, vital frenzy, and the luxury of live nature in the revolution [...]" (IV: 150-151). A few days later Kuzin was released.

Around 10 April, together with the Mandelstams, Kuzin left Moscow for Staryi Krym, to visit the widow of the writer Aleksandr Grin, Nina Nikolaevna. Later he would fondly remember this trip and the more than two weeks that they spent there together (Kuzin: 155).

In Crimea, Mandelstam studied Italian and immersed himself in reading and rereading the greatest Italian classics — Dante, Petrarch, Ariosto and Tasso. He subsequently translated Petrarch's sonnets, wrote a poem about Ariosto, and was planning on writing an article about Tasso. At the end of May 1933 he began working on his last major prose work, the essay, "Conversation on Dante."

"As I was taking the dictation of "Conversation on Dante," Nadezhda Iakovlevna would recall, "I would often note that he was inserting a lot that was personal into the article, and I would say: 'You are settling scores here.' He would reply: 'That is how it should be. Don't bother me...'" (NM-2: 248). Uncompromisingly "settling scores" with his many opponents (Blok especially), Mandelstam in his essay "reconciled" in absentia with those two poets with whom he had the sweetest and the most bitter memories of Crimea. In the fifth chapter of his essay, he benevolently quoted the émigré poet Marina Tsvetaeva (III: 239). Elsewhere in the essay he spoke warmly of Maksimilian Voloshin with whom he renewed his friendship in 1924 and who died on 11 August 1932.

While in Crimea, Mandelstam was a witness of the horrifying famine there and in other areas of the Ukraine and southern Russia. In order to crush the peasants' opposition to collectivization, the authorities confiscated all of their grain reserves in 1932, and by winter there was a massive famine. Mandelstam reacted to it by writing a civic poem, "almost in Nekrasov's style," which a year later would figure in the criminal case against him. The protocol of the interrogation that took place on 25 May 1934 contains Mandelstam's words: "By 1930 a major depression had taken over my political consciousness and social wellbeing. The underlying social reason for this depression was the liquidation of the kulaks as a class. My perception of this process is expressed in my poem, 'Kholodnaya vesna' ['Cold Spring']" (Polianovsky: 90).

On 28 May 1933, the Mandelstams moved to the Koktebel Dom Tvorchestva [House of Creativity]. Andrei Bely and his wife, Klavdiia Nikolaevna, were staying there as well. Andrei Bely and Osip Mandelstam have never been close. Long before, during the time of Mandelstam's first debuts, Bely spoke approvingly of the beginning poet's experiments with Russian meters. Then he became quite disparaging of Mandelstam's poetry, which the latter was inclined to interpret as manifestations of the anti-Semitic views characteristic of Symbolist poets of Bely's generation. Bely certainly should have been dismayed by Mandelstam's scathing remarks on Bely's prose works. Despite these critical comments, Mandelstam firmly believed that Bely's late novels were "the height of Russian psychological prose" (the formula used in Mandelstam's essay, "Literary Moscow. The Birth of Plot," II: 262).

On 7 June 1933, Andrei Bely complained in a letter to Petr Zaitsev from Koktebel': "Everything would be great, if it weren't for…the Mandelstams (husband and wife); as fate would have it, we have been assigned the same table as they have (here the tables are for four); and so we are forced to have breakfast, lunch, tea, and supper with them. It should be noted that they are the only ones out of the 20+ guests whom we find unpleasant and alien" (Andrei Bely 1994: 324). Bely was even more harsh in a letter to Fedor Gladkov: "…It is difficult with the Mandelstams; < … > they engage in very "intelligent," tedious, and elaborate conversations with winking, with "what," "you understand," "yet," "you don't say;" while I don't understand "anything"; in other words, I find M[andelstam], for some reason, exceptionally unpleasant; and we stand on diametrically opposed poles" (Andrei Bely 1994: 326-327). In his Koktebel' diary, Bely had written something so harsh about the couple he shared his table with, that his wife considered it best to destroy this fragment.

The poet and dramaturgist, Anatoly Mariengof, who was resting at the same time as Bely and Mandelstam in Koktebel described the situation as follows: "The administration […] placed them in the dining-room at the same table. Such good intentions completely ruined the summer for both. Osip Emil'evich's outdated style of declamation and terrible pronunciation of Italian words, the words of Dante and Petrarch, incredibly irritated Andrei Bely. Mandelstam, being sensitive, understood everything right away. And this, in its turn, made him very much upset" (Mariengof: 495). The memoirist very accurately portrayed Andrei Bely's uneasiness of Mandelstam's seditious "winks" in risky political conversations conducted precisely at the moment when the elderly writer was at pains to demonstrate his loyalty to the Soviet regime. But when it comes to Mandelstam, Mariengof was wrong: Osip Emil'evich, apparently, believed that his relations with Bely were greatly improving. In Nadezhda Iakovlevna's memoirs, Mandelstam's contacts with Bely in Koktebel' are referred to almost as a friendship: "...they would meet, though furtively, and would enjoy their conversations. In those days O.M. had written the 'Conversation on Dante', and he was reading it to Bely" (NM-1: 182).

In May 1933, while the Mandelstams were in Crimea, the Leningrad journal, "Zvezda" ["Star"], published "The Journey to Armenia." On 17 June, already after the Mandelstams' return to Moscow, a scathing review of Mandelstam's prose was placed in "Literaturnaia Gazeta." On 30 August, "Pravda" followed suit. It said: "From Mandelstam's images one gets the scent of an old, musty, imperialistic chauvinist, who, while lavishing praises upon Armenia, glorifies it for being exotic, for its past slavery, but does not write a single word about its present [...] The old Petersburg Acmeist poet O. Mandelstam disregarded the Armenia that is rapidly blooming and cheerfully building socialism" (Mandelstam 1990b: 421).

In September 1933, the Mandelstams visited Leningrad, where they met once again with Anna Akhmatova. She recalled: "He had just learned Italian and he was raving about Dante. He read the 'Divine Comedy' by heart in full pages. We began to speak about 'Purgatory', and I read him a piece from the XXX song (the appearance of Beatrice) [...] Osip began to cry. I became frightened — 'What is wrong?' — 'No, nothing, it is just these words and your voice'" (Akhmatova 1989a: 134).

Mandelstam also read his "Conversation on Dante" at Akhmatova's. Some of the best literary scholars and poets were in attendance that evening: Viktor Zhirmunsky, Iury Tynianov, Benedikt Livshits, Lidiia Ginzburg... The latter recorded her impressions in her notebooks: "Not tall, Mandelstam is thin, with a narrow forehead, a small hooked nose, the sharp lower half of his face is in an unkept almost grey beard, his gaze intense and it is as if he does not notice trifles. He speaks tucking up his toothless mouth, in a singing voice, with the unusually refined intonation of Russian speech. He is overwhelmed with rhythms (just as he is overwhelmed with ideas) and beautiful words. As he reads, he sways and moves his hands; he breathes with great delight in time to his words, and reminds one of a coryphaeus behind which appears the dancing choir. [...] He speaks in the language of his poems: inarticulately (bellowing, with "that..." constantly intersecting his speech), and is not embarrassed to use lofty, grandiose expressions. Never misses an opportunity to sparkle with wit and to joke" (Ginzburg: 119-120).

His manuscript "Conversation on Dante" was rejected by the "Writers' Publishing House in Leningrad."

The Mandelstams moved into a cooperative two-room apartment in October 1933. It was here that Osip Emil'evich would write in November 1933 his two suicidal poems: "The Apartment is as Silent as a Sheet of Paper..." and "We live not feeling the country beneath us..."

5.

The Mandelstams had dreamed of their own private living quarters for many years. They had spent much energy in the effort to obtain an apartment in the writers' house on Nashchokinsky Lane. "The house was one of the very first cooperatives, and each potential candidate for residency was carefully selected by the writers themselves" (Gershtein: 40). As Mandelstam put it, it was practically for the first time that he began to feel like a writer. But instead of rejoicing at the new apartment, the poet was overcome by a heavy sense of shame and remorse. Almost for the first time in his life Mandelstam felt like some traitor, not only toward the circle of his "worn out with suffering and underfed" audience, but also toward the large masses of homeless and famished peasants that he had seen recently while travelling to Crimea. And the cost of his betrayal, the new apartment in the Nashchokinsky Lane, was for him the equivalent of Judas' thirty silver coins.

Unwillingly adding fuel to the fire, Boris Pasternak, whose own living arrangements were not settled, tried to cheer the poet up while visiting the Mandelstams: 'So, now that you have an apartment, you can write

CHAPTER FOUR

From left to right: Aleksandr Mandestam, Maria Petrovyh, Emil, Nadezhda, and Osip Mandelstam, Anna Akhmatova. 1934

poetry', he said, as he was walking out the door. 'Did you hear what he said?' O.M. was furious" (From N.Ia. Mandelstam's memoirs, NM-1: 176).

Thus discussion resumed as to how a poet should build his relations with contemporary reality, a discussion that grew out of the argument between Mandelstam and Pasternak over the "Gornfeld case." "I refuse to have anything in common with Boris Leonidovich, as he has a trade union ticket in his pocket," is how Lidiia Ginzburg epitomizes one of Mandelstam's retorts of that time (Ginzburg: 117). According to her, Pasternak expresses the concilliatory moods of the intelligentsia while Mandelstam expresses the consciousness of "intelligentsia in self-defense" (Ginzburg: 116). After Pasternak's visit, Osip Emil'evich began to feel the need to urgently act, accomplish something, write poetry: "reject the ticket."

Mandelstam's outburst found its expression in the poetical counterpart of his "Fourth Prose"—in his poem, "The Apartment is as Silent as a Sheet of Paper...". This time, the outburst was directed against himself.

Another sacrificial act of catharsis and self-release from the subjugation to Soviet "writing" was his uncompromisingly hostile satirical verse attacking Stalin personally. Mandelstam wrote it in November 1933 as Stalin's portraits had overflowed the Soviet newspaper pages and streets in connection with the celebration of the anniversary of the October revolution. Mandelstam was the first among his contemporaries in the USSR who dared express such satire aimed specifically at the Great Leader.

We live not feeling the country beneath us,
Our speech can't be heard ten steps away,

And if they dare to start talking,
They'll invoke at once the Kremlin mountaineer.

His fat fingers are as greasy as worms,
And his words are as heavy as a sledge-hammer,

His cockroach eyes are laughing,
And the tops of his boots are shining.

All around him a slew of thin-necked sycophants,
He preys on the services of half humans.

One whistles, another meows, a third whimpers,
Only he is free to call and prod,

He produces, like horseshoes, one decree after another:
Cuffing someone's groin, forehead, brow, or eye.

Each execution fills him with delight,
He has the wide chest of an Ossetian.

Mandelstam began reading this poem to those close to him, and then to those not so close. He considered it to be "not a document of personal perception and attitude, but a document of perception and attitude of a specific social group, most explicitly that of the old intelligentsia, which in these days considers itself to be the carrier and transmitter of the values of previous cultures" (from Mandelstam's interrogation protocol dated 25 May 1934; see: Polianovsky: 91-92). To each of the listeners he solemnly and sincerely announced that he or she would be the only keeper of the terrible secret. And then it turned out that the poem is known by others. Emma Gershtein recollects: "It seemed to me that all of this had been deeply buried. Before Mandelstam had been sentenced, I did not say a single word to any person about the poem, nor, of course, did I read it outloud. But once, in my company, the Mandelstams began to discuss it, and Nadia serenely announced that Nina Nikolaevna Grin preferred the other version. There you go! It turns out that I was not the only one privy to the secret" (Gershtein: 52).

It is known that, aside from Nadezhda Iakovlevna, Mandelstam had read his epigram to Evgeny Khazin's wife's brother, his own brother Aleksandr Mandelstam, Boris Kuzin, Emma Gershtein, Vladimir Narbut, Anna Akhmatova and her son, Lev Gumilev, Boris Pasternak, Viktor Shklovsky, Semen Lipkin, Nina Grin, Georgy Shengeli, Sergei Klychkov, Nikolai Khardzhiev, Aleksandr Tyshler, and Aleksandr Osmerkin. The text of the anti-Stalin epigram was also known about by the poet and translator, Maria Sergeevna Petrovykh, to whom Mandelstam had addressed a few love poems in 1934.

The Mandelstams had met this beginning poetess and translator through Anna Akhmatova, who had come to visit her old friends in their new apartment in the middle of November 1933. Mandelstam had chosen Anna Andreevna as his confidante: "...having lost his head, he would confide in Akhmatova that had he not been married to Naden'ka, he would have left and gone to live with only his new love," Nadezhda Iakovlevna wrote in her memoirs (NM-2: 222). And here is what Akhmatova herself wrote: "In 1933-1934, Osip Emil'evich was wildly, shortly, and unrequitedly in love with Maria Sergeevna Petrovykh. The poem "Turchanka" is dedicated, or, rather, addressed to her (the heading is mine), in my view, the best love poem of the 20th century" (Akhmatova 1989a: 128).

Arguably the most important event of the 1933/34 winter for Osip Emil'evich was the sudden death of Andrei Bely on 8 January. He reacted to it by writing several poems, one of which he passed on to Bely's widow. But she did not like it, finding it too "obscure."

In the middle of April 1934, the Mandelstams arrived in Leningrad. In the beginning of May, at the premises of the "Writers' Publishing House" Osip Emil'evich finally got the opportunity to get even with the president of the disgraceful court of justice in "the case of Sargidzhan vs Mandelstam," Aleksei Tolstoy. Elena Tager wrote down what happened as reported by Valentin Stenich:

"Mandelstam, seeing Tolstoy, went up to him with an extended hand, his intentions being so unclear, that Tolstoy did not even move away.

Mandelstam, once he reached him, slapped him slightly, as if stroking him on the cheek, and pronounced in his dramatic manner: 'I punished the executioner who issued a warrant for the beating of my wife'"(Tager: 241).

Fedor Volkenshtein offers a different version: "Mandelstam grew pale, then jumping back and turning gave Tolstoy a loud slap in the face.

'Here you go for your 'community court', he mumbled.

Tolstoy grabbed Mandelstam by the hand.

'What are you doing?!' Tolstoy hissed, 'Don't you realize that I can de-s-tr-oy you!'" (Volkenshtein: 56-57).

Volkenshtein adds to this: "I know and I swear to the reader that Tolstoy did not have anything to do with Mandelstam's subsequent arrest or what happened to him later" (Volkenshtein: 57) Mandelstam's action was widely discussed in literary circles. Ekaterina Petrovykh reports: "...the poet Perets Markish, upon hearing about the slap in the face with the look of utmost amazement lifted his finger upward with the words: 'Oh! A Jew slapped a Count in the face!!!'"(Osip and Nadezhda: 167).

CHAPTER FOUR

It is safe to assume that Mandelstam went to Leningrad especially for the purpose of punishing Tolstoy: having completed his act of vengeance, he returned to Moscow. In order to avert the consequences of his action, Mandelstam, together with his wife, rushed to Bukharin and told him about what had happened.

He also bombarded Akhmatova with telegrams and telephone calls persuading her to visit them in Moscow.

On the night of 13-14 May 1934 (the official NKVD records give a different date — the night of 16-17 May), Osip Emil'evich Mandelstam was arrested.

Chapter Five

THE FINAL YEARS (1934-1938)

1.

"The search [of the premises] took all night. They were looking for poems, throwing manuscripts out of the trunk they would walk all over them. We were all sitting in one room. On the other side of the wall, at Kirsanov's, a Hawaiian guitar was playing. The investigator found "Wolf" [the poem "For the Future Ages' Resounding Glory..."] in my presence and showed it to O.E. He silently nodded. Saying goodbye, he kissed me. They took him away at seven in the morning" (From Akhmatova's memoirs, Akhmatova 1989a: 137).

That is how Nadezhda Iakovlevna's tells the story: "There were five of them in all — three agents and two witnesses [...] The senior agent concerned himself with the trunk with the archives, while the other two conducted the search [...] It became morning of 14 May. All the guests, both called and uncalled, left. The uncalled guests took with them [to the internal prison at the Lubianka] the proprietor of the premises. We were left tête-a-tête with Anna Andreevna, just the two of us in an empty apartment still fresh with the traces of the night's debauch. It seems to me that we just sat there in front of each other and were silent" (NM-1: 17).

According to the protocol of O.E. Mandelstam's search and arrest, the following items were confiscated: "letters, notes with telephone numbers and addresses and manuscripts on separate sheets totaling 48 / forty eight / sheets.

The search was conducted by the operative agents Commissars Gerasimov, Veprintsev, Zablovsky" (Polianovsky: 78). The authorization to conduct the search and to arrest Mandelstam was issued by the deputy chairman of the OGPU, Iakov Agranov. The poet took with him "eight collars, a soap dish, a brush, seven different books," and 30 rubles (the prison receipt quoted in Polianovsky: 78).

In the morning, Nadezhda Mandelstam went over to her brother's Evgeny. Anna Andreevna went first to Boris Pasternak's and then to the Secretary of the Presidium of the Central Executive Committee, Avel' Enukidze and the writer, Lidiia Seifullina. Pasternak, upon learning about the arrest, in his own turn, appealed to Demian Bedny and Bukharin for help. The formerly Russian Symbolist poet who was appointed Ambassador of independent Lithuania in the USSR, Jurgis Baltrushaitis, also tried to appeal on Mandelstam's behalf. "The fuss and the noise raised around O.M.'s first arrest clearly played a part, because the case took a turn that was not typical. That is how Anna Andreevna sees it" (From Nadezhda Iakovlevna's "Memoirs," NM-1: 35). "By all this we probably succeeded in accelerating and mitigating the sentence" (Akhmatova 1989a: 138).

The Mandelstam case was turned over to the operative agent of the OGPU (Soviet secret police), Nikolai Khristoforovich Shivarov, who previously participated in underground communist activities in Bulgaria. He was the close friend of the writers Petr Pavlenko and Aleksandr Fadeev. The first interrogation took place on 18 May 1934.

Mandelstam, inherently incapable of playing the role of a conspirator and resisting rough pressure, apparently immediately chose to cooperate with the interrogator. Already in the very first, preliminary interrogation protocol, he admitted having belonged to the S.R. party as a youth (this was an incriminating fact both in 1934 and in 1938). From this protocol it also follows that the text of the poem, "We live not feeling the country beneath us," was willingly reproduced by him on his own. Mandelstam named the names of the seven who had heard his anti-Stalin epigram: (Aleksandr Mandelstam, Evgeny Khazin, Emma Gershtein, Anna Akhmatova and her son Lev Gumilev, David Brodsky, Boris Kuzin). The name of the poet translator, David Brodsky, he later had removed. During the next interrogation which took place on 19 May, two other people were named: Maria Petrovykh and Vladimir Narbut.

1934

One cannot help but note that Mandelstam had concealed many names from Shivarov. It can't have been simply an error of memory: it is difficult to imagine, for example, that the poet had forgotten about how he had read the poem: "We live not feeling the country beneath us..." to Boris Pasternak (After hearing the poem, Pasternak said: "What you have read to me has no connection to literature or poetry. It is not a literary fact, but a suicidal act that I do not approve of and in which I do not wish to participate. You did not read anything to me, I did not hear anything, and I ask you that you please do not read them to anyone else") (Pasternak: 95).

The conditions of Mandelstam's upkeep at the Lubianka prison were very difficult: the light in his cell was constantly turned on, day and night, as a result of which Mandelstam's eyelids became inflamed; his cellmate was a "sitting-hen" from the NKVD who wore Osip Emil'evich out with his endless conversations and scared him with predictions that Osip's relatives would also be arrested.

In a fit of despair the poet attempted to cut his veins with the blade that he took out of the heel of his boot. However, the suicide attempt was suppressed by the jailers.

The third and last interrogation took place on 25 May. On 27 or 28 May the interrogation was completed. Mandelstam received an unexpectedly mild sentence: three years of exile in the city of Cherdyn' in the Sverdlovsk oblast'. Nadezhda Iakovlevna was permitted to accompany her husband. Emma Gershtein recalls: "We were sitting at the Nashchokinsky [apartment] and waiting for Nadia's return [from the Lubianka]. She came back shaken, tormented:

"It's the poems. 'About Stalin', 'The Apartment', and the Crimean ('A Cold Spring...')" (Gershtein: 54). "It was over," Anna Andreevna writes. "Nina Ol'shevskaia went off to collect money for his departure. A lot was collected. Elena Sergeevna Bulgakova began to cry and put into my hands the entire contents of her purse" (Akhmatova 1989a: 139).

They travelled to Cherdyn' by train through Sverdlovsk. In Solikamsk they moved to a steamer and travelled on along the Kama, Vishera, Kolva. They arrived in Cherdyn' in early June 1934. Mandelstam was on the verge of mental illness, he was terrified of being executed. In order to avoid execution, on the first early morning upon arrival in Cherdyn' he attempted to commit suicide. Shaken, Nadezhda Iakovlevna telegraphed her mother in Moscow: "Osia is sick with traumatic psychosis yesterday he threw himself out of the window of the second floor but only sprained his shoulder his delirium has quietened the doctors obstetrician young internist say possible to transfer to psychiatric in Perm' consider it undesirable due to danger of new trauma caused by a provincial hospital = Nadia" (Freidin 1994: 15). Telegrams with similar contents were sent to Nikolai Bukharin and Aleksandr Mandelstam. Later it turned out that when jumping out of the window of the prison hospital, Mandelstam had broken his arm.

On 6 June, Aleksandr Emil'evich appealed to the OGPU with the request to have his brother transferred somewhere "near Moscow,

Leningrad, or Sverdlovsk without confining him to the hospital quarters" (Freidin 1994: 17).

On 10 June, the Mandelstam case received an unexpected turn: his sentence was reviewed. He received permission to change the place of exile. On 14 June, an official telegram was received in Cherdyn' re a three year administrative exile, upon the completion of this term, a deprivation of the right to reside in Moscow, Leningrad, and ten more cities of the USSR. The Mandelstams were summoned to the Cherdyn' commandant's office in order to select a new location of the exile. From Nadezhda Iakovlevna's "Memoirs": "We were not familiar with the provinces, we did not have any friends anywhere except for the forbidden twelve cities, plus the outskirts, which were also forbidden. Suddenly O.M. remembered that [an acquaintance of B.S. Kuzin's] the biologist Leonov from the Tashkent University had praised Voronezh, where he had been born. Leonov's father was a prison doctor. "Who knows, maybe we will need a prison doctor," said O.M. and our choice became Voronezh. The commandant wrote out the orders" (NM-1: 112).

Why did Osip Mandelstam's final sentence end up being milder than the initial one? Why was he allowed to exchange Cherdyn' for another city? We know now that it was the "Kremlin mountaineer" who personally got involved in the turn of the interrogation. "Preserve, but isolate," those were the orders that, according to word of mouth, were given to the handlers of Mandelstam's case. Nikolai Bukharin's intervention had played a significant role in this. After receiving Nadezhda Iakovlevna's telegram and Boris Pasternak's visit, Bukharin sent Stalin a long letter in which one section concerned Mandelstam: "About the poet Mandelstam. He was recently arrested and exiled. Before his arrest he visited me with his wife and expressed his fears of being detained in connection with his having fought (!) with A. Tolstoy, to whom he had given a 'symbolic slap' because he had apparently unjustly passed judgment in the case, where another writer had beaten his wife. I spoke with Agranov, but he was unable to tell me anything specific. And now I have received totally desperate telegrams from Mandelstam's wife, stating that he is psychotic, that he tried to jump out of a window, and so forth. My assessment of Mandelstam is that he is a first class poet, but absolutely uncontemporary, and he is absolutely not perfectly normal; he feels as though he is being harassed and so forth. As I am constantly receiving appeals on his behalf, yet I don't know what he is about or what his 'sin was', I decided to write you about this as well [...] P.S. Am writing about Mandelstam again because Boris Pasternak is totally upset over M[andelstam's] arrest and nobody knows anything" (Maksimenkov: 239).

Stalin responded with a resolution on this letter: "Who gave them the right to arrest Mandelstam? How despicable..." (Maksimenkov: 240). Stalin's "them" is, of course, especially touching. Perhaps by making the poet's lot milder, Stalin had wanted to play out the role of the enlightened, magnanimous leader.

Such speculation could be confirmed by the phone call that Stalin had made to Boris Pasternak. The record of this phone conversation is as follows. On 13 June 1934, the telephone rang in the communal apartment where the Pasternaks lived. Stalin began by assuring the poet that the Mandelstam case was being reviewed and that everything would be all right with him. Then he asked Pasternak why he had not taken up Mandelstam's cause either directly with him, Stalin, or with various writers' organizations. "I would have been crawling the walls if I had found out that my friend the poet had been arrested." Pasternak replied: "Writers' organizations haven't handled such cases since '27, and if I had not taken up the cause, you would not have heard anything." In response Stalin asked: "But isn't he your friend?" Pasternak tried to define the nature of the relations between him and Mandelstam, saying that poets, like women, are jealous of each other. "But he is a master, a master!" Stalin quoted the cliché description of Mandelstam so common in the Soviet press, which couldn't help but exacerbate Pasternak. "But that is all beside the point," he brushed it aside, "why do we keep going on and on about Mandelstam, yes about Mandelstam. For a long time I have wanted to meet with you and have a serious conversation." — "About what?" — "About life and death." The proposed subject of conversation, in its turn, did not especially make Stalin happy. Instead of replying to Pasternak, he hung up on him.

2.

The Mandelstams went to Voronezh via Moscow and arrived there on 25 June 1934. At first they stayed at the hotel "Tsentral'naia." "We were not given a separate room, but were provided with a cot each in the male and female sections. We lived on different floors, and I kept running up and down the stairs, because I was worried about how O.M. was feeling" (From N.Ia. Mandelstam's memoirs, NM-1: 145). However, the psychiatrist who was examining Osip Emil'evich did not find any traces of traumatic psychosis. On the other hand, Nadezhda Iakovlevna, who was exhausted from all that she had gone through, had contracted typhus and was taken to the hospital, where she spent a few weeks. By the end of August she came down with dysentery (on 31 October 1934 she would write to Marietta Shaginian out of a paroxysm of despair: "I believe the end is near. Perhaps it is a result of having had typhus and dysentery, but I have no strength left, I don't believe that we will be able to pull through this").

For the summer months the Mandelstams rented a glassed-in terrace close to a railroad station. Thus began their adaptation to life in Voronezh. In September 1934, Mandelstam addressed the head of the local Branch of the Union of Soviet Writer, Aleksandr Shver, with the request that he be given the opportunity to take part in the work of the writers' organization. A similar request was sent by Boris Pasternak in Moscow to the Department of Culture and Propaganda of the Central Committee of the Communist Party. On 20 November, a high party functionary, P. Iudin, sent a letter to Voronezh suggesting that Mandelstam be "gradually pulled into writers' work and used, to the extent possible, as a cultural force and be given the opportunity to earn a living" (Nerler 1991: 92).

The Union of Writers functionary, Olga Kretova, compiled a report about what mood the exiled poet was in: "In his discussions with communist-writers, members of the Governing Union, Mandelstam spoke about his enormous desire to embrace and comprehend Soviet reality, and asked for help in going to factories and kolkhozes, so that he could work with young writers.< ... > The editorial board of the oblast' literary journal, "Pod'em," allowed Mandelstam to advise beginning writers and to charge consulting fees [...] [Mandelstam] expects to begin working on a book about the old and new Voronezh" (Nerler 1991: 92).

Even if Kretova exaggerated or simplified the picture, it is clear that he made every effort to come to terms with the new reality. Similar determination seeps through a letter from Mandelstam to his father sent about a year later: "For the first time in many years I don't feel like a renegade, I am *living in society*, and I really do feel good [...] I want to see a whole lot of things, to master <Marxist> theory, to study... The same as you... We are young. We should enroll in the University..." (IV: 160). One memoirist testifies on Mandelstam during the Voronezh period: "Mandelstam spoke of Stalin favourably" (Roginsky: 43). But Mandelstam wouldn't be Mandelstam if his periods of optimistic acceptance of Soviet reality didn't alternate with periods of rebellion against it, with his alternate moods finding their way into his lyrics of that time.

In February 1935, the editorial board of the newspaper, "Kommuna," invited the poet to give a lecture about Acmeism "with the goal of revealing Mandelstam's attitude toward his past" (as formulated by the secretary of the party group of the Voronezh branch of the Union of Writers, Stefan Stoichev). "In his speech Mandelstam showed," Stoichev continues, "that he did not learn anything, he remains the way he was" (Nerler 1991: 93). It was precisely in this speech that the author of "Stone" defined Acmeism as "anguish for world culture," and said that he is renouncing "neither the living nor the dead." At the same time, Mandelstam "said that [he himself] had moved away from Acmeism" (Gydov: 34).

In the end of March 1935, Nadezhda Iakovlevna went to Moscow for almost a month. On 30 March, the young formalist scholar, a pupil of Tynianov, Sergei Rudakov, arrived in Voronezh. Like many other people who were from families of the pre-revolutionary nobility, he was exiled from Leningrad after S.M. Kirov's assassination. Rudakov met Osip Emil'evich on the third day of his arrival to Voronezh and immediately became a passionate companion, a stern assessor of Mandelstam's old and new poems, and a caring guardian. When he himself unexpectedly came down with scarlet fever, the roles were reversed. "I have lain for a day and a half at the M[andelstams]," Rudakov reported in a letter to his wife. "They are incredibly caring" (Rudakov: 115).

Nadezhda Iakovlevna had given part of Mandelstam's archives to Rudakov for safekeeping, as he had the idea to write a large book about Mandelstam. In a letter to Boris Kuzin dated 11 July 1942, she had called Sergei "the person dearest to me" (Kuzin: 678). These words echo the assessment given by Osip Emil'evich in a note to Rudakov dated 10 December 1935: "You are the greatest guy in the world" (IV: 161).

It was only much later, when scholars received access to the numerous letters from Sergei Rudakov written to his wife while in Voronezh, that it suddenly became apparent that the infinitely ambitious young scholar, who loved Osip Emil'evich and kept good relations with Nadezhda Iakovlevna, had experienced incredible pangs of hurt pride in the presence of the poet. First of all, Mandelstam had not appreciated Rudakov's poetry. Secondly, Mandelstam supposedly minimized Rudakov's role in the process of creating his own literary works. Thus, Sergei Borisovich would write with vexation to his wife about his joint work with Mandelstam over the poem, "Ariosto:" "Lika, I swear, the plan (quantity of stophes and lines in them, the theme of the strophes created out of half-line scraps) was mine. The entire composition, the face of the thing, is beautiful, svelte [...] Os'ka is embarrassed and... tries to pretend that I "only helped." This has become so offensive that I practically gave up and decided to drop everything and go away. Some kind of asinine stupidity, fear for one's own fame" (Rudakov: 72). That is how Rudakov describes in his letters to his wife Mandelstam's attitude toward him. For justice's sake, it should be noted that in these same letters Rudakov expressed about Mandelstam different, more heartfelt words: "Being near Mandelstam has given so much, that it is impossible to even surmise how much. It would be the same as if I were living with a live Vergil, or Pushkin, if worst came to worst (though some Baratynsky would not be enough)" (from a letter dated 17 April 1935, Rudakov: 43).

As in the case of Boris Kuzin, Sergei Rudakov's appearance "woke up" Mandelstam: early April 1935 marked a new period in Mandelstam's writing, the period of his Voronezh poems.

CHAPTER FIVE

"On 17, 18, 19, and 20 [April] Mandelstam worked like a maniac," Rudakov would tell his wife. "I have never seen anything like this in my life. You will see the results [...] At a distance it is impossible to measure or relate. I am standing before a working mechanism (perhaps even organism — it would be the same) of poetry. I see the same thing as in myself, though in the hands of a genius, which will mean much more than it is possible to understand now. There is no human anymore — there is Michelangelo [...] For the sake of 4 lines, literally 400 are pronounced. He does not see anything. He does not remember that some of these lines already belong to his earlier poems and repeats these lines again. Then by eschewing the old lines he creates new poems" (Rudakov: 44).

That is how were born the lyrics that Mandelstam considered to be his main achievement in poetry. In Voronezh, Mandelstam finally gave free rein to his inspiration. "He was working at the same time on different things," Nadezhda Iakovlevna reports. "He would often ask me to write down the first drafts of up to two or three poems at a time, which in his mind were already complete. I could not stop him: 'Understand, otherwise I won't be able to keep up'" (NM-2: 213). "It is amazing that the sense of space, breadth, deep breathing appeared in Mandelstam's poetry while in Voronezh, when he was not at all free," Akhmatova wrote in her memoirs (Akhmatova 1989a: 140).

On 22 April, Nadezhda Iakovlevna returned from Moscow and told Osip Emil'evich about the telephone conversation that Stalin had with Pasternak. "O.M. heard the detailed account and remained fully pleased with Pasternak, especially with his phrase about writers' organizations, which "have not handled this since 1927..." "He gave an exact reference," he laughed" (NM-1: 175). In the end of April, Osip Emil'evich and Nadezhda Iakovlevna began their joint work, "Goethe's Youth," which was meant to be performed on the local radio. The material was garnered from Goethe's book, "Poetry and Truth," with some of the fragments being quoted practically verbatim. Osip Emil'evich would choose for the radio compositions "episodes that were characteristic not only of Goethe's biography, but that of any poet" (NM-1: 248).

THE FINAL YEARS (1934-1938)

On 8 May 1935 Nadezhda Iakovlevna again left for Moscow. At the end of May, Osip Emil'evich finally received a three-month residence permit and his passport, which had been confiscated upon his arrest. On 3 June he wrote two poems inspired by his memory of Olga Vaksel'. She had married a Norwegian diplomat and moved to Oslo. It was there that Olga took her life in 1932. Mandelstam found out about Vaksel's death a long time ago; it was his work over "Goethe's Youth" that made him remember her again. Nadezhda Iakovlevna recalls: "We borrowed a few German biographies from the university library. As he was looking at the portraits of the women, Mandelstam suddenly noticed that they all seemed to resemble Olga Vaksel' in some way" (NM-2: 249).

Nadezhda Iakovlevna returned from Moscow on 14 June. During her absence, Mandelstam had spent time with, other than Rudakov, Iakov Iakovlevich Roginsky, the prominent anthropologist dispatched to Voronezh by the Moscow University. Among the topics they discussed were Lamarck, Darwin, and 18th century France. As Roginsky recalls, "we are sitting on the square with the monument to [the 19th century poet Aleksei] Kol'tsov. Mandelstam asks: "What do you think, will they ever mount a monument for me in Voronezh?" (Roginsky: 43-44).

During the summer of 1935, Mandelstam wrote a few reviews of books by contemporary poets. But a more serious challenge he confronted at that time was the newspaper "Kommuna's" assignment to visit a state farm and write about it. On June 22, together with his wife, he travelled to the Vorob'evsk district of the Voronezh oblast' to prepare a feature story about state farms. Not so long ago Mandelstam, in his 1933 anti-Stalin epigram, had vented his anger at the horrors of collectivization. Now he began to cherish the feeling of being a helper and an ally of the state. What was now required, he believed, were not wrathful invectives, but specific proposals for the improvement of the lives of the peasants. In Mandelstam's notebook there appeared, for example, such practical proposals: "It is necessary to: 1) Arrange for visiting lecturers for two-week long series of lectures on literature, party history, international education, technology and so forth [...] 4). Organize regular performances of amateur musicians (there are just a few solitary accordion players). Arrange for a short term choir instructor with the assistance of the radio committee" (III: 429-430). Upon his return from the visit to the state farm, Mandelstam told Sergei Rudakov that his hosts were surprised to discover in him a kind of high ranking official, a "boss" inspecting the place and giving recommendations and directions rather than an exiled intellectual who fell out of grace with the authorities (Rudakov: 78).

And yet just a few days later the pendulum swung into the opposite direction. The feature story about life on the state farm wasn't coming together for Mandelstam. Rudakov wrote to his wife on 2 August 1935: "He [Mandelstam]: "I am once again at the same crossroads. I am not being accepted by Soviet reality. Thank God that we are not being turned out. But I cannot do what they want me to do here. I can't do it like this: "look and see." It's not possible to stare like a bull at a cow and write. I have struggled with this all of my life. I cannot describe, only God or a bailiff can describe. I am not a feature-story writer. I can't do this. Why go to Vorob'evka in order to describe [...] I sinned three times against truth and myself: I wrote grovelling verses (about the pilots), which are cheerful, turbid, and empty. An ode without any real reason to celebrate anything, 'Oh! Oh!'—just meaningless exclamations. Wrote reviews under pressure and on ridiculous themes, and wrote a feature story. I hate myself. All that is loathsome rises within me from the bottom of my soul. Hunger has made me an opportunist. I was able to write a handful of really good poems but because of my subservience I have strained and lost my voice. It is the beginning of a vast emptiness" (Rudakov: 80). Mandelstam was right: the poems returned to him only later, in more than a year—in December 1936.

On 10 October 1935, upon the recommendation of the local section of the Soviet Writers Union, Mandelstam received a job at the Voronezh Bolshoi Soviet Theater. He was to assist the stage director with selecting and adjusting literary works for the stage. This position was similar to the one that Mikhail Bulgakov received after Stalin's telephone conversation with him in April of 1930. The new job promised the poet a relatively decent and stable salary. "He was a very quiet and modest person, he would quietly sit through performances and rehearsals," recalled an actor of the theater. "Surely he must have had his own point of view about the performances, and perhaps he might have shared it with the director of the theater or the stage director, but never with the troupe. And he also never read us, the actors, any of his poetry [...] It seemed as though he were afraid of spilling his own internal world" (Nerler 1997: 187).

Mandelstam's new position was comfortable both for him and the theater. "He was considered to be in charge of the literary side of the productions, but he hadn't a clue as to what he was supposed to be doing. In essence he just hung out and talked with the actors, and they liked him very much," recalls Nadezhda Iakovlevna (NM-1: 166). On 17 December 1935, Osip Emil'evich wrote to Rudakov in the hospital: "What do I have to say about myself? I am very tired. But my mood is solid, good. I have become friends with the Theater, where I do some work (not office work)" (IV: 162). On 18 December, Osip Emil'evich received a passport good for three years. That same day he went to rest at the Tambov sanatorium. From a letter he wrote to his wife in Moscow (she was there from 15 December 1935 through 15 January 1936): "The actors have grown attached to me. The stage directors started to ask me serious questions. I held up for a couple of days in the position. Then I collapsed. [...] We live on the high banks of the river Tsna. It is wide or else just seems to be as wide as the Volga. Then it becomes ink blue forest. The mildness and harmony of the Russian winter is cause for deep pleasure. Beautiful places" (IV: 163). In another letter, however, Mandelstam compared the sanatorium to a "penal battalion" (IV: 168).

He left for Voronezh earlier than expected, on 5 January 1936. Here an unpleasant surprise awaited him: the owners of the apartment took over his room while the Mandelstams were away. "He is very weak, barely walking. And then his nerves. He seeks a lodging every night" (from a letter from S.B. Rudakov to his wife, dated 12 January 1936) (Rudakov: 123). In the middle of Januray, Panov, who, apparently was reprimanded by the local NKVD, went to the directors of the Writers Union with apologies and invited the Mandelstams to move back in. Mandelstam accepted.

CHAPTER FIVE

On 5 February 1936, Anna Akhmatova, came to visit the Mandelstams in Voronezh. It was a very short visit. Already six days later, on 11 February, Akhmatova returned to Moscow. "It became so empty at the Mandelstams, almost to the point of tears," Rudakov wrote to his wife. "[...] Nadia with her mournful reminiscences. We are sitting with Osip at opposite corners of the room, for some reason angry with each other (jealousy!?)" (Rudakov: 145). Akhmatova commemorated her visit with the Mandelstams in her poem, "Voronezh," which ends in the following strophe that had not been published for a long time:

While in the room of the disgraced poet
Fear and the Muse are on duty in turn.
And night arrives,
Which knows not dawn.

On 13 March 1936 the Mandelstams moved to a new apartment, in the center of Voronezh. It is here that Emma Gershtein came to visit them during the May holidays: "On the second day, Osip Emil'evich began to feel badly. I went with him to the physician on duty at a clinic [...] Osip Emil'evich was extremely anxious" (Gershtein: 63). Mandelstam's health was worsening. On 27 May a council of physicians at the outpatient clinic № 1 concluded that Mandelstam was disabled and directed him to a commission for the disabled to determine the extent of his disability. On 18 June the poet was examined by a cardiologist who determined that he had "the heart of a 75-year-old, but that he would continue living" (Rudakov: 182). That same day the Mandelstams and Rudakov heard a radio broadcast on the occasion of Gor'ky's death. "For him Gor'ky (as indeed a real writer) was despite the point of whether or not "he 'wrote well'," noted Rudakov, "Gor'ky was Gor'ky" (Rudakov: 183).

In the middle of June, Mandelstam was informed about his being discharged from the theater as of 1 August (soon he would lose his job at the Radio Committee as well). On 20 June, Osip Emil'evich together with Nadezhda Iakovlevna went to rest at a datcha in Zadonsk. The Mandelstams were able to pay for their vacation thanks to the money provided by Akhmatova, Pasternak, and Evgeny Khazin. The writer

Iury Slezkin, who also was spending the summer in Zadonsk, wrote about his meeting with Mandelstam in a journal entry: "He is totally grey, with heart problems, exiled to Voronezh. He has decided to spend the summer in Zadonsk. I went with him to look for a rental. But he is unable to go anywhere as he is afraid of having a heart attack, he does not let his wife take a step anywhere without him, and his speech is erratic" (Nerler 1991: 93). In the beginning of July 1936, Sergei Rudakov came to visit the Mandelstams in Zadonsk in order to say farewell. "The parting was more than touching," wrote Rudakov to his wife on 8 July 1936) (Rudakov: 185).

In the fall of 1936 a new wave of repressions started sweeping the country. It was the advent of the Great Terror period (referred to as "Ezhovshchina"). Its vibrations were immediately felt even in the provincial Voronezh. "Beginning with the fall of [19]36 my situation in Voronezh harshly changed for the worse," Mandelstam complained in a letter, "Here is an accurate characteristic of the situation: it does not matter whether or not I am healthy or sick, it is impossible for me to get any kind of work in Voronezh. By the same token, my wife, who is living together with me, is absolutely unable to find any work in Voronezh" (IV: 179).

On 11 September, at a meeting of Voronezh writers devoted to issues of the struggle with class enemies on the literary front, Mandelstam's name came up more than once. A few decades later Olga Kretova thus described the event in her memoirs: "A disgraceful meeting took place during which we, 'fellow writers', attempted to excommunicate and isolate Mandelstam from literature, renounced him and those of his ilk and ostracized them. Some did this candidly and passionately, others — with bitterness and pain. Mandelstam looked drawn and turned into a complete knot of nerves, suffering from shortness of breath.

His wife, Nadezhda Iakovlevna, appealed for financial assistance. As a deputy of the secretary of the Writers' Union, I issued the following resolutions: 'Refuse,' 'Refrain'" (Kretova: 39).

In the beginning of September the Mandelstams were visited for the first time by Natalia Evgen'evna Shtempel'.

CHAPTER FIVE

3.

Natalia Shtempel' was a teacher of Russian language and literature at one of the Voronezh technical secondary schools. She was born lame. In her memoirs she describes her first visit with the Mandelstams: "Nadezhda Iakovlevna greeted me with a certain surprise (apparently the Mandelstams were not used to guests) and led me into the room. Osip Emil'evich was standing in the middle of the room and looking at me with curiosity. Embarrassed I mumbled something incoherent about Sergei Borisovich. "Oh, so this is who he has been hiding!" he exclaimed slyly and cheerfully. [Upon leaving Voronezh, the jealous Rudakov made Natalia Evgen'evna swear that she would not visit the Mandelstams] And immediately things became light and natural [...] Osip Emil'evich asked me whether or not I knew any of his poems by heart. I replied in the affirmative. 'Please read a few, it has been so long since I have heard my poems read', he said sadly and immediately became serious. I don't know why, but I read from "Stone": 'I have lost a gentle cameo, I don't know where, on the banks of the Neva...' My God, what happened after. Osip Emil'evich was indignant. He was the embodiment of wrath. I was struck by such a fierce reaction, such an unexpected change of mood. I was at a loss. The only thing that I remembered from the yelling was: 'You have read my worst poem!' Through tears I justified myself by saying: 'I am not to blame that you wrote it.' This seemed to calm him down, it even appeared as though he regretted his explosiveness. Then Nadezhda Iakovlevna got involved and said: 'Osia, don't you dare offend Natasha'" (Shtempel': 26).

Natalia Shtempel' fell absolutely in love with the Mandelstams. "We (Nadezhda Iakovlevna and I) were pulled into the orbit of the intense internal life led by Osip Emil'evich and we lived through him and his poetry," she would recall. "His new poems were a festive event, victory, and happiness" (Shtempel': 46). And this happened at a time when Mandelstam more than ever was sharply in need of spiritual support, when "everything was chopped off—no people, no ties, no work" (Shtempel': 57). It had almost gotten to the point that the poet was ready to recite his poems to totally unexpected listeners. "Osip Emil'evich has written some new poems," witnessed Natalia Evgen'evna, "he became animated and threw himself across the street from the house toward the pay phone, he dialed someone's number and began to recite his poems, and then angrily replied to whoever was on the other end of the line: 'No, listen, I have no one else to read to!' I was standing next to him and could not understand what was going on. It turned out that he was reciting to the NKVD investigator whose charge he was" (Shtempel': 27).

"Natasha is a master of the art of friendship," Mandelstam said (quoted in: Shtempel': 29). About his own attitude toward Natalia Shtempel' one can gather from the lyrical poems dedicated to her. She writes in her memoirs:

"Osip Emil'evich was sitting on the bed in his usual pose, with his feet under him, Turkish style. I sat down on the couch. He was serious and focused. 'Last night I wrote some poetry," he said, and read it. I was silent. 'What is it?' I did not understand the question and continued to be silent. 'It is a love lyric', he replied for me. 'It is the best of what I have written.' Then he gave me the sheet of paper <with these verses>.

1

Falling unwittingly to the hollow ground,
Her gait irregular and sweet
She walks — just barely leaving behind
Her light-footed friend and a young man.
Drawn as she is by restrained freedom
Inspired by such life in want.
And it might happen, sheer conjecture
Would seek to linger in her gait —
About how for us this spring weather
Is progenitor of the sepulchral arch,
Which will continue beginning forever.

CHAPTER FIVE

2

Some women belong to mother earth,
Every step of theirs resonant with sobbing,
Born to escort the resurrected and be
Always the first to greet the dead.
It is a crime to expect them to be tender,
Just as it is impossible to leave them.

Now — an angel, later — a sepulchral worm,
Afterwards — barely an outline...
What was once a step is now beyond reach...
Flowers are immortal. The sky is a whole.
And the future before us — a mere promise.

4 May 1937

Osip Emil'evich continued: "Nadiusha knows that I have written these poems, but I won't read them to her. When I die, please send them as my testament to the Pushkin House." And after a slight pause, he added: 'Now kiss me.' I went up to him and touched his forehead with my lips, he remained sitting like a statue. For some reason it was very sad" (Shtempel': 60-62).

Natasha Shtempel's acquaintance with the Mandelstams began with her reading of the worse, from the poet's point of view, love poem. The highest point of their acquaintance was the creation of his best, as the poet himself believed, love lyrics.

4.

In the end of October and early November 1936, the Mandelstams had moved to their last apartment in Voronezh. They had no work, they had no money. There were no prospects for improving the conditions of life in Voronezh. It was not possible to expect any help from Bukharin after he had learned that the true reason for Mandelstam's arrest in

1934 was his anti-Stalin epigram. Moreover, soon, on 27 February 1937, Bukharin was arrested right during the plenary proceedings of the Central Committee of the CPSU.

As one can judge by the extant letters from Mandelstam during the winter of 1936 and spring of 1937, the poet totally gave himself up to a sense of feverish despair. His poems of those days combine defiance with an almost childish entreaty for help. He wrote Nikolai Tikhonov on 31 December 1936:

"...I am extremely ill, I have been forgotten by everybody and am destitute. I am going to write the officials at the local NKVD in a few days and, if necessary, will write the government. Here in Voronezh I am living as if in the woods. People and trees are one and the same, no sense from either. I am literally physically perishing" (IV: 174). "You should know that ultimately it has been proposed that I live at the expense of relatives or check in to any hospital from where they will throw me out to an almshouse (with the homeless and the paralytics)," wrote Osip on 8 January 1937 to his brother Evgeny, who did not send money (IV: 175).

"You know that I am extremely ill, that my wife has been looking for work in vain. Not only can I get any medical treatment, but I cannot live: no means. I ask of you, though we are not at all close to one another" (From a letter to K. I. Chukovsky dated 9 (?) February 1937) (IV: 180).

"We have nothing to live on. I don't even have any ordinary acquaintances in Voronezh. Extreme hardship forces me to turn to completely unknown people, which is totally inadmissible and pointless" (From a March letter to N. S. Tikhonov) (IV: 181).

"...everything was taken away from me: my right to live, my right to labor, my right to receive medical treatment. I was put into the position of a dog" (From a letter to K. I. Chukovsky dated 17 April 1937) (IV: 185).

Such was the psychological background on which, beginning with 6 December 1936, were created the best poems by Mandelstam of the Voronezh period. One of them especially stands out. It is the poem "When I would take the coal for the highest acclaim..." (January-February 1937), referred to by the poet and his wife as "Ode." It was born out of the aspiration to glorify Joseph Stalin and the Stalin epoch. Whereas from Mandelstam's ephemeral prosperity of the early 1930's there emerged the anti-Stalin epigram, "We live not feeling the country beneath us," permeated with the feeling of a horrible overall destitution, the poet's personal plight in the winter of 1937 led him to write the "Ode," celebrating the great achievements and happiness of the whole nation.

The "Ode" begins with the depiction of an artist's—Mandelstam's—futile and fruitless attempts to create an adequate portrait of the national leader. To depict the leader faithfully, one needs to merge with his people, and in order to do this one must abandon all of one's previous delusions, repent for all of one's previous mistakes.

Having finished his ode to Stalin, Mandelstam read it everywhere, in Voronezh and in Moscow. He was driven by the hope that the "Ode" would save him. In vain. The reaction to this, one can say, crowning artistic achievement of Mandelstam's creative work on behalf of the officials was guarded. The topic was too sensitive to allow anyone to risk passing independent judgment without the supreme echelon's direct encouragament and authorization. Besides the subject matter itself, Mandelstam's style by no means met the requirements and criteria of "socialist realism." When the Union of Writers officials asked Petr Pavlenko to provide an expert evaluation of Mandel'stam's "Ode" he wrote: "...this poem as a whole is worse than some of its individual stanzas. It is full of incoherent speech, which is not appropriate when the subject is Stalin" (Nerler 1994: 14-15).

Mandelstam's "Poems about the unknown soldier" (1-15 March 1937) can be considered to be the poet's response to his own half-joking, half-serious question recently posed in a conversation with Iakov Roginsky, whether or not posterity will erect a monument to him. As in his "Ode," Mandelstam appears in his "Poems about the unknown soldier," surrounded by endless throngs of people—the traditional Horacean opposition between the "poet" and the "people" is cancelled. It is not he, Osip Mandelstam, who is worthy of a monument, but the "unknown soldier" representing millions who have been senselessly killed in all past and future wars. The fact that Mandelstam was thinking of Pushkin's "Pamiatnik" (Monument), his anniversary being celebrated in 1937, while working over his "Poems about the unknown soldier," becomes apparent when one reads the discarded ending.

But Mandelstam had a more topical "newspaper" purpose for the writing of his "Poems about the unknown soldier." It should be noted that in his 1923 essay about Auguste Barbier, he maintained that "the ability to use the topic of the day does not belittle it for one's inspiration, but rather increases the poet's merits" (II: 304).

On 12 February 1937, at a meeting of writers conducted in conjunction with the celebration of the Red Army day (23 February), the secretary of the USSR Writers Union, V.P. Stavsky, issued instructions to the masters of the word to pay more attention to the impending war. On 23 February, responding to this social commission, the Moscow paper, "Izvestia," published a long poem by Nikolai Zabolotsky, "War to war!".

Seven days later, Mandelstam began working on "Soldier." Like Zabolotsky, Mandelstam placed in the center of his poem the theme of the generation that still remembered the horrors of the First World War. Both poets address gas poisoning and the air raids as key events. Competition with Zabolotsky might well have provided Mandelstam with creative stimulus, especially because Zabolotsky figured in his conversations with Sergei Rudakov (see references to these discussions in Rudakov: 42, 70, 135).

5.

The term of Mandelstam's Voronezh exile expired on 16 May 1937. N. Ia. Mandelstam mentions their standing "without any faith or hope" in line at the local NKVD commandant's office: "'What does fate have in store for us?' O.M. whispered to me as he made his way to the window. There he said his last name and asked whether or not there was anything for him, as his term had ended. He was given a piece of paper. At first he could not figure out what it said, then exclaimed and returned to the window. "Does this mean that I am free to go wherever I want?" he asked. The attendant on duty snapped — they always snapped, it was their way of speaking with people—and we finally understood that O.M. had been returned his freedom" (NM-1: 258).

The Mandelstams quickly packed their belongings and went to Moscow. Here they were to meet with Anna Akhmatova, who was visiting the Ardovs at the Writers House on Nashchokinsky pereulok. "Osip was already quite sick, he spent a lot of time lying down," the poetess recalled. "He read me his new poems but did not let anyone record them. He spoke a lot about Natasha (Shtempel'), with whom he was friends in Voronezh [...] One of the two Mandelstam rooms was taken over by a person who was writing false denunciations against them [this was the essayist Nikolai Kostarev who had been moved to the Mandelstams' apartment in their absence], and soon it became impossible to appear at this apartment" (Akhmatova 1989a: 143). Nevertheless, initially the Mandelstams' mood was elated.

Liliia (Elikonida) Popova, whom the Mandelstams at that time saw almost every day, wrote to Vladimir Iakhontov in early June 1937: "How do I spend my time? Most of my time is spent at the Mandelstams. The Writers Union supports them, gives them money, Osip Emil'evich is being treated by physicians, in a few days his poems will be heard at the Union, at a special meeting [...] They have gotten to be very attached to me ("loved and respected by all"). <...> it looks as though he is twenty years younger after his exile, he looks like some wayward teenager and has written me some poems that he is hiding from Nadezhda Iakovlevna" (Shveitzer: 236).

It should be taken into consideration that the beautiful Liliia Popova was a fanatic supporter of Stalin and his politics, "a Stalinist of the touching type," as years later Nadezhda Iakovlevna would call her (NM-1: 243). For a short while, Mandelstam's feelings toward Liliia were practically inseparable from the feelings toward the Great Leader. Sobering came to him quicker than to many others. Already on 17 July 1937 Iakhontov's wife wrote down in her journal:

"I became upset and angry after two, even three, phone calls from M[andelstam]. It's this ceaseless, capricious egoism. Demanding from everyone, literally, unlimited attention to himself, his own troubles and pains.

In their atmosphere there is always "world history" happening, nothing less, and this "world history" is their personal fate, their biography.

In general, it is the disreputable, cheerless, eventless, closed fate of two people, one of whom has taken upon himself the role of a premier, the other — the everlasting classical mourner over him. His defender from the external world, and externally it is something that is deserving of bared teeth.

And thus, in everlasting conflict (one wonders whether or not this conflict would have existed before the October revolution. Most likely not)" (Shveitzer: 252).

During this period the Mandelstams had already been living for over two weeks in the city of Savelov on the Volga: in early June 1937 the militia demanded that Osip Emil'evich and Nadezhda Iakovlevna leave the capital within 24 hours. It turned out that after his exile, the poet did not have the right to live in Moscow.

In the middle of July it became clear that the presentation at the Writers Union that Popova triumphantly wrote Iakhontov about would not take place. At that time Natalia Shtempel' visited the Mandelstams in Savelovo.

To make ends meet, the Mandelstams were helped by Valentin Kataev and Evgeny Petrov, Solomon Mikhoels and Vladimir Iakhontov, Semen Kirsanov and Vsevolod Vishnevsky. In order to have enough money to live on, Osip Emil'evich and Nadezhda Iakovlevna went to Leningrad and received financial assistance from Mikhail Lozinsky, Iury Tynianov, Kornei Chukovsky, Mikhail Zoshchenko, Valentin Stenich while there. The Mandelstams stayed overnight at the Punins, in the Fountain house.

In November 1937 the Mandelstams moved to Kalinin. In a letter to the exiled Boris Kuzin dated 30 November, Nadezhda Iakovlevna related: "We are living now in a hut at the edge of town. Under our windows there are kitchen gardens, kitchen gardens, and kitchen gardens. It just snowed and the landscape now looks respectable [...] Kalinin itself is a nice town, but it is impossible to find any lodging in the center" (quoted as per: Kuzin: 520). In an earlier letter dated

6 November, Nadezhda Iakovlevna informed Kuzin some good news and some bad news about Mandelstam: "What is bad is that Osia is ill, he has sclerosis of the aorta and a bad heart condition. What is good is that he has been exceptionally active and has been working a lot" (Kuzin: 518).

By early spring good news had arrived: on 2 March, the Literary Fund provided the Mandelstams with two vouchers to the "Samatikha" sanatorium. Between 3 and 5 March, Osip Emil'evich and Nadezhda Iakovlevna traveled to Leningrad, where Mandelstam saw Akhmatova for the last time. "Woe followed in our footsteps everywhere we went," wrote Akhmatova in her "Sheets from a Journal," — "There was practically nowhere left for them to live. Osip was having a difficult time breathing, he kept gasping for air. I went somewhere to see them, but I don't recall where it was. Someone who had arrived after me said that Osip Emil'evich's father …had no warm clothes. Osip took off the sweater he was wearing under his jacket and asked that it be given to his father" (Akhmatova 1989a: 143).

And yet their stay at the sanatorium "Samatikha" perked Mandelstam up. On 10 March 1938 he sent a buoyant letter to Boris Kuzin: "Yesterday I grabbed a tambourine from the props at the House of Rest, and shaking and beating it, I was dancing in my room: that is how the new setting has affected me. 'I have the right to shake the tambourine with bells'" (IV: 199). On 16 April he wrote his father: "It's a very simple, modest, and remote place. 4 ½ hours along the Kazan' road, then 24 kilometers by horse. When we arrived there was still snow on the ground […] In any case, we got a lot of rest and peace over 2 months. We have 3 more weeks of this rest left. My health is better […] the most important thing: to work and to be together" (IV: 200).

In the meantime, the discussion of Mandelstam's fate was being conducted at the highest level of the literary establishment. On March 16, the head of the Union of Soviet Writers, V. Stavsky sent the following letter to the Commissar of Internal Affairs of the USSR, Ezhov:

"Esteemed Nikolai Ivanovich!

"In the writers' circles the issue of Osip Mandelstam is being discussed extremely nervously.

As is known, O. Mandelstam was exiled three or four years ago to Voronezh for writing disgraceful defamatory poetry and engaging in anti-Soviet agitation. His term was completed. Now he is living with his wife under Moscow (outside the limits of the "zone").

But in fact, he quite often visits his friends, primarily among the writers, in Moscow. They support him, collect money for him, treat him as a "martyr" — genius poet, unacknowledged by anyone. Valentin Kataev, I. Prut, and other writers spoke openly in his defense.

In order to attempt to take the strain off the situation, O. Mandelstam received material assistance from the Litfond. But that does not solve the Mandelstam problem.

The issue not only concerns him, as author of disgraceful defamatory poetry about the party leadership and the Soviet people. The issue also concerns the attitude of a group of leading Soviet writers toward Mandelstam. And I am appealing to you, Nikolai Ivanovich, with the request for help.

Recently O. Mandelstam wrote a series of poems. But they are not of exceptionally high value, according to the opinion of those comrades whom I have asked to look at them (including comrade Pavlenko, whose opinion is attached).

Once again I beseech you to help resolve the issue of O. Mandelstam.

With communist greetings

V. Stavsky"

(Nerler 1994: 13)

Attached to Stavsky's letter was the already quoted review of Mandelstam's poetry prepared by Petr Pavlenko, from which I adduce here a small excerpt: "While reading Mandelstam's old poems, I always felt that he was not a poet, but a versifier, a cold, cerebral compiler of rhymed works. Having read his most recent works, I am still unable to do away with this feeling" (Nerler 1994: 13).

CHAPTER FIVE

A photograph from Mandelstam's case. 1938

It turns out that Osip Emil'evich was not wrong in his prophetic dismay at the fellow writers' tribe, as it was specifically they who in the end destroyed Mandelstam. Early in the morning on 2 May 1938 the poet was arrested at the sanatorium "Samatikha." Nadezhda Iakovlevna recalls: "As soon as I came to, I began to collect things and heard the usual: "You have packed too many things—do you think he will be with us a long time? They will interrogate and then release…" No search took place: they just turned out the contents of the suitcase into a previously prepared bag. Nothing else [...] 'See me off on the truck to Cherusti', O.M. requested. 'Impossible', said the military solder, and then they left. All of this took place over twenty minutes or less" (NM-1: 427).

This time they dealt quickly with the investigatory formalities. The arrests had taken on such a massive extent that Mandelstam's case was being handled as a routine one, among hundreds of similar ones. There is just one protocol of his interrogation, dated 17 May 1938. It was conducted by investigator Shilkin.

"Question: You were arrested for anti-Soviet activity. Do you consider yourself guilty?

Answer: I do not consider myself guilty of anti-Soviet activity. < ... >

Question: The investigation is aware that while in Moscow you engaged in anti-Soviet activity about which you are withholding information. Provide veracious testimony.

Answer: I have not engaged in any kind of anti-Soviet activity (Nerler 1994: 18).

On 24 June Mandelstam was examined by the medical commission: "...does not suffer from mental disease, but is a person of a psychopathic constitution with the tendency of obsessive thoughts and fantasizing. Mental condition — OF SOUND MIND" (Nerler 1994: 20). On 20 July 1938 an indictment was concluded. On 2 August, Mandelstam was sentenced to penal labor camp for a term of five years, to begin with 30 April 1938. (Nerler 1994: 22). On 16 August, Mandelstam's documents were turned over to the Butyrsky prison for delivery to Kolyma. On 23 August he received a money transfer from Nadezhda Iakovlevna — 48 rubles. And in the beginning of September 1938, the poet was sent off on his final journey across the country in one of Stolypin's traincars — final destination: transit penal colony 3/10 of the Administration of North-Eastern Penal Labor Colonies.

6.

In 1949, the émigré Sergei Makovsky, the publisher of the journal "Apollon" before the revolution, in which Mandelstam had once made his literary debut, entered the following information compiled for him by a Western Slavicist: "After 'Tristia" there was another book published that included poems from 'Stone', 'Tristia', and new poems written already after the revolution [...] This final collection was published in 1927. But the poet continued to publish his poems in various Soviet journals, well up to '36 or '37, when he ran into trouble. Namely he had written an epigram about Stalin (three quatrains) and had read it to his fellow poets: to Pasternak at whose house it was, then three others. The GPU, however, became immediately aware of Mandelstam's political prank. He was arrested. Then there began appeals on his behalf. The case reached Stalin. Those who were appealing on Mandelstam's behalf were stating that despite the fact that he had not written much, he was the greatest genius of contemporary poets. Stalin apparently personally called Pasternak by telephone and asked him whether or not this was true. Pasternak was so taken aback by the phone call from the "father of the people" himself that he was unable to defend Mandelstam's reputation... Mandelstam was exiled to the south of Russia (perhaps to Erivan', to which he had dedicated one of his last poems). He remained in this exile up to '39, after which he was allowed to return to Moscow. During that time of his return, he read some of his poems which apparently astounded everyone with their brilliance. Later the poet again ended up somewhere in the provinces where he was when the war began. After the German troops attacked, out of fright he decided to run following his nose, he jumped out into the courtyard of the house where he was living and broke his leg. At that time the Germans were there and had shot him" (Makovsky 1997: 103, 131).

This muddled account shows how limited was the knowledge in the émigré community about the great poet's fate. Until the late 1950s Mandelstam's name was unmentionable in the Soviet press and as late as 1960s all sorts of legends about Mandelstam's death were circulating in the "samizdat" (one of them was the basis for Varlam Shalamov's short story "Cherry Brandy") (Shalamov: 75-76).

The true and full account of the last months of the poet's life became available only during the perestroika period. Osip Mandelstam had arrived in Vladivostok, to the colony on the Vtoraia river on 12 October 1938. According to the testimony of Iu. Moiseenko, "Some time around 2 or 3 November in honor of the anniversary of the October Revolution, a "letters day" was announced: the prisoners were allowed to write home [...] After breakfast, around eleven, a representative of the cultural-educational office showed up. Everyone was provided with half a page of a school notebook lined sheet of paper, pencils — six per barrack [...] Osip Emil'evich also left a letter. He wrote sitting, hunched over his planked bed" (Nerler 1994: 30).

Since Mandelstam did not know anything about the fate of Nadezhda Iakovlevna, he addressed his letter to his brother. In it he wrote that he had been given a term of 5 years. The letter continued:

"From Moscow's Butyrka the convoy departed on 9 September and arrived on 12 October. Health is very bad, emaciated almost to the bone, wasted, practically unrecognizable, though don't know if it makes sense to try and send things, food, or money. Though you might try. Am freezing without clothes.

Dear Naden'ka, don't know if you are still alive, my dearest. Shura please write me right away about Nadia. This is a transit point. They have not taken me to Kolyma. I might winter here. My dear ones, I kiss you all.

Osia.

Shurochka, I want to add that over the past few days I have been working, and this has improved my mood. From our colony, which is a transit one, they send on to permanent ones. Apparently I am in the "dropout" category, and I need to prepare for winter.

And I would like to ask: please send me a radiogram and money via telegraph."

(IV: 201)

Weakened both physically and morally, Osip Emil'evich was not ready for the harsh penal colony life, and the harsh penal winter.

Another witness reports: "Lice were dropping from Mandelstam. He had traded his coat for a few handfuls of sugar. We pulled together whatever we could for Mandelstam: rubber slippers, something else. He immediately sold everything and bought some sugar" (Nerler 1994: 37). From the testimony of D. Zlotinsky: "We began to (rather quickly) notice oddities of his behavior: he would tell us in confidence that he is afraid of death, that the colony's administration wants to poison him. We would attempt to dissuade him in vain, he was losing his mind right before our very eyes" (Nerler 1994: 42-43). From the testimony of D. Matorin: "I would say to Mandelstam: 'Osia, first of all, exercise; secondly, split your ration in three parts.' He would eat his food not like a human, devouring his ration in its entirety right away, which though small, was still 400 grams! I would say to him: 'Osia, save it.' He would respond: 'Mitia, they will steal it' [...] And another thing: he lost his spirit, and that means losing everything" (quoted as per: Nerler 1994: 49).

The denouement occurred on 27 December 1938. From the memoirs of Iu. Moiseenko: "In November we began to be tormented by pedigree white lice [...] Spotted fever had, of course, reached us also. Those fallen ill were taken away and never seen again. By the end of December, a few days before New Year's, we were taken to a bathhouse for sanitation. But there was no water there at all. We were told to undress and turn over our clothes to a heated cell. Afterwards we were taken to the other half of the building for dressing, where it was even colder. It reeked of sulphur and smoke. At that time two totally naked men fell unconscious. Immediately fierce locker room attendants ran up to them and took out of their pockets pieces of plywood, cord, and placed on each of the deadmen nameplates on which they had written their names: Mandelstam Osip Emil'evich, article 58 (10), term 10 years." And Morants from Moscow, I think it was Moisei Il'ich, with the same details" (Moiseenko: 3).

From the evidence of D. Matorin: "And then the thugs with the pliers took over, they quickly shooed me away. Before burying a dead man, they would tear out his crowns and golden teeth. With the help of soap, they would remove rings, if the ring didn't come off, they would chop the finger off. As far as I know, Mandelstam had golden crowns... And only after that would they bury them: in an undershirt, long johns, wrapped in a sheet they would be taken to a cemetery without a coffin. On the Vtoraya River of the first zone they would dig a trench — 50-70 cm. deep and place them in rows" (quoted as per: Nerler 1994: 50).

That is how Osip Emil'evich completed his journey on earth. It was followed by many years of practically total oblivion in his homeland.

Epilogue
NADEZHDA IAKOVLEVNA

Already by February 1939 Nadezhda Iakovlevna knew for sure that Mandelstam had perished in the camps. From then on and for the next two decades the goal of her life would become the preservation of her husband's unpublished works. "The poems live with me...That is a lot. Others don't have this," Nadezhda Iakovlevna wrote to Boris Kuzin on 8 July 1938 (Kuzin: 540). "She could recite the poetry and the prose by heart, memorizing them because she did not have faith in any secret storage places and because some of these works were simply too dangerous to keep — such as the epigram on Stalin; these she did not even dare to write down" (Polivanov: 5).

* * *

Nadezhda Iakovlevna spent most of the war in evacuation, in Tashkent, together with Anna Akhmatova. She continued to be intensely engaged over Osip Emil'evich's archives. E. Babaev recollects: "Among all the anxiety and terror that surrounded Nadezhda Iakovlevna, the biggest one was the "manuscript suitcase" which stood under the ottoman near the door. Everything that she could take with her during evacuation and wandering was stored in it. Just the very thought of the possibility of the disappearance of this suitcase made her fall into despair" (Babaev: 134).

In August 1946 a notorious resolution of the Party Central Committee was issued about the journals, "Zvezda," and "Leningrad," full of foul invective against Anna Akhmatova and her Acmeist past. Fearing for what was her only treausure, Nadezhda Iakovlevna decided to find a safer place for her husband's archives and turned them into the custody of a person with firmer standing in her own close circle, — the linguist, Sergei Ignat'evich Bernshtein. Mandelstam's papers remained in his custody through the fall of 1957 (the archives had also been, at different times, in the custody of Evgeny Khazin, Emma Gershtein, Ignatii Bernshtein, and Nikolai Khardzhiev). It was only from the late 1950s — early 60s that Mandelstam's poems of the 1930s began circulating in Russia, finally finding their reader. Copied over by hand innumerable times and then typed on the typewriter by hundreds of nameless enthusiasts, these poems began their wide wandering across the country.

In the West, already in the early 1950s, publications and republications of Mandelstam's poems as well as memoirs about him began appearing. The USSR kept an icy silence well up to 1957, when the limited-circulation newspaper, "Moskovsky literator" published in its 16 June issue an unsigned tiny notice that on 28 February 1957 a commission had been established to study the poet's literary heritage.

Then four years later, in the first issue of "Novyi Mir" for 1961, a chapter of the memoirs of a member of this commission, Il'ia Erenburg, was published. This was the first detailed account of Mandelstam's life to appear in the Soviet press. It was followed by publications of Mandelstam's late poems in the literary miscellany, "Den' poezii" [The Day of Poetry] (1962) and in the № 8 issue of the journal "Moskva" for 1964. In 1967, the publishing house "Iskusstvo" brought out Mandelstam's "Conversations about Dante," with a substantive afterword by L.E. Pinsky and annotations by Aleksandr Morozov. A full-fledged book of poems by Mandelstam had to wait well up to 1973.

In the meantime, two prominent Russian émigré scholars, Gleb Struve and Boris Filippov, initiated the mammoth task of collecting and publishing whatever Mandelstam texts could be discovered or smuggled out of the Soviet Union. Already in 1955 the New York based Chekhov Publishing House brought out a one-volume "Collected Works" by Mandelstam. This was the first book of the poet to appear after his 1928 Collected Poems. Struve and Filippov kept working on Mandelstam's literary legacy and their efforts resulted in the publication of four huge, heavily annotated volumes of Mandelstam's Complete Works. Thanks to their activities Mandelstam's poetry and prose enetered the canon of Western Slavic studies while the name of the poet was still reluctantly mentioned in the official Soviet press.

The appearance of the "American" Mandelstam edition made Nadezhda Iakovlevna sigh with relief. Finally, what had seemed to her to be an almost insurmountable task — making Mandelstam's poetry of the last period available to the reader — has been accomplished, albeit by roundabout way. Quite a large number of the Struve and Filippov books, despite a total ban on them in the Soviet Union, were brought to the country through various unofficial and secret channels. Together with a vast number of the *samizdat* works they formed what was later termed a second, alternative culture of the Soviet period.

Two memoir books written by Nadezhda Iakovlevna during these years also became part of this unofficial literature. Their manuscripts were sent abroad and brought out in Paris by émigré publishers. Along with Pasternak's "Doctor Zhivago" and Akhmatova's "Requiem," her books were a major contribution to the formation and growth of dissident intelligentsia in the USSR. Upon receiving the author's copies of her second book, Nadezhda Iakovlevna said that "she had fulfilled her duty and now wants to "join Os'ka," testifies Iu. Tabak (Tabak: 273). She also took steps to insure the preservation of her husband's papers. "I remember that once when we came to visit Nadezhda Iakovlevna, she said: "Now I can die peacefully. Osya's archives are in reliable hands," writes A. Arens (Osip and Nadezhda: 353). In 1973, the poet's archives had been sent through secret channels to Princeton University in the US.

She died on 29 December 1980 and was buried at the Starokuntsevskoe cemetery. Natasha Shtempel', who attended the funeral, writes, "I got the feeling that we were not only seeing Nadezhda Iakovlevna off, but were also paying final tribute to Osip Emil'evich. I shared my thoughts with those who were walking with me, and they responded that they too had the same feeling, that this is how it was" (Shtempel': 81).

Next to the oak cross over Nadezhda Iakovlevna's tombstone, the sculptor, Dmitry Shakhovskoy, had placed a right-angled symbolic granite stone in memory of Osip Mandelstam.

Bibliography

Adamovich 1989 — G. Adamovich, "Moi vstrechi s Annoi Akhmatovoi," *Zvezda*, 1989, № 6.

Adamovich 1996 — G. Adamovich. *S togo berega*. M., 1996.

Altman — M. Altman. *Razgovory s Viacheslavom Ivanovym*. SPb., 1995.

Andreev — V. Andreev, "Vozvrashchenie v zhizn'," *Zvezda*. 1969. № 5.

Andrei Bely 1988 — Andrei Bely. *Izbrannaya proza*. M., 1988.

Andrei Bely 1994 — Andrei Bely. [Pis'ma: P. Zaitsevu i F. Gladkovu], *Minuvshee: istoricheskii al'manakh*. 15. M.—SPb., 1994.

Arbenina — O. Arbenina, "O Mandelstame," *Tynianovskii sbornik. Shestye-Sed'mye-Vos'mye Tynianovskie chteniia*. M., 1998.

Argo — A. Argo. *Zvuchit slovo*. M., 1968.

Akhmatova 1989 — A. Akhmatova, "Avtobiographicheskaia proza," *Literaturnoe Obozrenie*, 1989, № 5.

Akhmatova 1989a — A. Akhmatova, "Listki iz dnevnika," *Requiem*. M., 1989.

Akhmatova 1989b — A. Akhmatova. *Poema bez geroia*. M., 1989.

Akhmatova 1996 — *Zapisnye knizhki Anny Akhmatovoi*. M.—Torino, 1996.

Averintsev 1991 — S. Averintsev, "Byli ochi ostree tochimoi kosy…", *Novyi Mir*, 1991, № 1.

Averintsev 1996 — S. Averintsev, "Sud'ba i vest' Osipa Mandelstama," *Poety*, M., 1996.

Babaev — E. Babaev. *Vospominaniia*. SPb., 2000.

Basalaev — I. Basalaev, "Zapiski dlia sebia," *Literaturnoe Obozrenie*, 1989, № 8.

Batiushkov 1978 — K. Batiushkov, "Vospominanie mest, srazhenii i puteshestvii," *Opyty v stikhakh i proze*. M., 1978.

Batiushkov 1989 — K. Batiushkov. *Sochineniia: v 2-kh tt*. Vol. 2. M., 1989.

B. Gasparov — B. Gasparov, "Izviniaius'," *Kul'tura russkogo modernizma. Stat'i, esse i publikatsii. V prinoshenie Vladimiru Fedorovichu Markovu*. M., 1993.

Bely i Razumnik — Andrei Bely i Ivanov-Razumnik. *Perepiska*. SPb., 1998.

Belza — I. Belza, "Vstrechi s O.E. Mandelstamom," *Nashe Nasledie*. 38 (1996).

Berberova — N. Berberova, "Iz peterburgskikh vospominanii: Tri druzhby," *Opyty*. [New-York]. 1953. Kn. I.

Berezov — R. Berezov, "Iz ocherka 'V Dome Gertsena'," *Novoe russkoe slovo*. [New-York], 1950. 3 September.

Berestov — V. Berestov, "Mandelstamovskie chteniia v Tashkente vo vremia voiny," *"Otdai menia, Voronezh…" Tret'i mezhdunarodnye Mandelstamovskie chteniia*. Voronezh, 1995.

Blok — A. Blok. *Dnevnik*. M., 1989.

Bobrov — S. Bobrov, [Review of "Tristia"], *Pechat' i revolutsiia*. 1923. № 4.

Bogomolov — N. Bogomolov. *Russkaia literatura pervoi treti XX veka. Portrety. Problemy. Razyskaniia*. Tomsk, 1999.

Boyadzhieva — Kh. Boyadzhieva, "Vospominaniia ob Osipe Mandelstame," *Al'manakh Poeziia. 57. 1990*. M., 1990.

Borisov — L.Borisov. *Za kruglym stolom proshlogo: Vospominaniia*. L., 1971.

Briusov — V. Briusov. *Sredi stikhov. 1894-1924*. M., 1990.

Bulgakov — M. Bulgakov. *Zapiski na manzhetakh*. M., 1988.

Chudovsky — V. Chudovsky, "Literaturnaia zhizn'. Sobraniia i doklady," *Russkaia Khudozhestvennaia Letopis'*, 1911, № 20.

Chukokkala — *Chukokkala. Rukopisnyi al'manakh Korneia Chukovskogo*. M., 2006.

Chukovskaia 1997 — L. Chukovskaia. *Zapiski ob Anne Akhmatovoi. 1938-1941*. Vol. 1. M., 1997.

Chukovskaia 2001 — L. Chukovskaia, "Dom poeta," *Druzhba Narodov*, 2001, № 9.

Chukovsky-1 — K. Chukovsky. *Dnevnik. 1901-1929*. M., 1991.

Chukovsky-2 — K. Chukovsky. *Dnevnik. 1930-1969*. M., 1994.

Deich — A. Deich, "Dve dnevnikovye zapisi," *"Sokhrani moiu rech'…"*. Vyp. 3/2. M., 2000.

Deich 1969 — A. Deich, *Den' nyneshnii i den' minuvshii*. M., 1969.

Eikhenbaum — B. Eikhenbaum. *O literature (Raboty raznykh let)*. M., 1987.

E. Livshits — E. Livshits, "Vospominaniia," *Literaturnoe Obozrenie*, 1991, № 1.

E. Mandelstam — E. Mandelstam, "Vospominaniia," *Novyi Mir*, 1995, № 10.

Erenburg 1966 — I. Erenburg, "Ludi, gody, zhizn'," *Sobranie sochinenii: v 9-ti tt*. Vol. 8. M., 1966.

Erenburg 1922 — I. Erenburg, [Review of "Tristia"], *Novaia Russkaia Kniga* (Berlin), 1922, № 2.

Feinberg — I. Feinberg, "O Mandelstame," *Voprosy Literatury*, 1991, № 1.

Fish — G. Fish, "Dirizher Galkin v tsentre mira," *Krasnaia Gazeta*, 1925, 30 iiunia. Vechernii vypusk.

Freidin 1989 — Arkhiv Mandelstama, *Dom Kino: Press-bulleten' tsentral'nogo Doma kinematografistov*. M., 1989. Dekabr'.

Freidin 1991 — Iu. Freidin, "'Ostatok knig': biblioteka O. E. Mandelstama," *Slovo i sud'ba. Osip Mandelstam*. M., 1991.

Freidin 1994 — Iu. Freidin, "Put' v Voronezh," *Mandelstamovskie dni v Voronezhe*. Voronezh, 1994.

Galushkin — A. Galushkin, "'Vy, veroiatno, znaete poeta O. E. Mandelstama...'. Nikolai Bukharin ob Osipe Mandelstame," *Russkaia Mysl'*. 2000, 8-14 iiunia.

Gardzonio — S. Gardzonio. *Stat'i po russkoi poezii i kulture XX veka*. M., 2006.

Gasparov 1987 — M. Gasparov, "Marshak i vremia," *Daugava* (Riga), 1987, № 11.

Gasparov 1993 — M. Gasparov, "Poetika 'serebryanogo veka'," *Russkaia poeziia serebrianogo veka. 1890-1917. Antologiia*. M., 1993.

Gasparov 1994 — M. Gasparov, "Lektsii Viach. Ivanova o stikhe v Poeticheskoi Akademii 1909 g.," *Novoe Literaturnoe Obozrenie*, 1994, № 10.

Gasparov 1995 — M. Gasparov, "Poet i kul'tura. Tri poetiki Osipa Mandelstama," in: O. Mandelstam. *Polnoe sobranie stikhotvorenii*. SPb., 1995.

Gasparov 1996 — M. Gasparov. *O. Mandelstam. Grazhdanskaia lirika 1937 goda*. M., 1996.

Gasparov 2000 — M. Gasparov. *Zapisi i vypiski*. M., 2000.

Gatov — A. Gatov, "Uroki masterstva," *Zhizn' i tvorchestvo O. E. Mandelstama*. Voronezh, 1990.

Gershtein — E. Gershtein. *Memuary*. SPb., 1998.

Gertsyk — E. Gertsyk. *Vospominaniia*. Paris, 1973.

Ginzburg — L. Ginzburg. *Zapisnye knizhki. Vospominaniia. Esse*. SPb., 2002.

G. Ivanov 1994 — G. Ivanov. *Sobranie sochinenii: v 3-kh tt*. Vol. 3. M., 1994.

Gladkov — A. Gladkov. *Pozdnie vechera. Vospominaniia, stat'i, zametki*. M., 1986.

Glukhov-Shchurinsky — A. Glukhov-Shchurinsky, "O. E. Mandelstam i molodezh'," *Zhizn' i tvorchestvo O. E. Mandelstama*. Voronezh, 1990.

Gollerbakh — "Mandelstam v arkhive E.F. Gollerbakha," *Slovo i sud'ba. Osip Mandelstam*. M., 1991.

Gonta — M. Gonta, "Iz vospominanii o Pasternake," in: N. Gromova. *"Uzel." Poety: druzhby i razryvy. Iz literaturnogo byta kontsa 20-kh — 30-kh godov*. M., 2006.

Gorbacheva — V. Gorbacheva, "Zapisi raznykh let," *Novyi Mir*, 1989, № 9.

Gornfeld — "Pis'mo A.G. Gornfel'da A.R. Paleiu," *"Sokhrani moiu rech'..."*. Vyp. 3/2. M., 2000.

Gornung — B. Gornung, "Zametki k biografii O. E. Mandelstama," *"Sokhrani moiu rech'..."*. Vyp. 3/2. M., 2000.

Grigor'ev, Petrova — A. Grigor'ev, I. Petrova, "O. Mandelstam na poroge 30-kh godov," *Russian Literature*, 1977, № 5.

Grishunin — A. Grishunin, "Blok i Mandelstam," *Slovo i sud'ba. Osip Mandelstam*. M., 1991.

Gromov — P. Gromov. *Napisannoe i nenapisannoe*. M., 1994.

Gumilev — N. Gumilev. *Sochineniia: v 3-kh tt*. Vol. 3. M., 1990.

Gurvich — E. Gurvich, "Chto pomnitsia," *"Sokhrani moiu rech'..."*. *Mandelstamovskii sbornik*. M., 1991.

Gydov — V. Gydov, "O. E. Mandelstam i voronezhskie pisateli (po vospominaniiam M. Ia. Bulavina)," *"Sokhrani moiu rech'..."*. *Mandelstamovskii sbornik*. 2. M., 1993.

Iakhontov — V. Iakhontov, [Zapis'iz dnevnika ot iuliia 1931 g.], *Pamiatnye knizhnye daty-1991*. M., 1991.

Ivnev — "Osip Mandelstam v 'Memuarakh' Riurika Ivneva," *"Sokhrani moiu rech'..."*. *Mandelstamovskii sbornik*. M., 1991.

Iz perepiski — "Iz perepiski N. Ia. Mandelstam s N. A. Struve," *Vestnik Russkogo Khristianskogo Dvizheniia*. № 133 (1981).

Kablukov — "O. E. Mandelstam v zapisiakh dnevnika i perepiske S. P. Kablukova," in: O. Mandelstam. *Kamen'*. L., 1990.

Karpovich — M. Karpovich, "Moe znakomstvo s Mandelstamom," *Osip Mandelstam i ego vremia*. M., 1995.

Kataev — V. Kataev. *Trava zabveniia*. M., 2000.

Katz, Timenchik — B. Katz, R. Timenchik. *Anna Akhmatova i muzyka. Issledovatel'skie ocherki*, 1989.

Katz — B. Katz, "Zashchitnik i podzashchitnyi muzyki," in: O. Mandelstam. *"Polon muzyki, muzy, i muki...". Stikhi i proza.* L., 1991.

Kaverin — V. Kaverin, "Vstrechi s Mandelstamom," *Schast'e talanta. Vospominaniya i vstrechi, portrety i razmyshleniya.* M., 1989.

Khardzhiev — N. Khardzhiev, "V Khlebnikove est' vse", *Ot Maiakovskogo do Kruchenykh. Izbrannye raboty o russkom futurizme.* M., 2006.

Khantsyn — I. Khantsyn, "O Mandelstame," *"Sokhrani moiu rech'...".* Vyp. 3/2. M., 2000.

Khelemsky — Ia. Khelemsky, "Vetvi odnogo stvola," in: M. Petrovykh. *Cherta gorizonta. Stikhi i perevody. Vospominaniia o Marii Petrovykh.* Erevan, 1986.

Khodasevich 1922 — V. Khodasevich, [Review of "Tristia"], *Dni* (Berlin), 1922, 13 noiabria.

Khodasevich 1997 — V. Khodasevich. *Sobranie sochinenii: v 4-kh tomakh.* Vol. 4. M., 1997.

Khudaverdian — A. Khudaverdian, "Vstrechi s poetom," *Literaturnaia Armeniia*, 1991. № 5.

Kochin — N. Kochin, "Mandelstam v 'Moskovskom komsomol'tse'," in: O. Mandelstam. *"I ty, Moskva, sestra moia, legka..." Stikhi, proza, vospominaniia, materialy k biografii. Venok Mandelstamu.* M., 1990.

Kofeinia — *Kofeinia razbitykh serdets. Kollektivnaia shutochnaia p'esa v stikhakh pri uchastii O. E. Mandelstama (Stanford Slavic Studies.* Vol. 12, 1997).

Kovalenkov — A. Kovalenkov. *Khoroshie, raznye... Literaturnye portrety.* M., 1966.

Kreps — E. Kreps. *O prozhitom i perezhitom.* M., 1989.

Kretova — O. Kretova, "Gor'kie stranitsy pamiati," *Zhizn' i tvorchestvo O. E. Mandelstama.* Voronezh, 1990.

Kupchenko 1987 — V. Kupchenko, "Osip Mandelstam v Kimmerii," *Voprosy Literatury*, 1987, № 7.

Kupchenko 1991 — V. Kupchenko, "Ssora poetov (K istorii vzaimootnoshenii O. Mandelstama i M. Voloshina)," *Slovo i sud'ba. Osip Mandelstam.* M., 1991.

Kuzin — Boris Kuzin. *Vospominaniia. Proizvedeniia. Perepiska.* Nadezhda Mandelstam. *192 pis'ma k B. S. Kuzinu.* SPb., 1999.

Kuzmin — M. Kuzmin. *Dnevnik. 1908—1915.* SPb., 2005.

Lakshin — V. Lakshin. *Otkrytaia dver': Vospominaniia i ocherki.* M., 1989.

Lavrov — A. Lavrov, [Gippius Vladimir Vasil'evich], *Russkie pisateli. 1800-1917. Biograficheskii slovar'.* Vol. 1. M., 1989.

Lavrov 2007 — A. Lavrov. *Russkie simvolisty. Etudy i razyskaniia*. M., 2007.

Lekmanov 2000 — O. Lekmanov. *Kniga ob akmeizme i drugie raboty*. Tomsk, 2000.

Lekmanov 2003 — O. Lekmanov. *Zhizn' Osipa Mandelstama. Dokumental'noe povestvovanie*. SPb., 2003.

Lezhnev — A. Lezhnev, "Literaturnye zametki," *Pechat' i Revolutsiia*, 1925, № 4.

Lerner — N. Lerner, [Review of "Shum vremeni"], *Byloe*, 1925, № 6.

L. Gornung — L. Gornung, "Iz vospominanii ob Osipe Mandelstame," in: O. Mandelstam. *"I ty, Moskva, sestra moia, legka...". Stikhi, proza, vospominaniia, materialy k biografii. Venok Mandelstamu* M., 1990.

Lindeberg — O. Lindeberg, "Vospominaniia Vl. Gippiusa ob A. Bloke (po arkhivnym istochnikam)," *Aleksandr Blok i mirovaia kul'tura. Materialy*.Velikii Novgorod, 2000.

Lipkin — S. Lipkin, "Ugl', pylaiushchii ognem," *Osip Mandelstam i ego vremia*. M., 1995.

Lisnyanskaia — I. Lisnianskaia. *Khvastun'ia. Vospominatel'naia proza*. M., 2006.

Livshits — B. Livshits. *Polutoraglazyi strelets. Stikhotvoreniia. Perevody. Vospominaniia*. L., 1989.

LN — *Literaturnoe Nasledstvo*. Vol. 92. Book 3. M., 1982.

Lopatto — M. Lopatto, "Pis'ma V. Edzhertonu ot 30 ianvaria i 14 iiunia 1972 g.," *Piatye Tynianovskie chteniia: Tezisy dokladov i materialy dlia obsuzhdeniia*. Riga, 1990.

Luknitskaia — V. Luknitskaia. *Nikolai Gumilev. Zhizn'poeta po materialam domashnego arkhiva sem'i Luknitskikh*. L., 1990.

Luknitsky — "Mandelstam v archive P. N. Luknitskogo," *Slovo i sud'ba. Osip Mandelstam*. M., 1991.

Lundberg — E. Lundberg. *Zapiski pisatelia. 1917-1920*. L., 1930.

Lur'e — A. Lur'e, "Osip Mandelstam," *Osip Mandelstam i ego vremia*. M., 1995.

Lyons — E. Lyons. *Moscow Carousel*. New York, 1935.

Maari — G. Maari, "Posleslovie k publikatsii stikhov Mandelstama," *Literaturnaia Armeniia*, 1966, № 1.

Makovsky 1995 — S. Makovsky, "Osip Mandelstam (fragment)," *Osip Mandelstam i ego vremia*. M., 1995.

Makovsky 1997 — S. Makovsky, "Ob Osipe Mandelstame," *Daugava* (Riga), 1997, № 2.

Maksimenkov — L. Maksimenkov, "Ocherki nomenklaturnoi istorii sovetskoi literatury (1932-1946). Stalin, Bukharin, Zhdanov, Shcherbakov i drugie," *Vorposy Literatury*, 2003. Iiul'- Avgust.

Malmstad — D. Malmstad, "Edinstvo protivopolozhnostei. Istoriia vzaimootnoshenii Khodasevicha i Pasternaka," *Literaturnoe Obozrenie*, 1990, № 2.

Mandelstam 1990 — O. Mandelstam. *Kamen'*. L., 1990.

Mandelstam 1990a — O. Mandelstam. *Sochineniia: v 2-kh tt*. Vol. 1. M., 1990.

Mandelstam 1990b — O. Mandelhstam O. *Sochineniia: v 2-kh tt*. Vol. 2. M., 1990.

Mandelstam 2002 — O. Mandelstam. *Shum vremeni*. M., 2002.

Manfred — A. Manfred, [Review of "Stikhotvoreniia"], *Kniga i Revolutsiia*, 1929, № 15/16.

Mariengof — A. Mariengof. *Bessmertnaia trilogiia*. M., 1999.

Maiakovsky — V. Maiakovsky. *Polnoe sobranie sochineni*: v 13-ti tt. Vol. 12. M., 1959.

Mets 2005 — A. Mets. *Osip Mandelstam i ego vremia. Analiz tekstov*. SPb., 2005.

Mets 2006 — O. Mandelstam, "O prirode slova." Vstupitel'naia stat'ia i primechaniia A. Metsa, *Russkaia Literatura*, 2006, № 4.

Mindlin — E. Mindlin. *Neobyknovennye sobesedniki. Kniga vospominanii*. M., 1968.

Minchkovsky — A. Minchkovsky, "On byl takim," *Aleksandr Prokof'ev: vspominaiut druz'ia*. M., 1977.

Mints — Z. Mints. *Aleksandr Blok i russkie pisateli*. SPb., 2000.

Mitsishvili — N. Mitsishvili. *Perezhitoe*. Tbilisi, 1963.

Mochulsky — K. Mochulsky, "O. E. Mandelstam," *Osip Mandelstam i ego vremia*. M., 1995.

Moiseenko — Iu. Moiseenko, "Kak umiral Osip Mandelstam," *Izvestiia*, 1991, 22 February.

Musatov — V. Musatov. *Lirika Osipa Mandelstama*. Kiev, 2000.

Naiman — A. Naiman. *Rasskazy o Anne Akhmatovoi*. M., 1989.

Nappel'baum — I. Nappel'baum, "Slepaia lastochka," *Literaturnoe Obozrenie*, 1991, № 1.

Narbut — V. Narbut, "Viacheslav Ivanov. "Cor ardens". M., 1911," *Novyi Zhurnal dlia Vsekh*, 1912, № 9.

N. Chukovsky — N. Chukovsky, "O Mandelstame," *Literaturnye vospominaniia*. M., 1989.

Nerler 1989 — P. Nerler, "Osip Mandelstam v Narkomprose v 1918-1919 godakh," *Voprosy Literatury*, 1989, № 9.

Nerler 1991 — P. Nerler, "On nichemu ne nauchilsia... (O. E. Mandelstam v Voronezhe: novye materialy)," *Literaturnoe Obozrenie*, 1991, № 1.

Nerler 1994 — P. Nerler. *"S gur'boi i gurtom...". Khronika poslednego goda zhizni O. E. Mandelstama.* M., 1994.

Nerler 1994a — P. Nerler. *Osip Mandelstam v Geidelberge.* M., 1994.

Nerler 1997 — P. Nerler, "Chut' mertsaet prizrachnaia stsena...", *Al'manakh Poeziia*, 1997, № 7.

Nerler 2001 — P. Nerler, "Materialy ob O. E. Mandelstame v amerikanskikh arkhivakh," *Rossika v SShA. 50-letiu Bakhmet'evskogo arkhiva Kolumbiiskogo universiteta posviashchaetsia.* M., 2001.

NM-1 — N. Mandelstam. *Vospominaniia.* M., 1999.

NM-2 — N. Mandelstam. *Vtoraia kniga.* M., 1999.

N. Tabidze — N. Tabidze, "Pamiat': glava iz knigi," *Dom pod chinarami.* Tbilisi, 1976.

Obolenskaia — "Osip Mandelstam v Krymu letom 1916 goda. Neizvestnoe pis'mo Iulii Obolenskoi," *Russkaia Mysl'*, 1996. 25 aprelia-1 maia.

Odoevtseva — I. Odoevtseva, "Na beregakh Nevy," *Zvezda*, 1988, № 3.

Ofrosimov — O. Ofrosimov, "O Gumileve, Kuzmine, Mandelstame... (Vstrecha s izdatelem)," *Novoe Russkoe Slovo* (New-York), 1953. 13 dekabria.

Olesha — Iu. Olesha. *Kniga proshchaniia.* M., 2001.

Onoshkovich-Iatsyna — A. Onoshkovich-Iatsyna, "Dnevnik 1919-1927," *Minuvshee. Istoricheskii al'manakh.* 13 (1993).

Osip i Nadezhda — *Osip i Nadezhda Mandelstamy v rasskazakh sovremennikov.* M., 2002.

Osmerkina-Gal'perina — E. Osmerkina-Gal'perina, "Moi vstrechi (fragmenty)," *Osip Mandelstam i ego vremia.* M., 1995.

Parnis 1991 — A. Parnis, "Mandelstam v Petrograde v 1915-1916 godakh. Materialy k ikonografii poeta," *Literaturnoe Obozrenie*, 1991, № 6.

Parnis 1991a — A. Parnis, "Shtrikhi k futuristicheskomu portretu O. E. Mandelstama," *Slovo i sud'ba. Osip Mandelstam.* M., 1991.

Pasternak 1992 — B. Pasternak. *Sobranie sochinenii: v 5-ti tt.* Vol. 5. M., 1992.

Pavlovich — N. Pavlovich, "Vospominaniia ob Aleksandre Bloke," *Prometei.* Vyp. 11. M., 1977.

Perepiska Pasternaka — *Sushchestvovan'ia tkan' skvoznaia. Boris Pasternak. Perepiska s Evgeniei Pasternak.* M., 1998.

Piast — V. Piast. *Vstrechi.* M., 1997.

Pimenov — V. Pimenov. *Svideteli zhivye*. M., 1978.

Poliakova — S. Poliakova. *"Oleinikov i ob Oleinikove" i drugie raboty po russkoi literature*. SPb., 1997.

Polianovsky — E. Polianovsky. *Gibel' Osipa Mandelstama*. SPb.—Paris, 1993.

Polivanov — M. Polivanov, "Predislovie," in: N. Mandelstam. *Vtoraia kniga*. M., 1990.

Prishvin — M. Prishvin, "Sopka Maira (fragment)," in: O. Mandelstam. *"I ty, Moskva, sestra moia, legka..." Stikhi, proza, vospominaniia, materialy k biografii. Venok Mandelstamu*. M., 1990.

Proust — M. Prust. *Po napravleniu k Svanu*. Per. N. Liubimova. M., 1973.

PSE — *Pisateli sovremennoi epokhi. Bio-bibliograficheskii slovar'russkikh pisatelei XX veka*. Vol. 1. M., 1992.

Punin 1922 — N. Punin, "Tristia", *Zhizn' Iskusstva*, 1922. 17 oktiabria.

Punin 2000 — N. Punin. *Mir svetel liuboviu. Dnevniki. Pis'ma*. M., 2000.

Pushkin — A. Pushkin. *Polnoe sobranie sochinenii: v 10-ti tt*. Vol. 10. L., 1978.

Roginsky — Ia. Roginsky, "Vstrechi v Voronezhe," *Zhizn' i tvorchestvo O. E. Mandelstama*. Voronezh, 1990.

Ronen — O. Ronen, "Osip Mandelstam," *Literaturnoe Obozrenie*, 1991, № 1.

Rubakin — A. Rubakin. *Nad rekoiu vremeni*. M., 1966.

Rudakov — "O. E. Mandelstam v pis'makh S. B. Rudakova k zhene (1935-1936)," *Ezhegodnik Rukopisnogo otdela Pushkinskogo Doma. 1993. Materialy ob O. E. Mandelstame*. SPb., 1997.

Rusanova — A. Rusanova, T. Rusanova. *Vstrechi s Akhmatovoi i Mandelstamom*. Voronezh, 1991.

Sedykh — A. Sedykh. *Dalekie, blizkie*. M., 1995.

Shalamov — V. Shalamov. *Kolymskie rasskazy*. SPb., 2004.

Shershenevich — V. Shershenevich, "Velikolepnyi ochevidets. Poeticheskie vospominaniia 1910-1925 gg.," *Moi vek, moi druz'ia i podrugi. Vospominaniia Mariengofa, Shershenevicha, Gruzinova*. M., 1990.

Shklovsky — V. Shklovsky. *"Eshche nichego ne konchilos'...".* M., 2002.

Shtempel' — N. Shtempel. *Mandelstam v Voronezhe*. M., 1992.

Shumikhin — S. Shumikhin, "'Mandelstam byl ne po plechu sovremennikam...'. Pis'ma Nadezhdy Mandelstam k Aleksandru Gladkovu," *Russkaia Mysl'*, 1997, 12-18 iunia.

Shvarts — E. Shvarts. *Zhivu bespokoino... Iz dnevnikov*. L., 1990.

Shveitser — V. Shveitser, "Mandelshtam posle Voronezha," *Voprosy Literatury*, 1990, no. 4, pp. 235-253.

Sinani — I. Sinani, "Psikhiatr Boris Naumovich Sinani," *"Sokhrani moiu rech'…"*. Vyp. 3/2. M., 2000.

Slepian — D. Slepian, "Chto ia vspomnila o N. S. Gumileve," *Zhizn' N. Gumileva. Vospominaniia sovremennikov*. L., 1991.

Smol'evsky — A. Smol'evsky, "Olga Vaksel' — adresat chetyrekh stikhotvorenii Osipa Mandelstama," *Literaturnaia Ucheba*, 1991, № 1.

Sokolova — N. Sokolova, "Razroznennye stranichki," *Sokhrani moiu rech'*. Vyp. 3/2. M., 2000.

Soloviev — V. Soloviev. *Literaturnaia kritika*. M., 1990.

Tabak — Iu. Tabak, "K stoletiiu so dnia rozhdeniia N.Ia. Mandelstam," *Smert' i bessmertie poeta. Materialy mezhdunarodnoi nauchnoi konferentsii, posviashchennoi 60-letiiu so dnia gibeli O. E. Mandelstama (Moskva, 28-29 dekabria 1998 g.)*. M., 2001.

Tabidze — *Russkii literaturnyi avangard. Materialy i issledovaniia*. Trento, 1990.

Tager — E. Tager, "O Mandelstame," *Osip Mandelstam i ego vremia*. M., 1995.

Tenishevets — *Tenishevets*, 1907, № 1.

Terapiano — Iu. Terapiano, "Vstrechi. Fragment," *Osip Mandelstam i ego vremia*. M., 1995.

Tikhonov — N. Tikhonov, "Ustnaya kniga: dvadtsatye gody," *Sobranie sochinenii*. Vol. 6. M., 1986.

Timenchik 1988 — R. Timenchik, ["Kamen'", 1913], *Pamiatnye knizhnye daty-1988*. M., 1988.

Timenchik 1994 — R. Timenchik, "Evreiskie motivy v russkoi poezii nachala XX veka (Tri predvaritel'nykh zametki)," *Tynianovskii sbornik. Piatye Tynianovskie chteniia*. M., 1994.

Timenchik 1998 — R. Timenchik, "O trudakh i dniakh Akhmatovoi," *Novoe Literaturnoe Obozrenie*, 1998, № 29.

Timenchik 2000 — R. Timenchik, "Osip Mandelstam v Batume v 1920 godu," *"Sokhrani moiu rech'…"*. Vyp. 3/2. M., 2000.

Timenchik 2005 — R. Timenchik. *Anna Akhmatova v 1960-e gody*. M.—Toronto, 2005.

Toddes — E. Toddes, "Poeticheskaia ideologiia," *Literaturnoe Obozrenie*, 1991, № 3.

Tsvetaeva 1995 — M. Tsvetaeva, "Istoriia odnogo posviashcheniia," *Osip Mandelstam i ego vremia*. M., 1995.

Tsvetaeva 2001 — M. Tsvetaeva. *Neizdannoe. Zapisnye knizhki: v 2-kh tt.* Vol. 2. M., 2001.

Tsvetaeva. Vol. 6 — M. Tsvetaeva. *Sobranie sochinenii: v 7-mi tt.* Vol. 6. M., 1995.

Tsvetaeva. Vol. 7 — M. Tsvetaeva. *Sobranie sochinenii: v 7-mi tt.* Vol. 7. M., 1995.

Tynianov — Iu. Tynianov. *Poetika. Istoriia literatury. Kino.* M., 1977.

Ustinov — A. Ustinov, "1929 god v biografii Mandelstama," *Novoe Literaturnoe Obozrenie*, 2002, № 58.

Vas. Gippius — V. Gippius, "Tsekh poetov," *A. Akhmatova. Desiatye gody.* M., 1989.

Vatsuro — V. Vatsuro. *S. D. P. Iz istorii literaturnogo byta pushkinskoi pory.* M., 1989.

VChK — *Iz istorii Vserossiiskoi Chrezvychainoi komissii. 1917-1921 gg. Sbornik dokumentov.* M., 1958.

Vechtomova — E. Vechtomova, "Sotvorenie mira," *Aleksandr Prokof'ev: vspominaiut druzia.* M., 1977.

Veidle — V. Veidle, "Pevchie iamby," *Umiranie iskusstva.* M., 2001.

Vidgof — L. Vidgof. *Moskva Mandelstama. Kniga-ekskursiia.* M., 1998.

Vil'mont — N. Vil'mont. *O Borise Pasternake: Vospominaniia i mysli.* M., 1989.

Vitkovich — V. Vitkovich. *Dlinnye pis'ma. Sto istorii v doroge.* M., 1967.

V. Ivanov — V. Ivanov, "Vselenskoe delo," *Russkaia Mysl'*, 1914, no. 12.

V. Lur'e — V. Lur'e, "Iz vospominanii," *Zhizn' Nikolaia Gumileva.* L., 1991.

Volkenshtein — F. Vol'kenshtein, "Tovarishcheskii sud po isku Osipa Mandelstama," *"Sokhrani moiu rech'…". Mandelstamovskii sbornik.* M., 1991.

Vol'pin — N. Vol'pin, "Osip Mandelstam," *Literaturnoe Obozrenie*, 1991, № 1.

Z. Gippius — Z. Gippius. *Zhivye litsa.* Vol. 2. L., 1991.

Zenkevich — M. Zenkevich, "Beseda s L. Shilovym i G. Levinym," State Literary Museum (Moscow).

Zubakin — B. Zubakin, [Pis'ma V. Piastu], *Filologicheskie Zapiski*, Voronezh, 3 (1994).

Index of Names

....

Adamovich, **Georgy Viktorovich (1892-1972)**, Acmeist poet and literary critic, translator, memoirist. Emigrated in 1923. — 29, 86

Aduev (Rabinovich), **Nikolai Al'fredovich (1895-1950)**, Soviet poet, playwright, satirist, wrote librettos for musical comedies. Graduate of the Tenishev school. Was a member of the constructivists in the 1920's. — 107

Aeschylus (525-456 B.C.), ancient Greek dramatist. — 50-52

Agranov, **Iakov Saulovich (1893-1938)**, leading collaborator of the VChK-OGPU-NKVD [All-Russian Extraordinary Commission — United State Political Directorate — People's Commissariat of Internal Affairs]. Arrested in 1937. Executed by shooting. — 136, 139

Akhmatova, **Anna Andreevna (1989-1966)**, poet. — 2, 25, 28, 29, 32, 34, 35, 45, 46, 49, 53, 54, 59-61, 63, 66, 74, 78, 86, 87, 89, 91, 93, 96, 103, 111, 122, 123, 126, 130, 132, 135, 136, 144, 148, 156, 158, 165, 167

Aleksandr I (1777-1825), Emperor of Russia from 1801 through 1825. — 58

Aleksandr II (1818-1881), Emperor of Russia from 1855 through 1881. — 58

Altman, **Moisei Semenovich (1896-1986)**, literary scholar, studied under Viacheslav Ivanov. — 77

Andersen, **Hans-Christian (1805-1875)**, Danish author. — 25

Andreev, **Leonid Nikolaevich (1871-1919)**, Russian prose writer. From 1917 on lived at his datcha on Chernaya Rechka in Finland, thereby becoming an émigré when Finland declared independence. — 26

Andreev, **Vadim Leonidovich (1903-1976)**, Russian poet, prose writer. Son of L.N. Andreev. — 26

Andronikashvili (Andronikova), **Salomeia Nikolaevna (1888-1982)**, The addressee of poems by O. Mandelstam, A. Akhmatova, and M. Tsvetaeva. — 57, 59, 60, 74

Annensky, **Innokenty Fedorovich (1855-1909)**, Russian poet and literary critic. Taught classical languages and Russian literature at the gymnasium where Akhmatova and Gumilev studied. — 22, 23, 25, 28, 86, 90

INDEX OF NAMES

Apostolov, N., head of the political investigation. — 70

Arbenina-Gil'debrandt, Olga Nikolaevna (1897/98-1980), artist, actress. Addressee of poems by Gumilev, Mandelstam, Livshits, Kuzmin. — 73-75

Ardovs — family of Viktor Efimovich Ardov (Zigberman) (1900-1976), Soviet writer and satirist, a close friend of A. Akhmatova. — 156

Arens, Anna Evgen'evna (1892-1943), wife of N.N. Punin. — 167

Ariosto, Lodovico (1474-1533), Italian poet. — 124

Averbakh, Leopold Leonidovich (1903-1937), literary critic, Communist Party Functionary, Head of the Russian Association of Proletarian Writers. Executed by shooting. — 107

Averintsev, Sergei Sergeevich (1937-2004), scholar, specialist in Classical Antiquity and in the poetry of Viacheslav Ivanov and Osip Mandelstam. — 4, 31, 96

Babaev, Eduard Grigor'evich (1927-1995), literary scholar, friend of A. Akhmatova and N. Ia. Mandelstam. — 165

Babel, Isaak Emmanuilovich (1894-1940), writer. Arrested in 1939, executed by shooting. — 106

Bagritsky (Dzyubin), Eduard Georgievich (1895-1934), poet. — 107

Balmont, Konstantin Dmitrievich (1867-1942), Symbolist poet, translator, essayist. — 28

Balmont-Bruni, Nina (1900-1989), daughter of the poet K. Balmont and wife of L. Bruni. — 57

Baltrushaitis, Jurgis (1873-1944), Russian and Lithuanian poet. Participated in the Russian Symbolist Movement. Served as Lithuania's plenipotentiary to the USSR from 1921-1938. Lived in Paris since 1939. — 136

Baratynsky, Evgeny Abramovich (1800-1844), poet. — 28, 143

Barbier, Auguste (1805-1882), French poet. — 58, 155

Batiushkov, Konstantin Nikolaevich (1787-1855), Russian poet. — 35, 86, 120, 121

Baudelaire, Charles Pierre (1821-1867), French poet. — 19, 21

Bedny, Demian (Pridvorov Efim Alekseevich) (1883-1945), Russian poet. — 136

Beilis, Menahem Mendel Tovievich (1874?-1934), a Jew from Ukraine who was brought to trial for a blood libel accusation in Kiev in 1913. — 34

INDEX OF NAMES

Bely, **Andrei (Bugaev Boris Nikolaevich) (1880-1934)**, writer and poet, Symbolist theorist. — 35, 90, 98, 124-126, 131

Benedict XV (1854-1922), born **Giacomo Paolo Giovanni Battista della Chiesa**, reigned as Pope from 3 September 1914 to 22 January 1922. — 48

Berdiaev, **Nikolai Aleksandrovich (1874-1948)**, Russian theologian and religious philosopher. — 79

Bernshtein, **Ignatii Ignat'evich (1900-1978)**, writer. — 166

Bernshtein, **Sergei Ignat'evich (1892-1970)**, linguist. — 166

Berzen, **Richard Andreevich (1869-1958)**, St. Petersburg architect. Built the Tenishev school. — 13

Blagoi, **Dmitry Dmitrievich (1893-1984)**, Soviet literary scholar. — 79

Bliumkin, **Iakov Grigor'evich (Simha-Iankel Gershevich) (1898-1929)**, member of the party of the left Socialist Revolutionaries, in 1918 served as member of the All-Russia Extraordinary Commission (VChK), on 6 July 1918 assassinated the German Ambassador to Russia, Count V. Mirbach. — 63, 64, 71, 72

Blok, **Aleksandr Aleksandrovich (1800-1921)**, Russian poet, Symbolist. — 16, 28, 35, 37, 52, 72, 73, 75, 77, 78, 99, 124

Blokh, **Iakov Noevich (1892-1968)**, owner of the publishing house, "Petropolis." — 80

Bobrov, **Sergei Pavlovich (1889-1971)**, poet and writer. — 83, 94

Borodin, **Sergei Petrovich (1902-1974)**, Soviet writer. — 120, 131

Botsianovsky, **Vladimir Feofilovich (1869-1943)**, writer. — 22

Braun, **Fedor Aleksandrovich (1862-1942)**, philologist, specialist in German studies, Dean of the Faculty of History and Philology of the Saint Petersburg University. — 50

Briger, **N.**, Tenishev school teacher. — 14

Briusov, **Valery Iakovlevich (1873-1924)**, poet, Symbolist theoretic, critic. — 3, 4, 16, 20, 21, 28, 37, 38, 79, 84, 94

Brodsky, **David Grigor'evich (1895-1966)**, poet, translator. — 136

Brown, **Clarence (1929-2009)**, American Slavist, author of the first Mandelstam biography. — 4

Bruni, **Nikolai Aleksandrovich (1891-1938)**, Graduate of the Tenishev school, member of the "Guild of Poets." — 47, 54

Bugaev, **B.N.** — see **Bely A**.

Bugaeva Klavdiia Nikolaevna (1886-1970), wife of Andrei Bely. — 124

INDEX OF NAMES

Bukharin, Nikolai Ivanovich (1888-1938), Party leader. Member of the Central Committee of the Politburo 1924-1929. Editor of "Izvestia" 1934-1937. Arrested and shot. — 98, 100, 108, 111, 118, 132, 136, 138, 139, 152, 153

Bulgakov, Mikhail Afanas'evich (1891-1940), writer. — 146

Bulgakova Elena Sergeevna (1893-1970), M.A. Bulgakov's wife. — 138

Burliuk, David Davidovich (1882-1967), poet and artist. One of the founders of Russian Futurism. Lived in the USA from 1922. — 43

Burliuk, Nikolai Davidovich (1890-1920), poet, brother of David Burliuk. — 43

Catullus, Gaius (ca. 84 BC—ca. 54 BC), Roman poet. — 52

Chaadaev, Petr Iakovlevich (1794-1856), philosopher. — 44, 48, 49

Chebotarevskaia, Aleksandra Nikolaevna (1870-1925), translator. — 37

Cherubina de Gabriak (Vasil'eva, Elizaveta) (1887-1928), Russian poetess. — 21

Chukovsky, Kornei Ivanovich (Korneichukov, Nikolai Vasil'evich) (1882-1969), writer, literary scholar. — 10, 43, 44, 121, 153, 157

Chukovsky, Nikolai Korneevich (1904-1965), writer, son of Kornei Chukovsky. — 2, 3,

Coster, Charles de (1827-1879), Belgian writer. — 103, 107

Dante Alighieri (1265-1321), Italian poet. — 69, 124-126, 166

Darwin, Charles Robert (1809-1882), English naturalist. — 113, 119, 145

Deich, Aleksandr Nikolaevich (1893-1972), literary scholar. — 65

Del'vig, Anton Antonovich (1798-1831), Russian poet. Friend of Pushkin. — 28

Derzhavin, Gavrila Romanovich (1743-1816), poet. — 86

Dobiash, Aleksandr Antonovich (1875-1932), physicist, Tenishev school teacher. — 14

Dobroliubov, Aleksandr Mikhailovich (1876-1945), Decadent poet. Founder of a religious sect. — 15

Dolinov (Kotliar), Mikhail Anatol'evich (1892-1936), minor Russian poet. — 54

Dostoevsky, Fedor Mikhailovich (1821-1881), writer. — 86

Dreyfus, Alfred (1859-1935), French officer, Jew, accused of treason in the anti-Semitic Dreyfus Affair. — 106

INDEX OF NAMES

Dutley, Ralf, German scholar, Mandelstam specialist. — 4

Dzerzhinsky, Felix Edmundovich (1877-1926), headed the All-Russia Extraordinary Commission to Combat Counter-revolution and Sabotage — usually called the Cheka (based on the Russian acronym VChK). — 64

Efron, Elizaveta Iakovlevna (1885-1976), drama teacher, stage director, sister of S. Ia. Efron. — 55

Efros, Abram Markovich (1888-1954), art historian, literary critic. — 88

Eikhenbaum, Boris Mikhailovich (1886-1959), literary scholar. — 122, 123

Eliseev, merchant family dynasty, in 1858 purchased the Chicherin house on 15 Nevsky Prospekt. From 1919-1928 the building served as House of the Arts. — 75

Enukidze, Avel' Safronovich (1877-1937), Soviet political activist. From 1922-1935 served as Secretary of the Central Executive Committee of the USSR. Arrested in 1937 and executed by shooting. — 136

Erenburg, Il'ia Grigor'evich (1891-1967), writer, poet, journalist. — 71, 75, 83, 166

Erenburg, Lubov' Mikhailovna (1900-1970), artist, wife of I. Erenburg. — 69

Evdokimov, Ivan Vasil'evich (1887-1941), writer. — 99

Evreinov, Nikolai Nikolaevich (1879-1953), theater director, playwright, drama theorist and historian. — 68

Ezhov, Nikolai Ivanovich (1895-1940), People's Commissar for Internal Affairs (head of the NKVD) from 1936-1938, responsible for organizing massive purges. Arrested in 1939; executed by shooting. — 149, 158

Fadeev, Aleksandr Aleksandrovich (1901-1956), Soviet writer, one of the leaders of RAPP (Russian Association of Proletarian Writers), General Secretary of the Soviet Writers Union from 1946 to 1954. — 107, 136

Fedin, Konstantin Aleksandrovich (1892-1977), Soviet writer. During the 1920's belonged to the Petersburg Literary Group, "Serapion Brothers." — 96, 107

Filippov (Filistinsky), Boris Andreevich (1905-1991), literary scholar, writer, poet. Emigrated after WWII, has lived in the US since 1950. Edited the collected works of Kluev, Mandelstam, Akhmatova, and Voloshin. — 166, 167

Filonov, Pavel Nikolaevich (1883-1941), Russian avant-garde artist. — 34

INDEX OF NAMES

Fondaminskaia, Amalia Osipovna (?-1935), member of a family of leading figures of the Russian Socialist Revolutionary intelligentsia. — 19

Freidin, Iury L'vovich (1942–), literary scholar. Mandelstam specialist. — 4

Gasparov, Mikhail Leonovich (1935-2005), Russian literary scholar. — 4

Gavronskaia, Lyubov' Sergeevna, member of a family of leading figures of the Russian Socialist Revolutionary intelligentsia. — 19

Gedroits, Vera Ignat'evna (1870-1932), writer, member of the "Guild of Poets," the first woman-surgeon in Russia. — 106

Gerasimov, collaborator of the OGPU [United State Political Directorate]. — 135

Gerd, V.A., Tenishev school teacher. — 14

Gershenzon, Mikhail Osipovich (1869-1925), Russian literature scholar. — 48

Gershtein, Emma Grigor'evna (1903-2002), literary scholar, close friend of Anna Akhmatova and Mandelstam. — 2, 4, 10, 72, 113, 130, 136, 138, 148, 166

Gershuni, Grigory Andreevich (1870-1908), one of the leaders of the Socialist Revolutionaries. — 19

Gertsyk (Lubny-Gertsyk), Evgeniia Kazimirovna (1878-1944), translator, literary critic. — 21

Gertysk (Lubny-Gertsyk), Adelaida Kazimirovna (1874-1925), poet, prose writer, translator. — 21

Gidaspov, Dmitry (1870-1938), Russian Orthodox priest. — 14

Ginzburg, Lidiia Iakovlevna (1902-1990), literary scholar. — 35, 126, 128

Gippius, Vladimir Vasil'evich (1876-1941), poet, literary scholar. Taught at the Tenishev school. Participated in the "Guild of Poets." — 14-16, 20, 28, 30, 31

Gippius, Zinaida Nikolaevna (1869-1945), Symbolist poetess. One of the founders of the Religious-Philosophical Society. Emigrated in 1920. — 15, 24, 28

Gladkov Fedor Vasil'evich (1883-1958), Soviet writer, socialist realism classic. — 125

Gladkov, Aleksandr Konstantinovich (1912-1976), playwright, theatre expert, screenwriter, author of memoirs. — 121

Goethe, Johann Wolfgang (1749-1832), German poet. — 113, 144, 145

Gonta, Maria — screen actress. Wife of the poet, D. Petrovsky. — 67

Gor'ky, Maksim (Aleksei Maksimovich Peshkov) (1868-1936), writer. General Secretary of the Union of Soviet Writers in 1933-1936. — 148

Gorbacheva, Varvara Nikolaevna, wife of poet S. Klychkov. — 67

Gornfeld, Arkadii Georgievich (1867-1941), literary scholar, translator. — 8, 103-105, 107, 128

Gornung, Lev Vladimirovich (1902-1993), poet and translator, literary scholar, author of memoirs. — 78, 79

Gorodetsky, Sergei Mitrofanovich (1884-1967), poet. — 32, 34-37, 39, 54, 77

Gratsianskaia (Aleksandrova), Nina Osipovna (1904-1990), poetess. — 76

Grevs, Ivan Mikhailovich (1860-1941), historian of Roman and Medieval history. — 14

Grin, Nina Nikolaevna (1894-1970), wife of the writer A.S. Grin. — 123, 130

Gronsky (Fedulov), Ivan Mikhailovich (1894-1985), Party functionary, editor of the newspaper, "Izvestia" (1925-1934) and of the journal, "Novy Mir" (1935-1937). — 117, 118

Gruzdev, Il'ia Aleksandrovich (1892-1960), literary scholar. Member of the literary group "Serapion Brothers." — 96

Gumilev, Lev Nikolaevich (1912-1992), son of Akhmatova and Nikolai Gumilev, historian. — 130, 136

Gumilev, Nikolai Stepanovich (1886-1921), poet, literary critic, founder of the literary group, "Guild of Poets" and of the literary movement, Acmeism. Arrested in 1921 and executed by shooting. Was the husband of Anna Akhmatova from 1910-1918. — 21, 22, 28-30, 32, 34-37, 39, 43, 46, 53, 54, 73, 75, 77-79, 91, 111

Hamsun, Knut (1859-1952), Norwegian writer. Nobel Prize winner in literature (1920). — 20

Hauptmann, Gerhart (1862-1946), German writer. Nobel Prize winner in literature (1912). — 20

Hippocrates (nr. 460 B.C.—nr. 370 B.C.), Greek doctor. — 14

Iakhontov, Vladimir Nikolaevich (1899-1945), actor. — 117, 156, 157

Iashvili, Paolo (Pavel Dzhibraelovich) (1895-1937), Georgian poet. Committed suicide in anticipation of his arrest. — 71

Ionov (Bernshtein), Il'ia Ionovich (1887-1942), Party functionary, director of publishing house. — 107

Iudin Pavel Fedorovich (1899-1968), Party functionary. — 141

Ivanov, Georgy Vladimirovich (1894-1958), poet. Became member of the "Guild of Poets" in 1917, then emigrated in 1922. — 26, 30, 33, 34, 44, 64, 76

Ivanov, Viacheslav Ivanovich (1866-1949), Symbolist poet, philosopher, classical philologist. — 21, 22, 24, 27, 28, 30, 32, 37, 39, 47, 77, 86

Ivanov, Vsevolod Viacheslavovich (1895-1963), writer, member of the literary group, "Serapion Brothers." — 107

Ivanov-Razumnik (Razumnik Vasil'evich Ivanov) (1878-1946), historian. — 107

Ivnev, Riurik (Kovalev Mikhail Aleksandrovich) (1891-1981), Russian poet. Joined the imagists in the 1920's. — 33, 65

Joyce, James (1882-1941), Irish writer. — 33

Kablukov, Sergei Platonovich (1881-1919), teacher of mathematics at Petersburg gymnasiums, active participant in the Religious-Philosophical society in Petersburg; friend of Mandelstam's. — 27-29, 47, 51-53, 55, 57

Kalinin, Mikhail Ivanovich (1975-1946), Soviet political functionary. Served as Secretary of the Central Executive Committee of the USSR in 1937. — 157

Kannegiser, Leonid Ioakimovich (1896-1918), young poet, assassin of the first Soviet Secret Police Chief, Moisei Uritsky. Executed by shooting. — 62

Kariakin, Vasily Nikitich (1872-1938), translator. — 103-105

Karpovich, Mikhail (1888-1959), historian. Russian History Professor at Harvard since the 1940's. Editor of the New York journal, "Novy Zhurnal". — 1-20, 33

Kataev, Valentin Petrovich (1897-1986), Soviet writer. — 79, 107, 157, 159

Kaverin (Zil'ber), Veniamin Aleksandrovich (1902-1989), writer. Member of the literary group, "Serapion Brothers," since the 1920's. — 50-52, 97

Kerensky, Aleksandr Fedorovich (1881-1970), Head of the Provisional Government in 1917. — 60

Khalatov, Artemii (Artashes) Bagratovich (1894-1937), Head of the Gosizdat in the 1930's. — 98

Khardzhiev, Nikolai Ivanovich (1903-1996), literary and art historian. Published Mandelstam in 1973. — 4, 34, 121, 122, 130, 166

Khazin, Evgeny Iakovlevich (1893-1974), brother of N. Ia. Mandesltam. Literary critic. — 89, 130, 136, 148, 166

Khazina, N.Ia. — see **Mandelstam N.Ia.**

Khlebnikov, Velimir (Viktor Vladimirovich) (1885-1922), Futurist poet. — 34, 43, 79, 99, 111, 120-122

Khodasevich, **Vladislav Felitsianovich (1886-1939)**, poet, literary critic. Emigrated in 1922. — 50, 56, 76, 83

Khodotov, **Nikolai Nikolaevich (1878-1932)**, dramatic actor. — 71

Kipling, **Joseph Rudyard (1865-1936)**, English writer and poet. Nobel prize winner in literature (1907). — 116

Kirov (Kostrikov), **Sergei Mironovich (1886-1934)**, Soviet Communist Party leader. — 142

Kirsanov (Kortchik), **Semen Isaakovich (1906-1972)**, poet, member of the group, "Lef." — 123, 135, 157

Klavdiia Nikolaevna — see **Bugaeva K.N.**

Kliuev, **Nikolai Alekseevich (1884-1937)**, poet, representative of the new peasant movement in Russian 20th century poetry. Executed by shooting. — 38

Klychkov, **Sergei Antonovich (1889-1937)**, poet. Arrested and executed by shooting. — 119, 130

Kol'tsov, **Aleksei Vasil'evich (1809-1842)**, Russian peasant poet. Lived in Voronezh. — 145

Konevskoi (Oreus), **Ivan Ivanovich (1877-1901)**, poet, one of the founders of Russian Symbolism. — 15

Kostarev, **Nikolai Sergeevich (1914-1983)**, Soviet poet and songwriter, children's book writer. — 156

Kozakov, **Mikhail Emmanuilovich (1897-1954)**, Soviet writer. — 107

Kretova, **Olga Kapitonovna (1903-1994)**, Voronezh writer. — 141, 142, 149

Kruchenykh, **Aleksei Eliseevich (1886-1968)**, Futurist poet. — 39, 43, 44

Kudasheva, **Maia (Maria) Pavlovna (1895-1985)**, poetess and translator, Romain Rolland's wife. — 68

Kusevitsky, **Sergei Aleksandrovich (1874-1951)**, conductor. — 53

Kuzin, **Boris Sergeevich (1903-1975)**, biologist, friend of Mandelstam's in the 1930's. — 53, 113, 114, 119, 120, 123, 130, 136, 139, 143, 157, 158, 165

Kuzmin, **Mikhail Alekseevich (1872-1936)**, poet. — 24, 33, 59, 80

Kuzmin-Karavaev, **Dmitry Vladimirovich (1886-1959)**, social activist, expelled from Russia in 1922, Catholic priest. — 47

L'vov-Rogachevsky (Rogachevsky), **Vasily L'vovich (1873-1930)**, literary critic. — 79

Lamarck, **Jean-Baptiste (1744-1829)**, French naturalist. — 120-122, 145

INDEX OF NAMES

Landsberg, Leonid Emmanuilovich (nr. 1899-1957), lawyer. — 78

Legran, Boris Vasil'evich (1884-1936), Soviet diplomat. Director of the Hermitage from 1930-1934. — 78

Lenin (Ul'ianov), Vladimir Il'ich (1870-1924), founder of the Soviet State (1917-1924). — 60, 89, 110

Leonov, Leonid Maksimovich (1899-1994), writer. — 107

Leonov, Nikolai Dmitrievich, biologist. — 139

Lermontov, Mikhail Iur'evich (1814-1841), poet. Author of the first Russian psychological novel, "Hero of our Time." — 9, 86

Lerner, Nikolai Osipovich (1877-1934), literary historian, Pushkin scholar. — 53

Lesgaft, Emilii Frantsevich (1870-1922), geographer and teacher. — 14

Lezhnev, Isai Grigor'evich (1891-1955), journalist. Editor of the journal, "Rossia" from 1922-1926. From 1935-1939 served as the head of the department of literature and art of the newspaper "Pravda". — 88

Lika — see **Rudakova-Finkelshtein L.S.**

Liliia — see **Popova E.E.**

Lipkin, Semen Izrailevich (1911-2003), poet, translator. — 67, 87, 121, 130

Liuba — see **Erenburg L.M.**

Livshits, Benedikt Konstantinovich (1886-1938), poet, translator. Began as a futurist. Friend of Mandelstam's. Executed by shooting. — 43-46, 96, 107, 126

Lozinsky, Mikhail Leonidovich (1886-1955), translator, translated Dante's "Divine Comedy." Member of the "Guild of Poets." Friend of Akhmatova's. — 33, 34, 157

Luknitsky, Pavel Nikolaevich (1900-1973), writer, poet, author of memoirs about Akhmatova. — 61, 89, 99, 108

Lunacharsky, Anatoly Vasil'evich (1875-1933), People's commissar of education until 1929. Died on his way to Madrid, where he had been assigned as Ambassador. — 62, 64

Lur'e (Lourie), Artur Sergeevich (1891-1966), composer, one of the participants of the Russian avant-garde in music. From 1918-1921 headed the department of music of the Narkompros (MUZO). Moved to Berlin in 1922, later lived in France. Since 1941 lived in the US. — 53

Lutik — see **Vaksel' O.A.**

Lyons, Eugene (1898-1985), American journalist in the USSR. — 110

INDEX OF NAMES

Maiakovsky, **Vladimir Vladimirovich (1893-1930)**, Futurist poet. — 43, 44, 90, 111, 114

Makovsky, **Sergei Konstantinovich (1877-1962)**, poet, artistic critic, publisher. Edited the journal, "Apollon" from 1909-1917. Emigrated after the revolution in 1917. — 23, 24, 37, 161

Makridin, **Nikolai Vasil'evich (1882-1942)**, engineer specializing in reclamation. — 71

Malein, **Aleksandr Iustinovich (1869-1938)**, classical philologist, historian, professor of the Petersburg Institute of History and Philology. — 52

Mallarmé, **Stéphane (1842-1898)**, French poet. — 28

Mandelstam (Verblovskaia), **Flora Osipovna (1866?-1916)**, O. Mandelstam's mother. — 8, 10, 24, 33, 56

Mandelstam, **Aleksandr Emil'evich (1892-1942)**, O. Mandelstam's brother, bibliographer. — 8, 56, 64, 65, 67, 68, 71, 116, 130, 136, 138

Mandelstam, **Aleksandr**, brother of Morits Mandelstam, a distant relative of O. Mandelstam, medical specialist. — 7

Mandelstam, **Emil' (Khatskel') Veniaminovich (1852?-1938)**, O. Mandelstam's father. — 8, 10

Mandelstam, **Evgeny (1898-1979)**, O. Mandelstam's brother, physician, screenwriter. — 7, 8, 10, 12, 30, 40, 57, 76, 96, 115, 153

Mandelstam, **Morits**, brother of Aleksandr Mandelstam, a distant relative of O. Mandelstam, medical specialist. — 7

Mandelstam, **Nadezhda Iakovlevna (1899-1979)**, O. Mandelstam's wife. — 2-4, 10, 14, 23, 24, 27, 29, 33, 61, 62, 65-67, 75-77, 79, 84, 87-93, 95, 96, 98, 106, 108, 109, 113, 115, 118-120, 124, 126, 128, 130, 135, 136, 138, 139, 141-145, 147-150, 155-158, 160, 161, 163, 165, 167

Mariengof, **Anatoly Borisovich (1897-1962)**, Imagist poet. — 125, 126

Markish, **Perets Davidovich (1895-1952)**, Jewish poet. Arrested in 1949 for being a member of the presidium of the Jewish Anti-Fascist Committee. Executed by shooting. — 131

Marot, **Clément (1497-1544)**, French poet. — 50

Marshak, **Samuil Iakovlevich (1887-1964)**, poet, translator. — 131

Matorin, **Dmitry Mikhailovich (1911-?)**, Leningrad sportsman. O. Mandelstam's fellow-inmate. — 163, 164

Mayne Reid (1818-1883), English writer. — 107

Melies, **George (1861-1938)**, French film director. — 46

Merezhkovsky, Dmitry Sergeevich (1866-1941), novelist, Symbolist poet, religious thinker. — 16, 24, 27

Michelangelo (1475-1564), Italian sculptor, painter. — 144

Mikhoels (Vovsi), Solomon Mikhailovich (1890-1948), actor, director of the Moscow State Jewish Theater. — 95, 157

Mindlin, Emilii L'vovich (1900-1981), writer. — 68

Mirbach, Wilhelm von (1871-1918), German diplomat, appointed German Ambassador to Russia in April 1918. Assassinated by the Left Socialist-Revolutionaries, Iakov Bliumkin and Nikolai Andreev. — 64

Mitia — see **Matorin D.M.**

Mitsishvili, Nikolaz (1894-1937), Georgian poet. — 70

Mochulsky, Konstantin Vasil'evich (1892-1948), literary scholar, philosopher. Graduated from the Petersburg University in 1910. Emigrated in 1919. Lived in Paris. — 50

Moiseenko, Iury Illarionovich (1914-?), prisoner of the transit colony on the Vtoraia river. — 162, 164

Molotov (Skriabin), Viacheslav Mikhailovich (1890-1986), Communist party leader. — 115

Morgulis, Aleksandr Osipovich (1898-1938), writer, translator. — 119

Morozov, Aleksandr Anatol'evich (1932-2008), literary historian, Mandelstam scholar. — 4, 166

Mravian, Askanaz Artem'evich (Arutiunovich) (1885-1929), Party functionary. Commissar of Education from 1923. Also served as the deputy chairman of the Council of People's Commissars of the Armenian SSR. — 109

Nabokov, Vladimir Vladimirovich (1899-1977), Russian-American writer. — 15

Nadiradze, Kolau Galaktionovich (1895-1990), Georgian Symbolist poet. — 71

Nadson, Semen Iakovlevich (1862-1887), poet. — 17, 28

Naiman, Anatoly Genrikhovich (1936-), poet, young friend of Akhmatova. — 34

Napoleon Bonaparte (1769-1821), French Emperor from 1804-1814 and from May-June 1815. — 75

Narbut, Vladimir Ivanovich (1888-1944?), Acmeist poet. Member of the "Guild of Poets". — 39, 43, 44, 130, 136

INDEX OF NAMES

Nerler (Polian), Pavel Markovich (1952–), literary scholar. Founder of the Mandelstam Society. — 4

Neumann, Karl Friedrich (1793-1870), German orientalist, born under the name of Bamberger, later converted to Protestantism and took the name of Neumann. Served as Professor of Armenian and Chinese at the University of Munich from 1831 until 1852. — 25

Nicholas II (1868-1918), Emperor of Russia from 1894 to 1917. — 21

Nietzsche, Friedrich (1844-1900), German philosopher and poet. — 9

Nikonov, V.N., teacher at the Tenishev School. — 14

Novikov, Nikolai Ivanovich (1744-1818), writer, journalist, book publisher. — 16

Novinsky, Aleksandr Aleksandrovich (?-1958?), commander of the Port of Feodosia. — 68, 70

Ol'shevskaia, Nina Antonovna (1908-1991), Ardov's wife, actress, friend of A. Akhmatova. — 138

Olesha, Iury Karlovich (1899-1960), writer. — 107

Osmerkin, Aleksandr Aleksandrovich (1892-1953), artist, author of A. Akhmatova's portrait. — 130

Ostrogorsky, Aleksandr Iakovlevich (1869-1908), director of the Tenishev School. — 18

Ozerov, Vladislav Aleksandrovich (1769-1816), playwright and poet. — 49

Palei, Abram Ruvimovich (1893-1995), writer. — 105

Parnakh (Parnokh), Valentin Iakovlevich (1891-1951), poet, translator. — 100

Parnok (Parnokh), Sophia Iakovlevna (1885-1933), poetess, Valentin Parnakh's sister. — 54, 97, 100

Pasternak, Boris Leonidovich (1890-1960), poet. — 12, 86, 87, 89, 91, 94, 95, 97, 104, 107, 108, 114, 122, 127, 128, 130, 136, 137, 139, 140, 141, 144, 148, 161, 162, 167

Pavlenko, Petr Andreevich (1899-1951), Soviet writer. — 136, 154, 159

Pavlovich, Nadezhda Aleksandrovna (1895-1980), poetess. — 49, 72

Pedenko, N.K., artist, teacher at the Tenishev school. — 14

Petrarch (Petrarca, Francesco) (1304-1374), Italian poet. — 124, 125

INDEX OF NAMES

Petrov (Kataev), Evgeny Petrovich (1902-1942), writer, V.P. Kataev's brother. — 157

Petrovykh, Ekaterina Sergeevna, sister of the poetess, Maria Petrovykh. — 131

Petrovykh, Maria Sergeevna (1908-1979), poet, translator. — 130, 136

Piast, Vladimir Alekseevich (1886-1940), Symbolist poet. — 99, 120

Pil'niak (Vogau), Boris Andreevich (1894-1938), writer. — 107

Pinsky, Leonid Efimovich (1906-1981), literary historian specializing in Western European literature of the 17th and 18th centuries. — 166

Plotnikov, Mikhail Pavlovich (1892-1938), writer, folklorist. — 119

Popova, Elikonida Efimovna (1903-1964), wife of the actor, V.N. Iakhontov. — 117, 156, 157

Prishvin, Mikhail Mikhailovich (1873-1954), writer. — 4

Proust, Marcel (1871-1922), French writer. — 39

Prut, Iosif Leonidovich (1900-1996), Soviet playwright. — 159

Punin, Nikolai Nikolaevich (1888-1953), art historian. — 29, 72, 83, 157

Pushkin, Aleksandr Sergeevich (1899-1837), poet. — 3, 13, 33, 49, 121, 143, 152, 154

Radishchev, Aleksandr Nikolaevich (1749-1802), writer, author of "A Journey from St. Petersburg to Moscow." — 16

Radlova, Anna Dmitrievna (1891-1949), poet, translator. — 59

Raskol'nikov (Il'in), Fedor Fedorovich (1892-1939), Soviet diplomat, writer, and journalist. — 64

Reisner, Larisa Mikhailovna (1895-1926), writer, revolutionary, participant of the Russian Civil War. — 64

Rittenberg, Sergei Aleksandrovich (1899-1975), literary critic, lived in Vyborg. — 64

Rodenbach, George (1855-1898), Belgian writer. — 20

Roginsky, Iakov Iakovlevich (1895-1986), anthropologist. — 145, 154

Ronen, Omry (1937–), American Slavist, Mandelstam scholar. — 4

Rozanov, Vasily Vasil'evich (1856-1919), religious philosopher, literary critic and journalist. — 20

Rozen, Nils I., Protestant pastor from Helsinki who baptized Mandelstam. — 30

INDEX OF NAMES

Rubakin, A., Mandelstam's acquaintance, student of the Tenishev School. — 14

Rudakov, Sergei Borisovich (1909-1944), literary scholar, poet. Friend of O. and N. Mandelstam during the Voronezh exile. — 53, 142, 144, 146-150, 155

Rudakova-Finkelshtein, Lina Samoilovna (1907-1977), wife of S.B. Rudakov. — 143

Sargidzhan, Amir — see **Borodin S.P.**

Savinkov, Boris Viktorovich (1879-1925), leader of the Fighting Organization of the Socialist-Revolutionary Party. — 19

Sazonov, teacher of physics at the Tenishev School. — 14

Schiller, Johann Christoph Friedrich (1759-1805), German poet. — 8

Seifullina, Lidiia Nikolaevna (1889-1954), Soviet writer. — 136

Selvinsky, Il'ia (Karl) L'vovich (1899-1968), poet, founder of the constructivist literary movement. — 107

Serge, Victor (Kibal'chich Viktor L'vovich) (1890-1947), took active part in the Comintern. Joined the anti-Stalin opposition in 1923. Arrested in 1933 and deported to Orenburg. Was released in 1936 and departed the USSR. — 118

Shaginian, Marietta Sergeevna (1888-1982), Soviet poet and prose writer. — 123, 141

Shakhovskoy, Dmitry Alekseevich (1902-1989), poet, published his poetry under the pen name of Strannik. Took his monastic vows in the 1920's as Ioann, later became priest and eventually Archbishop of San Francisco. — 94

Shakhovskoy, Dmitry Mikhailovich (1928–), sculptor, author of the monument to O. Mandelstam in Moscow. — 167

Shalamov, Varlam Tikhonovich (1907-1982), prose writer and poet, author of "Kolyma Tales." — 162

Shengeli, Georgy Arkad'evich (1894-1956), poet, literary scholar. — 65, 130

Shershenevich, Vadim Gabrielevich (1893-1942), poet, founder of Russian Imagism. — 76

Shilkin, P., Second Lieutenant and investigator who interrogated Mandelstam on 17 May 1938. — 160

Shivarov, Nikolai Khristoforovich, investigator of the OGPU [United State Political Directorate]. — 136, 137

Shklovsky, Viktor Borisovich (1893-1984), writer, literary scholar. — 130

INDEX OF NAMES

Shtempel', Natalia Evgen'evna (1910-1988), teacher, friend of the Mandelstams in Voronezh. — 149-152, 156, 157, 167

Shura, Shurochka — see **Mandelstam A.E.**

Shver, Aleksandr Vladimirovich (?-1938), Editor-in-Chief of the Voronezh newspaper, "Kommuna." — 141

Sinani, Boris (1889-1910), O. Mandelstam's childhood friend from school. — 15, 17, 18, 26, 27

Skriabin, Aleksandr Nikolaevich (1871-1915), composer. — 52, 53, 87

Slepian, Doriana Filippovna (?-?), actress and dramatist. — 3

Slezkin, Iury L'vovich (1885-1947), writer. — 149

Sluchevsky, Konstantin Konstantinovich (1837-1904), Russian poet, prose writer, playwright, and translator. — 16

Sologub (Teternikov), Fedor Kuz'mich (1863-1927), Symbolist poet, prose writer. — 16, 20, 24, 37, 99

Soloviev, Vladimir Sergeevich (1853-1900), philosopher. — 9

Stalin (Dzhugashvili), Iosif Vissarionovich (1879-1953) — 110, 129, 130, 136, 138-140, 142, 144-146, 153, 154, 156, 161, 162, 165

Stavsky (Kirpichnikov), Vladimir Petrovich (1900-1943), journalist, general secretary of the Writers Union of the USSR. — 155, 158, 159

Stenich (Smetanich), Valentin Iosifovich (Osipovich) (1898-1938), poet, translator. Executed by shooting. — 131, 157

Stoichev, Stefan, in 1935 served as secretary of the party group of the Voronezh section of the Soviet Writers Union. — 142

Stolypin, Petr Arkad'evich (1862-1911), Prime Minister of Russia from 1906-1911. Was the initiator of the massive resettlement of peasants from European Russia to Siberia, for which purpose a special type of railcar was introduced nicknamed the "Stolypin railcar." In Soviet times, these railcars were used for the transport of incarcerated convicts and exiles. — 161

Strauss, Richard (1864-1949), German composer. — 20

Struve, Gleb Petrovich (1898-1985), Russian émigré literary scholar. Edited, with Filippov, Mandelstam's Collected Works. — 166, 167

Sudeikin, Sergei Iur'evich (1884-1946), Artist and set-designer. Member of the "Mir iskusstva" movement. One of the organizers of the cabaret, "Brodiachaia sobaka" [Stray Dog]. Lived in Paris from 1920, later moved to New York. — 60

Sudeikina, Vera Arturovna (1888-1982), wife of Sudeikin, later of Igor Stravinsky. — 60

INDEX OF NAMES

Tabidze, Nina Aleksandrovna (1900-1965), wife of T. Iu. Tabidze. — 70

Tabidze, Titsian Iustinovich (1895-1937), Georgian poet. — 70, 71

Tager, Elena Mikhailovna (1895-1964), writer, poet. — 131

Tatlin, Vladimir Evgrafovich (1885-1953), Russian avant-garde artist. — 93

Tenishev, Viacheslav Nikolaevich (1843-1903), founder of the actual Tenishev School in St. Petersburg (1896). — 13

Terapiano, Iury Konstantinovich (1892-1980), Russian poet, literary critic. Emigrated in 1920, lived in France from 1922. — 65

Tibullus, Albius (ca. 54-19 BC), Roman poet. — 52

Tikhonov, Nikolai Semenovich (1896-1979), Soviet poet and prose writer, member of the literary groups, "Serapion Brothers" and "The Islanders." — 108, 115, 118, 122, 153

Timenchik, Roman Davydovich (1945–), literary scholar specializing in Russian literature of the early 20th century. — 4, 52, 57,

Tiutchev, Fedor Ivanovich (1803-1873), poet. — 20, 21, 47, 48

Toddes, Evgeny Abramovich (1941–), literary scholar specializing in Russian literature of the early 20th century. — 4, 37, 58

Tolstoy, Aleksei Nikolaevich (1882-1945), writer. — 21, 28, 29, 120, 131, 132, 139

Tolstoy, Lev Nikolaevich (1828-1910), writer. — 20, 26

Trotsky (Bronshtein), Lev Davydovich (1879-1940), Soviet Communist leader. Assassinated by an agent of the NKVD. — 110

Tsereteli, Grigory Filimonovich (1870-1938), Georgian Classical Philologist. — 50-52

Tsvetaeva, Anastasia Ivanovna (1894-1993), Russian writer, sister of the poet, Marina Tsvetaeva. — 60

Tsvetaeva, Marina Ivanovna (1892-1941), poet. — 12, 54-56, 60, 76, 86, 94, 95, 104

Tsygal'sky, Aleksandr Viktorovich (1880-?), Head of counter-intelligence in Feodosia, poet. — 70

Tugan-Baranovsky, Mikhail Ivanovich (1865-1919), economist, sociologist, historian. — 14

Tvardovsky, Aleksandr Trifonovich (1910-1971), poet, editor of the journal, "Novy Mir" from 1950-1954 and 1958-1970. — 109

Tynianov, Iury Nikolaevich (1894-1943), writer, one of the founders of the "formalist theory" in literary scholarship. — 50, 51, 86, 87, 121, 126, 142, 157

Tyshler, Aleksandr Grigor'evich (1898-1980), painter. — 29, 30, 130

INDEX OF NAMES

Uksha, Susanna Al'fonsovna (1885-1945), poetess, translator. — 78

Uritsky, Moisei Solomonovich (1873-1918), from March 1918 served as head of the Petrograd ChK. Assassinated by the poet, Leonid Kanegieser. — 62

Vaksel', Olga Aleksandrovna (1903-1932), actress, the addressee of love poems by Mandelstam. — 66, 91, 93, 145

Vasilenko, S.V., Mandelstam scholar. — 4

Venediktov, A.G., member of the board of the publishing house "Zemlia I fabrika" — 104

Vengerov, Semen Afanas'evich (1855-1920), literary historian. — 10

Veprintsev, collaborator of the OGPU [United State Political Directorate]. — 135

Verblovskaia, F.O. — see **Mandelstam F.O.**

Vergil (Publius Vergilius Maro) (10-19 B.C.), Roman poet. — 143

Verlaine, Paul (1844-1896), French poet. — 19, 20, 21, 25, 64

Viazemsky, Petr Andreevich (1792-1878), poet. — 49

Vishnevsky, Vsevolod Vital'evich (1900-1951), Soviet playwright. — 157

Volkenstein, Fedor Fedorovich (1908-1985), physicist, stepson of Aleksei Tolstoy. — 131

Voloshin (Kirienko-Voloshin), Maksimilian Aleksandrovich (1877-1932), poet, artist. — 24, 53, 54, 56, 68, 69, 70, 78, 91, 124

Vygodsky, David Isaakovich (1893-1943), translator and literary critic. Arrested in 1938. Died in the gulags. — 83, 98

Wrangel, Petr Nikolaevich (1878-1928), one of the leaders of the White Army movement during the Russian Civil War. — 67, 69, 73

Zablovsky, collaborator of the OGPU [United State Political Directorate]. — 135

Zabolotsky, Nikolai Alekseevich (1903-1958), poet. — 155

Zaitsev, owner of a boarding house in Tsarskoe Selo. — 93

Zaitsev, Petr Nikanorovich (1889-1970), publisher and literary critic. — 125

Zaks, Art Iakovlevich (1878-1938), local history specialist, teacher at the Tenishev school. — 14

Zaslavsky, David Iosifovich (1880-1965), Soviet journalist. — 107, 108

INDEX OF NAMES

Zel'manova-Chudovskaia, **Anna Mikhailovna (1891-1952)**, artist, author of the portraits of Akhmatova and Mandelstam. — 44-46, 59

Zelinsky, **Kornelii Liutsianovich (1896-1970)**, critic. — 107

Zenkevich, **Mikhail Aleksandrovich (1891-1973)**, poet, one of the cofounders of the "Guild of Poets". — 22, 43, 44, 118

Zhirmunsky, **Viktor Maksimovich (1891-1971)**, literary scholar. — 20, 26

Zlotinsky, **David Isaakovich**, author of the letter to Il'ia Erenburg about meeting Mandelstam in the penal colony. — 163

Zoshchenko, **Mikhail Mikhailovich (1895-1958)**, writer, member of the group "Serapion Brothers." — 107, 157

LaVergne, TN USA
04 February 2010
172129LV00004B/5/P